Teaching Tenses

Ideas for presenting and
practising tenses in English

Rosemary Aitken

Pearson Education Limited
Edinburgh Gate, Harlow,
Essex CM20 2JE, England
and Associated Companies throughout the world.

Printed in Malaysia, PA

Contents

WITHDRAWN

How to use this book

This book is intended to help you, as a teacher of English as a Foreign language (E F L), to teach common verb tenses and patterns more efficiently and clearly. Some of the material in the book may surprise you. To begin with, the explanations and commentary may seem self-evident, or the phonetic realisations may seem unnecessary. If this is so, please try to bear with me. The material in the book is designed to be of help to several groups: **the experienced native speaker** seeking a possible new approach to add to his armoury, **the novice teacher**, who speaks English with native speaker intuition, but has not yet fully analysed what it is that he does know, or why he says what he says, and also the non-native **E F L teacher abroad**, who speaks English excellently, and yet wishes to understand the subtler differences in usage and idiom which the native speaker takes for granted.

The organisation of the materials may not be what you expect – the placement of the present perfect in the section devoted to the present tense, for example. This is because you are reading a handbook for teachers, not a conventional grammar book, and the tenses are ordered in a way intended to make the concepts easier for you and your students, regardless of what grammatical purists might argue.

Lastly, I am aware that as a E F L teacher you are more likely to be female than male. Nevertheless, I have referred to 'the teacher' as 'he' throughout the text because writing 'he/she' is clumsy, 'they' is ungrammatical, 'one' is impersonal, and 'it' is insulting! If you are a female, please excuse my use of 'he' and regard this as a courtesy to the minority reader.

Please read this section of the book carefully. It is designed to help you to analyse common verb tenses and patterns, and their underlying concepts, and to choose appropriate contexts for making those concepts clear to your students. It is central to all that follows.

The rest of the book focuses closely on individual tenses and verb patterns. It is not intended to be read at one sitting, but to be dipped into for individual verb patterns. Of course, in a book of this length it is impossible to give all the possible verb patterns, with all their meanings, but the book does hope to cover most of the major ones. It will give you practical working principles, not a complete scholarly analysis. For this you need a good comprehensive grammar, and this book will work most successfully if you have one to refer to.

You will find an **analysis** of the usual forms and functions of each of the verb patterns discussed, together with a note on common phonetic problems. Then the book gives you a list of **suggested contexts** for teaching each of the functions. Although these contexts are tried and tested, they are not the only ones. The textbook which you use may well have others. Use this book to examine the examples given by your text, and see if you can see why the author has chosen them. It has been known for a good, clear textbook to be obscured by a muddled class teacher. There are times when you might feel that the textbook itself could be clearer. This book will show you how to choose clear contexts; use the ideas given here as a basis, and modify and add to them to create your own repertoire.

There is also a short section on **learner error** for each tense, one dealing with errors of **form**, and the other with common errors of **function**. The book cannot hope to deal with every possible mistake – every day learners invent new ways of getting things wrong! On the other hand, these sections do offer explanations for some of the more common errors, and by referring to them you may be able to work out why your own students make the errors that they do.

How to organise a tense for teaching

The problem of teaching tenses

Many teachers find that tenses are far more difficult to teach than, say, vocabulary; although planning a lesson around a tense is obviously easier, actually teaching it may be a different matter. Despite their best efforts, students consistently misuse, misunderstand and misapply tenses. Let us examine some of the reasons why this might be so.

Some of this mislearning is probably inevitable. Students of a foreign language have a great many things to remember at once, and mistakes are almost bound to occur, especially where the mother tongue leads the learner to expect something else. Ways in which this may happen will be discussed later, under the individual tenses. Some of the mistakes, however, are undoubtedly caused by the teacher, sometimes by his failure to understand fully the nature of the tense he is teaching, where the pitfalls are, how it differs from the mother tongue, why an English speaker selects one tense rather than another, and how to choose examples and illustrations which help, rather than hinder, understanding.

It is relatively easy for a student to learn the names of things in a foreign language; tedious, but relatively easy. You see a table or a chair and you learn the word for it. There is likely to be a mother tongue equivalent of some sort.

Even here, however, it can be a useful exercise to examine the boundaries of meaning. Take a piece of paper and a pencil and make a list, in English, of all the names of pieces of furniture designed for sitting on. You should have a list that runs into the teens at least. Then ask yourself, what are the dividing lines? What is the difference between a stool and a chair? Why is this object a bench and not a pew? See what guides you in your choice of name for each object, and you will begin to see the complexities of the concepts which are inherent in a language. Now compare that list with a similar list from another language which you know, if you can. You will see that there are distinctions in English which do not occur in the other language, and possibly vice versa. Nevertheless, it is possible to clarify and demonstrate the differences between all these words, once you have identified them for yourself, because the objects themselves are visible and concrete. Even if you invent a totally new object, lets call it a "woodle", once a student has been introduced to it, seen one and knows what it does, he will learn the name for it fairly easily and be able to identify a "woodle" when he sees one.

Verb tenses are more difficult, because the concept boundaries are less easily visible. The concept *eat* is comparable to the concept 'chair'; this is a piece of vocabulary, and no more difficult to grasp than many others. The difference between I *eat* and I *am eating* is a good deal more problematic; and much of the problem arises because English native speakers take it for granted that there is a distinction, while speakers of other languages take it for granted that there is none. Just as no photograph, drawing or object will enable a student to identify a 'pew' until he grasps the concept that it is in a church, miming someone eating an apple will not help to identify the concept of I *eat*, although it may help with I *am eating*. I *eat* is used more for routines and not for actions being carried out 'now'. All native speakers know this, but few of them recognise that they know it. As a teacher it is important that you understand the 'subconscious' contexts of different verb tenses, so that you can identify them and make them clear to your students.

Problems with verb tenses also arise because many teachers assume that all cultures share the same attitudes and concepts of the relationship between time and tense. Most Western cultures for instance, would regard the following diagram as representing the sequence of past, present and future time:

It is important to recognise, however, that other cultures and therefore other languages may conceptualise time in a completely different way. Consider the second diagram, which loosely represents the time/tense concept in one of the languages from the Indian sub-continent.

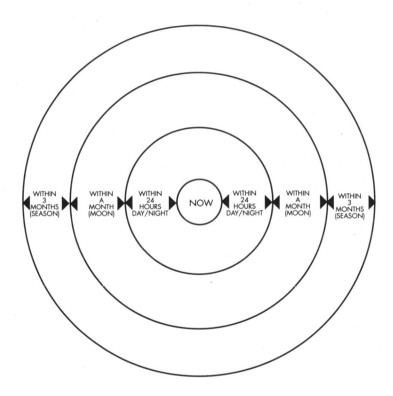

Here, what is important is not the 'past' nor 'future' concept of the tense, but the distance from 'now', so that actions which took place, and actions which will take place within twenty-four hours of 'now', will require the same tense; those at a greater distance, another, and so on.

To many English teachers this seems, at first sight, a very difficult and illogical concept, and raises questions as to how one would distinguish the future from the past. The answer, of course, is a time marker – a separate phrase or word which makes the time reference clear. This seems a very clumsy device to many English speakers, until they realise that English actually uses the same device itself. The two statements, I'm *working* and I'm *working this evening*, use the same tense; one to refer to the present, and one to the future. The difference lies, not in the tense, but in the time marker only.

Preparing to teach a tense

There are some basic steps which it is helpful to follow in planning a tense for teaching purposes. It may help to remember the (imaginary) word CASSIAL, to remind you of these guidelines:

C (choose) **A** (analyse) **S** (sequence) **S** (select) **I** (identify context) **A** (auxiliary materials) **L** (learner error)

C A S S I A L

Let us look at these steps in greater detail, and see what they entail, and why they are important.

C Choose

On the whole, this is self-explanatory. Choose which tense you propose to teach. Often, in fact, the choice will be made for you by the textbook or syllabus. It is important that there is a deliberate choice. This is one area of language which you cannot fall upon by accident, because it happens to turn up in a reading text, for example. The criteria for that choice may vary with circumstance, but will probably break down into a list something like this:

- Do my students need this tense? (for speaking or writing.)
- Is it a frequently used tense and in which contexts would you find it?
- Can I demonstrate and contextualise (rather than explain) its meaning and concept, using language the students already know?
- Does it build naturally on tenses and structures which my students already know?
- Does it give me the basis to teach other structures which my students need to know?
- All other things being equal, is this tense the simplest way of expressing the concept in question?

A Analyse

Ideally, make a list of all the uses of the tense that you can think of, and try to work out for yourself the differences between them (this book will help you with this task). Compare your chosen tense with other, similar tenses, and decide what distinctions there are between them; that is, work out the concepts of the tense. Then check your findings against a good grammar book; you may find that your own notes help to clarify what the experts say. (Don't miss this step or you will certainly omit some uses and there is always a perceptive student who will ask you about something that you haven't covered.)

Now, look at the tense in all its persons, not forgetting the negative and interrogative forms. Ask yourself if the conversational spoken form is identical to the written form. (Again, this book will give you this information at a glance.) If you examine these forms you can often see where problems are likely to arise. (For instance, we say He *isn't walking* but not *I amn't walking.* We can see that learners may be tempted to create such a form; it would be logical.)

It is a good idea to look at the pattern of more than one verb, (*walk, run and go*, for example) and watch carefully for any unexpected variations which may create difficulties for learners. These variations may take several forms:

Variations of form

We all know, for example, that I *eat* becomes *he eats* and I *can* becomes *he can*. (He *cans*, of course, means something different!) But the fluent or native speaker may sometimes fail to notice that he does know this, it has become second nature. Learners, however, do not possess this instinct, and will not make these changes appropriately unless you point them out, and you cannot point them out until you are aware of them. This book will try to alert you to major problem areas of form.

Variations of sound

Here again, the teacher's familiarity with the language may prevent him from anticipating the problems which seem perplexing to the foreign student. Consider the following random list:

he waits ... he watches ... he wears ... he closes ... he carries

If asked to pick the 'odd man out', many thoughtful people will select *carries*, on the grounds that *carry* changes the *y* to *ies* in the third person. A few perceptive souls will spot that *watch* actually adds *es* rather than *s*, and so adds a whole new syllable to the third person. If we begin to concentrate on sound we notice that the addition of the *s* to *close* has the same effect; *closes* becomes two syllables. Even *wears* / z / is different from *waits* / s /! So there is no odd man out – all are different, (except that phonetically *carries* follows the same rule as *wears*).

Students often mispronounce or fail to distinguish sounds because of phonetic realisations of which fluent speakers are no longer consciously aware. This book will help you to identify some of the chief minefields.

Variations of function

We have to decide for teaching purposes, not only what a tense looks like (form), or sounds like (phonetic realisation), but what it does – its function.

Part of the analysis of any tense should be to note down the question (or questions) to which the tense is the most natural answer. This can sometimes be a surprising exercise, and is rarely the simple interrogative form of the tense itself. (The words I *swim* are not usually an answer to *Do you swim?* The realistic answer to that is probably *yes*, or *no*, or *yes I do*.) You will want your students to practise using the tense in a realistic way, and this will involve teaching them an appropriate question form. You will find a section under each tense suggesting some **questions to draw the target** (i.e. questions which will require the students to answer in the desired tense).

Here is an example to think about: what is the question which realistically requires the answer I *swim*?

In analysing function we must also be aware that idiomatic use can throw up unpredictable usages. He *eats* is a statement in the simple present tense, and must be true of almost every human being. He *drinks*, on the other hand, often carries connotations of drinking alcohol, and to excess; and it is perfectly idiomatic to make the biologically impossible statement I *don't drink*.

S *Sequence*

Having completed our analysis we shall almost certainly find that every tense has several functions, and there may be additional problems with irregular forms, or the phonetic realisations of a rule. It is rarely possible to teach all forms, functions and variations of a tense in one lesson; and the more elementary the level, the smaller the proportion of the whole one can teach. These different functions (and forms if necessary) must be sequenced for teaching purposes, once again starting with the most common functions, and moving to the least usual.

Note: In some cases, a decision might be taken not to teach a particular form as a tense at all, but to introduce it in a lesson devoted to conversational expressions. For instance, *would* might be introduced quite early, not as part of a tense but as part of a lesson on requests, *I'd like a cup of tea, please*.

There is often no one right answer to the problem of sequencing, although the list of criteria given under **Choose** may help you to decide on a desirable order. Nevertheless, there are vexed questions. Should a teacher sequencing the simple past begin with the most common verbs (probably irregular), or the common pattern enabling students to perceive a rule? Textbooks and syllabi are divided on the subject. What is important is that the teacher does not attempt to teach all forms at once, and that he does not, for instance, believe that he has covered the simple past, when his students simply know the main irregular forms.

S *Select*

Again this is really self-explanatory. Once the sequence is decided, we must select which function we propose to teach to our particular students. Interestingly, different functions of a tense may be taught at quite widely differing levels. The present simple for habit, for instance, is commonly taught at elementary level, while its use for scientific truth may not be taught until intermediate stage, (unless of course the class consists of learners studying science!) In the same way, students' needs usually dictate the order and the selection of items. Students learning English in the U.K. will have different needs from those learning in a school environment in a different country.

I Identify the context

We have now chosen our tense, analysed it, and decided which forms and functions are appropriate to our students' level, and in what order they are to be taught. If we wish to teach effectively, however, we must also identify a teaching context. This should fulfil certain important criteria:

- It should be a context in which native English speakers would genuinely use the tense.
- It should make the concept of the tense clear, preferably in a way which can be demonstrated, or illustrated, or explained in the tenses which the students already possess. (If we wish to teach *used to* for discontinued habit in the past, we need a context which shows a) it was in the past, b) it was habitual, and c) it is discontinued. If any of those elements is missing the concept of the tense has not been taught.)
- It is good practice to test the concept of a new tense immediately after teaching it, preferably in language which does not require the new form: *Did he ride a bicycle in the past? Did he ride it often? Does he ride a bicycle now?*

A Auxiliary materials

In order to make the context and concept clear, auxiliary materials (pictures, diagrams, picture sequences, timetables) may be helpful.

The photocopiable section (see page 175) provides additional material which ties in with the contexts suggested for practice in the text. In addition to providing activities for consolidation, the material is a useful resource bank of visual aids which the teacher can use flexibly.

L Learner error

As we have already said, no one can predict what new errors a learner will produce. However, there are patterns of error which the classroom teacher should be alive to:

- Some errors are caused by 'mother tongue interference'; the native language behaves in ways which are not applicable to English, but the learner treats them as equivalents. This is notably more common in tenses where there is some overlap of meaning, or where the form suggests equivalence (especially the present perfect).
- Errors are caused by 'false patterning'; a rule already learned in English is applied to situations where it is not appropriate.
- Many errors, are caused by 'interlanguage'; a stage where the learner rejects a straightforward translation in favour of something which 'sounds more English', but which may not actually conform to the rules of either English or his mother tongue. These errors are unpredictable, but encouraging. A learner who makes them is beginning to develop a 'feeling' for the target language.

Present Section

Points to Ponder

- ### For trainee teachers

  What exactly is the difference between I *eat cornflakes* and I *am eating cornflakes*?
  What about I *eat more cornflakes these days* and I *am eating more cornflakes these days*?
  What is 'present' about the present perfect in the sentence, I *have eaten my dinner*.

- ### For teachers' workshops

  Which do you prefer to teach first, the present simple or the present continuous? Why?
  Would the type of class you were teaching make any difference to your choice?

- ### For non-native teachers

  How do the present tenses in English differ in concept from the present tenses in your own native language?

Tenses which have a relationship to present time

In this section you will find the tenses usually referred to as 'present' in grammars and reference works, the present simple and the present continuous. These tenses are discussed chiefly in their relation to present time and their use as future time markers is touched on only briefly here, but examined more fully under a separate listing (see page 63, Future).

Some readers will be surprised to find the present perfect and the present perfect continuous included in this section, but they are here because they have a relationship to present time. In fact this is probably their most important feature, unlike apparently similar tenses in other languages. It may help to clarify the nature of both these tenses if they are seen as describing actions which relate to the present rather than merely another form of 'past' tense. That is why the present perfect is called the **present** perfect.

The present emphatic (I **do** *walk* etc.) is not included in this section because it can be found in full in a separate section under Emphatic Tenses (Appendices, page 159). However, it is important that teachers do recognise a distinction between this and the normal form of the present simple. The Emphatics Section also includes a fuller discussion of stress and intonation, and the use of tag questions. This is not exhaustive, but should provide a guide for general teaching purposes. It has been given under Emphatic Tenses because intonation patterns become clearer when stressed, and broadly speaking, are very similar for all tenses.

PRESENT CONTINUOUS: analysis

Full Form	(Spoken Form)			Negative Form		(Spoken Form)	
I	am ('m)			I	am ('m)	not	
he				he			
she	is ('s)	looking		she	is ('s)	not	looking
it				it	(isn't)		
you				you			
we	are ('re)			we	are ('re)	not	
they				they	(aren't)		

Question Forms	
Are you looking?	Aren't you looking?
(*neutral question*)	(*expects answer 'yes'*)

Tag Questions	
You're looking, aren't you?	You're not looking, are you?
(*expects answer 'yes'*)	(*expects answer 'no'*)
I'm looking, aren't I?	I'm not looking, am I?
(*no form* amn't I**)	(*expects answer 'no'*)
(Also I'm looking, am I not?	
expects answer 'yes', very formal)	

Questions to draw the target

What am I doing? What are you doing?

What am I doing? ————————————⟶ You're *fishing* (or short answer: *Fishing*).
(only meaningful if the answer represents a guess)

What are you doing? ————————————⟶ I'm *reading* (*Reading*).
(only meaningful if the questioner cannot see or guess)

Is he (verb) or (verb)?
Is *he reading or writing?* ————————⟶ He's *reading* (*Reading*).

Why is he (verb)?
Why is he digging? ————————————⟶ He's *planting potatoes*.

Why has he got a (noun)?
Why has he got a hammer? ——————⟶ He's *mending the fence*.

Why is he/what's he doing+ place?
Why is he / what's he doing at the station? ——⟶ He's *waiting for a train*.

Notes

1 The spoken negative has two possible forms: He *isn't looking*, tends to be more neutral; *He's not looking*, more emphatic. To avoid confusing the student it is important not to interchange the two forms indiscriminately at an early stage.

2 **Stative and Dynamic Verbs.** Some verbs rarely take the present continuous form at all; these can be loosely defined as verbs which describe a state of affairs beyond the person's immediate active control, (If someone *is* a man, *has* a car, *knows* French, *hears* music, (as distinct from listening to it), or *likes* apples – there is little he can actually do to change this at the moment). These verbs are often called stative verbs, as distinct from dynamic verbs, where the person is actively doing something. However, even verbs which are usually stative, can take the present continuous, but they often mean something different.

The most common stative verbs are:

a **To Be.** Rarely occurs in the present continuous form except with adjectives of behaviour: *You are being silly*, which suggests a temporary, and deliberate act, or for mime and pretence: *I'm being an aeroplane*.

b **To Have.** In British English the verb *To have* in the present continuous may have two meanings:

• Where *have* implies present enjoyment or experience: *I'm having a bath*. This is dynamic and so is regular. For this usage American English prefers: *I'm taking a bath/a drink*.

• Where *have* indicates possession. This is stative and in the present continuous always carries a future meaning: *I'm having a new coat*. Have for health, is always regarded as stative: *I am having a cold* is therefore future, and suggests deliberate pretence (I'll deliberately pretend to have a cold because I don't want to go to work). British colloquial English prefers *I've got* to *I have* in stative senses; *I've got a cold* rather than I *have a cold*.

c **Verbs describing involuntary sensation** (*smell, see, hear*). These usually take the present simple, but the present continuous form exists for particular effect:

• Pretence: *I'm smelling roses* (used when someone is miming the act of smelling roses).

• A developing condition: *I'm not seeing very well these days* (I feel that my eyesight is getting worse).

• To suggest a progressive event: *I'm feeling sick* as opposed to I *feel sick*.

• To suggest deliberate action. This usage is often found with think/hope etc.:
  I'm thinking of going to the theatre tonight.
  I'm hoping to arrive at 6 o'clock.

3 Spelling:

a Verbs ending in vowel-consonant-*e* commonly drop *e* before *ing*: I *come*, I'm *coming*.

b Verbs ending in a short vowel followed by a single consonant commonly double the consonant before *ing*: I *run*, I'm *running*, (compare: I *sew*, I'm *sewing*).

c Verbs ending in *y* obey the rule and add *ing*, but verbs ending *ie* commonly change to *y* before *ing*: I *carry*, I'm *carrying*; I *tie*, I'm *tying*.

4 Stress on the auxiliary, or on the negative will produce an emphatic form of this tense:
  I **am** *doing my best*; I'm **not** *being silly*.

5 Phonetics:

a The contracted form *he's* is sometimes heard as *his*; *it's* as *is*.

b The last sound of the contracted auxiliary is lost when the following verb begins with the same consonant and may cause problems for beginners; *I'm mending*, *I'm ending*; *I'm meeting*, *I'm eating*; *he's sleeping*, *he's leaping*; *you're riding*, *you're hiding* etc.

c In verbs ending with *o*, a distinct /w/ sound is pronounced before *ing*: *going*.

M eaning and Function

It may be helpful to view the present continuous when used as a present tense as dealing with actions which began before the moment of speaking, are expected to continue past it, but are essentially transitory.

A *Temporary action* which began before the time of speaking, is continuing across it, and is not yet complete: I'm *walking at this moment.*

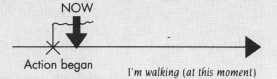

I'm walking (at this moment)

B *Temporary course of action*, fairly recently begun, currently engaged in, but not expected to be permanent: I'm *living in London.*

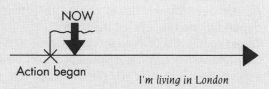

I'm living in London

C *Temporary habit* not necessarily engaged in at the moment of speech, but temporarily contracted for: I'm *watering his plants while he's away.*

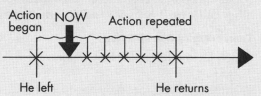

I'm watering his plants while he's away

D *Regrettable habit* with *always* (This is confusing for students as habit usually requires present simple.) I'm *always losing my keys.* This suggests that the speaker is constantly in a state of having lost the keys. (The action is repeated, but transitory; compare – I *always lose my keys*).

E *With verbs of hoping* etc. A more polite alternative to the present simple, especially in letters, invitations etc: We *are looking forward to seeing you;* I *am hoping to see you soon.* (Compare; I *hope to see you soon.*)
However, the present continuous is arguably most often used as a future tense (See page 65, Future Section)

F *Future action* (with future time marker). For plans already undertaken, and preliminary arrangements made. If other people are involved, arrangements are generally agreed between the parties.
I'm *picking her up at six* (she is expecting me).
We're *leaving tomorrow* (we have packed, bought our tickets etc).

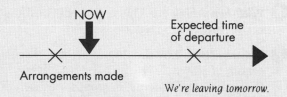

We're leaving tomorrow.

(Note: The time marker may be implied by earlier sentences and contexts. Verbs of sensation (e.g. *enjoying*) cannot be used in this future sense.)

a The verb *to have* in the sense of possession, I'm *having a red jumper,* can only have a future meaning and does not require a time marker.
b The form I'm *going to* (*London*) appears to be a present continuous and time marker, but may be a contracted form of the *Going to* future. (See page 69, Going to Future.)

Suggested Contexts

Ⓐ *Temporary individual action*:

This can be used to teach the meaning of individual vocabulary.

- Any clear mimed action. Beware of ambiguities: I'm *singing* probably means I *was singing*. If you choose I'm *talking* it becomes impossible to guess the meaning. I'm *sitting* can mean I'm *seated*.
- A series of pictures or a context (railway station) showing characters doing a variety of activities. (**See** *photocopiable page* **4**). These are also useful for practice. Once the students know or have seen all the pictures, the teacher chooses one and hides it. Students try to guess which: Is *he swimming*? No. Is *he running*? Yes. Then students select a picture, and guess in pairs or small groups.
- A video freeze-frame. (If well chosen, an activity stopped in mid-action can be identified or guessed, depending on the level of the students.)
- Taped sound effects. Students guess what 'X' is doing to produce the sounds they hear (practice only).
- Contrastive work with the present simple, based on pictures of people at work. What *does he do*? He's *a doctor*. What *is he doing*? He's *looking at the child*.
- For later revision, examine unusual methods of doing things, using mimes, or film and pictures of other cultures. What *is he doing*? He's *rubbing sticks together*. Why? He's *making fire*.

Ⓑ *Temporary course of action*:

- Role/play on the topic of a temporary stay (e.g. in England) *Where are you staying*? *Are you doing much shopping*?
- A similar context, or study habits, can be used for class questionnaires.

Ⓒ *Temporary habit*:

- Using an office, or similar context, give a list of jobs usually carried out by one employee, but shared among other staff when he is on holiday. Establish who is fulfilling these tasks by using an information gap exercise. Who's *making the coffee/buying the stamps/posting the letters while he's away*? (**See** *photocopiable page* **3**.)
- Role-play, in pairs. One student 'becomes' a customer asking for the manager, but gets a junior in his absence. (Intermediate.)

Ⓓ *Regrettable habit*, with *always*. This is probably best taught as an idiom, at intermediate or advanced level.

Ⓔ **With *hope/think*** etc. This is probably best taught as part of series on letter-writing, polite, formal conversation and invitations.

Ⓕ *Future action.* This should be taught as a specific future. It is important to identify the pre-arranged nature of plans.

- Diary context. Students, in groups are given different fixed engagements in their diaries, and asked to agree a date for example an informal dinner party, I *can't come on Monday*, I'm *babysitting* etc.
- Students are given the 'diary' of e.g. a pop-star and try to find times for an interview appointment.
- A contrastive lesson with other futures, showing that this tense denotes plans less easily changed than some others (see also page 63, Future Section).

Learner Error: Form, Spelling and Pronunciation

1 Students attempt to make present continuous forms of stative verbs when these are not appropriate, especially *to have* for possession: *I am having a cold* for I *have a cold*; and verbs of sensation *I am smelling fish* for I *smell fish*.

2 Contracted forms create difficulties for beginners. Students have been known to avoid using the contracted form because they regard it as slovenly. They need to be reassured that this form is the accepted norm in conversation.

a He's may be heard as his or is: What's he doing? *His swimming. Is swimming.*

b You're may be interpreted as your: *Your swimming, his swimming, my swimming.*

c The last letter of the contracted auxiliary is lost or assimilated in native speech, and as a result verbs are sometimes misheard, and misunderstood or mis-produced: I'm meeting / I'm eating; He's taking / *he's staking*, or *he staking*. (This can be avoided by choosing verbs carefully at an early stage.)

d We're is sometimes misheard by false beginners as where or were or vice versa.

3 Spelling (*comeing, runing* etc.) may be a persistent problem.

4 The two variant forms of the spoken negative (you aren't/you're not) may cause problems if teachers are unaware of this. Beginners may be taught one version, and find that the teacher is inadvertantly using the other in classroom interaction.

5 The tag/question form, I am, aren't I? Aren't I coming? etc. appears grammatically confusing. Am I not is a possible written form, but is not commonly used in conversation now, unless for particular effect.

Learner Error: Meaning and Function

1 Many languages have a single present tense covering contexts of both present continuous and present simple in English.

a Where the L1 tense resembles the present simple (e.g. French), students may avoid the present continuous altogether: Where is she?* She plays tennis.*

b Where the L1 tense resembles the present continuous, students may use that in all contexts (e.g. Indian languages): *I am hoping you are well.*

2 Some languages (e.g. Arabic) have no separate verb for To be and may produce forms such as *He running*; others (e.g. Spanish) have a form which parallels the present continuous in some senses (often that of single, interrupted action).

3 Statements such as I'm sitting (down) may cause problems, because in many languages (e.g. French) the state of being seated, and the action of sitting require different forms. Students may attempt to mark this in English with I'm sat or by a present continuous/present simple distinction.

4 Intermediate students have difficulty in distinguishing the stative and dynamic uses of To have for possession, and verbs of sensation: I am having a bath, I am having a cold.

5 The always idiom (I am always losing my key./I always lose my keys.), can cause problems for those who feel they have understood the distinction between simple and continuous tenses.

6 The future usage is confusing to many students, who prefer to use will.

a Used inappropriately it can sound rude: Would you like to come out tonight? I'm studying. The student may not intend the unarguable nature of the rejection.

b When the time marker is now the tense is not seen as future, but I'm leaving now actually means imminently.

c Students attempt to make future versions of verbs of sensation etc: We're going out to dinner. We're having a Chinese meal. *We're enjoying it.*

7 Students may avoid or misunderstand the present continuous in when, while and if clauses, where the action is often repeated. They may substitute the present simple in all cases and produce: I listen to the radio when I wash the dishes for I listen to the radio when I'm washing the dishes.

PRESENT SIMPLE: analysis

Full Form		(no contracted Spoken Form)	Negative Form		(Spoken Form)	
I you we they	walk		I you we they	do not (don't)		walk
he she it	walks		he she it	does not (doesn't)		

Question Forms	
Do you walk to school? (*neutral question*)	Don't you walk to school? (*expects answer 'yes'*)
Tag Questions (greatly affected by intonation patterns)	
You walk to school, don't you? (*expects answer 'yes'*)	You don't walk to school, do you? (*expects answer 'no'*)

Questions to draw the target

What do you do (+ time marker) (adverbial) (place)?

What do you do on Tuesday(s)?
- *best/usually?*
- *at school?* ————————————————————→ *I/We study.*

Do you (verb) or(verb)?
Do you walk or drive to school? —————————→ *I walk.*

How do you (+ verb, especially of process)?
How do you get to school? ————————————→ *I walk.*

What do you do? (requesting instruction)
What do you do? ——————————————————→ *You put the disc in the slot and push the*
(*How does it work?*) *button.*

Notes

Form:

1 In conversational English the question *What do you do?* is usually an enquiry about a person's occupation or profession, e.g: *What does he do? He's a doctor.*
(The impersonal *'you'* form, requesting instruction is more suitable for a post elementary level.)

2 In the negative the present simple is the same as the present emphatic (see page 160, Appendices), except for stress. Students may produce an emphatic answer instead of a neutral one by giving too much stress to *don't* or *doesn't.*

3 Adding a *do* auxiliary in the statement form produces the present emphatic instead of the present simple. (I *do walk* for I *walk.*)

4 Full verbs which also act as auxiliaries: *To Be, To Do, To Have.*

a In the full (statement) form:

The verbs *To Be* and *To Have* form irregular present tenses. I *am/you are/**he is** /we are/they are.* I *have/you have/* **he has**/*we have/they have.*
To Do is regular, obeying the spelling rules for verbs ending in *o,*

b In the negative:

* *To Be* is always irregular; I *am not/you are not/he is not/we are not/they are not.* There are two contracted forms *I'm not/you're not/he's not/we're not/they're not*; and *I'm not / (the form I amn't is now obsolete) you aren't/he isn't/we aren't/they aren't.* The absence of *amn't* leads to a very irregular tag question: *I'm late* **aren't I** ? The form *I'm late, am I not?* exists but is considered too formal for most interactions.

* *To Have* in British speech usually forms a negative on the pattern: I *haven't/you haven't/he hasn't/we haven't/they haven't.* American speech, however, forms a negative on the regular pattern, and this is becoming more widely adopted: I *don't have/you don't have* etc. Note that in any sentence where *have* refers to possession British English commonly substitutes the present perfect form *have got* in conversational or idiomatic uses, in both the negative and statement form. Hence: I *don't have a car* (American); I *haven't got a car* (British), I *haven't a car* (formal).

* *To Do,* when it is a full verb in its own right, forms a regular negative; e.g. I *do my homework,* I *don't do my homework* not *I don't my homework.**

5 Spelling: some verbs change the spelling before the third person *s*;

a Verbs ending in consonant- *y* commonly change to *ies*: I *hurry/he hurries,* I *try/he tries* etc.

b Verbs ending in sibilant clusters (*ss/sh/ch/tch, x*) commonly add *es* in third person: I *pass/he passes*; I *wash/he washes*; I *reach/he reaches*; I *watch/he watches*; I *box/he boxes.* This additional syllable is commonly pronounced / iz / (see note 6).

c Verbs ending in single *o* commonly add *es* in third person: I *go/he goes*; I *do/he does.*

6 Phonetics:

a Verbs which end in *se, ce, ze,* sibilant clusters or *dge* pronounce final *es* as /iz/
e.g. *he close, he voices, he freezes/he passes, he washes, he touches, he watches, he judges.*

b Verbs which end in the sounds /k/p/t/f/ pronounce *s* as /s/ in the third person.
e.g. *he hops, he hopes, he walks, he wakes, he pats, he hates, he sniffs.*

c Verbs ending in other consonants or vowels pronounce *s* as /z/ in third person.
e.g. *he rubs, he frees, he hugs, he pulls, he hums, he runs, he woos, he roars, he bows, he loves.*

d The third person *he does* is phonetically irregular: I *do* /du:/ but *he does* /dʌz/.

Meaning and Function

Many grammars give a long list of realisations of this tense; essentially it may be helpful to see it as a timeless tense for actions which are always, repeatedly or generally true; or actions encapsulated in a single instant (with no reference to past or future). (Compare the present continuous, where the action has commenced, is in progress,not yet completed, and likely to be transitory.)

(A) The tense is used to denote truths:

a **Habitual truths:** *He smokes 40 cigarettes a day.*
b **Eternal and unvarying truths:** *Jesus lives. The Koran says …*
c **Recurrent truths:** *The sun rises in the east.*
d **Permanent human truths:** *I like sweets. I live here* (Compare: *I'm living here temporarily.*)
e **General truths:** *English people drink a lot of tea.*
f **Mathematical and scientific truths:** *Two and two make four. Water boils at 100°c.*
g **Internal truths**: verbs of *thinking, knowing, wishing* etc; expressing a mental state:
I think he's very nice. I know it's here.

(B) **It is used for giving instructions, directions, or demonstrations**, often with the impersonal *you*; *You beat the eggs, and then you add the flour.* In many situations the *you* is dropped, giving the imperative, which gives direct instructions; *Beat the eggs and then add the flour.*
Nowadays many demonstrations, especially on T.V. use the more conversational form; *I beat the eggs and then I add the flour.*
The form *one beats the eggs*, although grammatically correct, is very formal, and is now rare in conversation.

(C) **The present simple is often used as a narrative device**, for dramatic effect in certain situations.
• In commentaries, especially those about activities where the action is swift, e.g. football: *He passes the ball to Clark, he swerves, aims and scores.* (Compare this with commentary on horseracing, where the action is sustained; *Pink Satin is coming up on the rails, he's overtaking Rover Boy, but Little Nell is pulling away …*)
• In headlines and captions, (*Reagan meets Gorbochev*). Perhaps the tense is seen as encapsulating a dramatic truth. (Note that when the present simple is used for headlines and captions, punctuation and grammar are often irregular. Articles are often omitted, and all or most of the words may begin with capital letters, or be printed wholly in capitals.)
• In very informal or colloquial spoken narrative: '*This man goes into a restaurant and he says, "Do you serve frogs?" The waiter says, "Yes", so he says, "Right, I'll have a coffee for myself and some flies for my frog."'* (Note that this use is not regarded as very educated.)

(D) **In describing feelings and senses**, especially sudden ones, over which the speaker has no control.
I feel sick (suddenly, but certainly); (compare: *I'm feeling sick*, continuing state and less urgent).
I hear bells etc. (suddenly) (Compare; *I can hear bells.*)

(E) **With a future time marker the tense gives a 'timetable future**; usually for schedules (especially transport); *My bus leaves at three.*

(F) **After when, to form a time clause**. This usually occurs with:
• The main verb in the present e.g. *I catch a bus when it rains. When you heat ice, it melts.*
This creates the general condition expressing habitual, general or eternal rules. *When* in such sentences can be replaced by either *if* or *whenever* without changing the meaning.

- The main verb in the future. Most commonly the verb is in the *will* future, *When I get home, I'll make tea*, but other forms are possible; *You're going to laugh when you see him*.
In this usage the *when* clause has a future time reference.

Special Note: Some usages, especially *To be*, *To have* for possession, are sometimes referred to as stative uses, because they describe a 'state of affairs' rather than an action.

Suggested Contexts

a *Habitual truths* :

- Use a picture series showing a daily routine. Introduce pictures in the present continuous: *It's eight o'clock, what's he doing now?* Then contrast this with real time; *Is it eight o'clock now? Is he eating breakfast now? No, he eats breakfast every day at eight o'clock* etc. (This method requires previous knowledge of the present continuous, and the ability to tell the time.)(**See photocopiable pages 1 and 2**.)
- Use a weekly timetable (e.g. school) in the same way. (Note: English native speakers should take care not to interchange *on Tuesday* and *on Tuesdays* when introducing this to beginners.)
- Use a calendar, showing seasonal activities, in the same way. (Note: Take care that activities are the kind engaged in regularly.)
  The following should be used for practice only as the tense is not fully contextualised:
- Collect pictures of different sports equipment, (or similar) and allocate them to different imaginary characters, or to the students themselves: *X rides a horse. Does Y play tennis? No, he plays football*.
- Use a tabulated chart which shows the frequency of events and adverbs of frequency; *Does he ever play cricket? Yes, sometimes. Football? No, never*.
- Elicit a list of habitual activities: *What do you do on Saturday night? I (sometimes) go to the disco*.

b and c *Eternal and recurrent truths:*

- Scientific contexts, especially geographic ones: *The earth spins. (Is is doing it now? Yes.) The sun rises. (Is it doing it now? No.)*
- Holiday brochures, especially those giving descriptions of places, prices, and services.
- Reading maps.
- Reading timetables.

d *Permanent human truths:*

Often introduced functionally, for survival, in certain set phrases. (*Do you like sugar? Where do you live?*) The form of the rest of the tense can be taught from these phrases, but the time reference cannot. Post elementary students may need to distinguish the two uses.

e *General truths* :

Comparisons are a useful device here, but note that a short answer is sometimes the natural response to direct questions. Interpreting graphs, information gap work or writing can avoid this.

- Comparing customs: *What do you do in summer in India? What do English people do?*
- Reading graphs/tables/timetables: *Women live longer than men. This bus is quicker/leaves earlier*.

f   *Mathematical and scientific truths:*

- Probably more appropriate for intermediate students and for English for Special Purposes (E.S.P.) learners. They can be taught from simple sums, but there are a number of idiomatic pitfalls. (e.g. *Two twos are four; twice two is four; put down three and carry one.*)
- Survival idioms are taught at an early stage, and functionally: *What does that come to? That costs 5p. How much is it?* etc.

g   *Internal truths:*

Some verbs require this pattern, and they are required for survival.

- May be taught as Ad above and in same lessons: *Do you want a cup of tea?*
- Other verbs may be taught transactionally in quizzes, (*Do you know?*) or discussion, (*Do you think?*).

B *Giving instructions* etc.

a   The imperative may be taught transactionally, (students are asked to do things) and need not form part of a specific lesson. Practise by using activities requiring the students to follow directions.

- Treasure hunts using real space, or maps. *Turn left at the corner, what is opposite …? What number is the house with the green gate?*
- Folding a paper hat, assembling items in a given order, or drawing a picture.

b   For the impersonal *you: You put the potatoes in the water and boil for 5 minutes.*
(If the same action produces the same result regardless of who does it – the *you* is impersonal.)

- Giving and asking directions based on a street map; *You turn left.*
- Students explain how to do things, or use equipment: *You put the flour in the bowl.*

c   For the impersonal *one.* Teach at post elementary levels only, for written work.

C *Narrative uses:*

Probably best taught at higher levels.
Commentaries, headlines and captions may be taught as part of a series of lessons on newspapers. Students write headlines/captions. The present used informally in a spoken narrative form might be taught for recognition only.

D *Feelings and senses, especially sudden ones:*

These can be taught functionally. They may be isolated for a separate lesson on comparing tenses at post elementary level.

E *Timetable future:*

(Best taught after other future tenses, and contrasted with them.)
It may be taught as a future tense at intermediate stage, using timetables, brochures, travel information. For practice, students decide on a destination, route, times etc. then explain their 'timetable' to others.

F *In 'when' clauses:*

a   General condition.

- May be used transactionally in general knowledge quizzes (especially where the questions are devised by students): *When do birds fly south? In Autumn/When it gets cold.* (N.B. Invites short answers.)
- Elicit facts about seasons, customs or scientific truths; *When do they hatch? When the monsoon begins* or practise in written work;. *The eggs hatch when the monsoon comes.*

b   With the main verb in the future (this can only be taught when other futures are known).

- Use for checking the relationship between future events. (Note: *When will he know? When he gets home.*)

Learner Error: Form, Spelling and Pronunciation

1 The third person *s* seems counter to the English plural rule. (**S** is the common plural noun ending, but marks a singular verb.) Students may:

a omit it altogether: *He come.*

b add it to the plural verb instead: *They comes.*

c add it to the written form but not pronounce it (especially where a final *s* is not pronounced in the mother tongue, e.g. French).

2 The *do* auxiliary in negative and interrogative forms is often omitted, on the pattern of L1 or by analogy with *to be*: *You not go*, *You gon't*, *You walk?* *Walk you?* or even *Is you walk?* It is most often omitted with the base verb *To do*: * Did you your homework? I didn't it.*

3 Conversely, the *Do* auxiliary may be inserted in the statement, forming an unwanted emphatic, I **do** *walk.*

4 Phonetics:

a In the early stages the question forms may create problems. *Does he* and *does she* are not discriminated; *do we* is often heard as *do he*.

b /s/z/iz/ endings are used indiscriminately. (They may even be interpreted as gender markers on the L1 pattern (e.g. Arabic speakers), because many 'female' occupations take /iz/; *she washes/brushes*. Hence, they may produce *she comiz*.)

5 Spelling variations create problems: *he gos, she watchs.*

6 Once the tense is learnt, the rules may be applied to *To be*. *You don't be, don't you be* etc.

Learner Error: Meaning and Function

1 Many languages have a single present tense covering the contexts of both present simple and present continuous in English.

a When the L1 tense resembles the present simple, (e.g. French) students tend to use the present simple in all contexts; *Where is she? She plays tennis?*

b Where the L1 tense resembles the present continuous, (Indian languages) students tend to avoid the present simple altogether; *I am hoping you are well*. *I am playing tennis at five every day.*

2 Students may use the stative (present simple) form of *to have, to be* or verbs of perception, when the dynamic (present continuous) form would be appropriate, and vice versa. At an intermediate stage this may require a specific lesson.

3 Some Eastern languages have a tense marking eternal (religious) truth. Speakers of these languages avoid using the same tense to deal with personal (trivial) habit. Hence: *God lives. I am living.*

4 Future clauses with *when* are often made on the mother tongue pattern: *I'll make tea when I will get home* (because both events are future).

PRESENT PERFECT: analysis

Full Form (Spoken Form)			Negative Form (Spoken Form)		
I you we they	have ('ve)	a) walked	I you we they	have not (haven't)	walked
		b) drunk			drunk
he she it	has ('s)	b) run	he she it	has not (hasn't)	run

a *Regular verbs*: use a past participle identical in form to the past simple. b *Irregular verbs*: use a past participle which usually differs in form from the past simple.

Question Forms	
Have you walked? (*neutral unless stressed*)	Haven't you walked? (*expects answer 'yes'*)

Tag Questions	
You've walked, haven't you? (*expects answer 'yes'*)	You haven't walked, have you? (*expects answer 'no' or expresses surprise*)

Questions to draw the target

What have you done (+ time marker)?

What have you done today? ———————⟶ *I've written three letters.*
- since 3 o'clock?

Why are you (+ verb/adjective)?
Why are you walking? ———————⟶ *I've missed my bus.*
- annoyed?

Note: Adjectives of physical state often require the present perfect continuous.

What have you done?
What have you done? ———————⟶ *I've broken a cup* (short answer: *Broken a cup*).

What has happened? (in the story)
What has happened? ———————⟶ *He's fallen down a hole.*

Why do you think ...?
Why do you think you are qualified for the job? ——⟶ *I've worked in an office before.*

How do you know ...?
How do you know about that film? ———————⟶ *I've seen it / I've read about it.*

Notes

1 Form:

Regular verbs form a past participle with *ed* – similar to the simple past form.

Irregular verbs:

a Some form a past participle which is similar to the (irregular) past simple: I *make/I made/I had made*; I *think/I thought/I had thought*.

b Many form a past participle which adds an *en*. This may be added to the base verb form:
I *eat/I ate/I have eaten*: I *fall/I fell/I have fallen*: I *am/I was/I have been* (root form *be*).
This ending may be modified:

– to *n* especially where the base verb ends with *e* or *ow*:
I *take/I took/I have taken*. I *know/I knew/I have known*.

– to *ne* where the base verb ends in *o*: I *do/I did/I have done*. I *go/I went/I have gone*.

c The *en* ending may be added to the past version of the base verb:
I *choose/I chose/I have chosen*; I *forget/I forgot/I have forgotten*; I *break/I broke/I have broken*.

d The past participle may be identical to the present or base form of the verb:
I *run/I ran/I have run*; I *come/I came/I have come*; I *put/I put/I have put*.

e The past participle may be formed by interior vowel change and be different from either base or past forms:
I *drink/I drank/I have drunk*; I *sing/I sang/I have sung*; I *sink/I sank/I have sunk*.
There are no easily discernible rules to guide foreign learners, and apparently similar verbs may produce past participles on different patterns: I *forget/I forgot/I have forgotten*; I *get/I got/I have got*. (But N.B. American usage I *have gotten*.)

2 Phonetics:

a The stress is on the past participle, not on the auxiliary *have* except in the emphatic form.

b The contracted *s* may be lost, *she stolen it,* or understood as *is*, *He is walked.*

c The contracted form *ve* is sometimes realised as *of* or *half*.

3 Note: The form I *have been* (derived from *to be*) is used and perceived as the present perfect of *to go* in some circumstances: He *has been to London* (He went to London and returned) but He *has gone to London* (and that is where he is now). Note: There is no form *I *am to London.**

Meaning and Function

The Present Perfect shows the present situation in relation to past action; that is, how the past is relevant to now.

A **For uncompleted action where both actor and results remain** (with a time marker showing past reference):

a A single, continuous action: London *has stood beside the Thames for hundreds of years*.
(Compare past simple forms e.g. London *stood* which suggests that London no longer exists.)

b A repeated or habitual action or truth: My *mother has always played tennis*.

B **For an action which took place in an identified period of time, which is not yet over:** I've read a book *this morning* (it is still 'this morning') compare: I *read a book this morning* (it may be afternoon now). The usage suggests that the activity has some present consequence; I've *seen her this morning* (she is probably still here). Compare: I *saw her this morning* (but now she may be anywhere).

C **For an action which took place in the past; but whose results are still present;** I've spilt the milk (it's still on the floor). Have *you finished your lunch*? (are you now full/free?).

D **For an action (single or repeated) which took place in the past, but which still relates to the present:**

I've studied French (and remember it. Therefore I can help you, empathise with you, or tell you about it). Compare: I studied French (but am making no present claim about it, unless perhaps you ask); I've seen that film (and I remember it, therefore I can discuss it with you/advise you about it/do not wish to see it again); Compare: I saw that film (but I am making no present claim about it).

E **With the time markers 'just',' yet', 'already', 'still',** the present perfect can also indicate the attitude of the speaker.

Just: a vague time marker showing that the time is either 'now' or very close to it, (Compare He's just setting off, I'm just going.) With the present perfect it is used to indicate immediate past time, whose results are very clear:

I've just washed the floor (so it's still wet). He's just finished breakfast (so he's ready for school). He's just left (so you are too late to speak to him). Sometimes this is strengthened to only just: He's only just left (so if you hurry you'll probably catch up with him).

N.B. With any tense just may also mean 'simply'. Hence: I've just given up may mean I gave up a moment ago or I've simply given up.

Yet: suggests that the speaker believes that the result of the action should or could be present 'now'.

* With questions: Have you painted my fence yet? (You promised to paint the fence, is it finished, how long will you take to finish it?).
  It also occurs with negative questions, as a reproof: Haven't you painted my fence yet? (I expected you to do it before now. Do it soon).
* With negatives: I haven't painted the fence yet (I intended to paint the fence before this moment, but I haven't done it. I intend to paint the fence soon).

Already suggests that the speaker believes that the action is over, and that the present result is surprisingly quick. It is used in:

* Statements: He's already eaten it (There is none left. That was surprisingly quick).
* Questions: Have you already seen it? (What a pity. We could have seen it together).
* It is rarely used in negatives, except after if and when or as a question or exclamation:
  Hasn't the train gone already? (that is surprising). It hasn't gone already! (Bother!)
  Note that in American usage the past simple commonly follows these time markers, with the same meaning. Hence: He just left. Did you make your bed yet? He ate it already.

Still: expresses the speaker's surprise that the action continues to affect the present moment. It is used chiefly with:

* Negatives: He still hasn't left (I am surprised that he is here now).
* Have got: Have you still got that hat? (I am surprised that you did not throw it away long ago, or, it must be very old by now).
  Note: American usage prefers the present simple with still: He still isn't gone. Do you still have that hat?

Always can be used as a time marker for actions continued up to the present time: Have you always lived in London? (I know you live in London now, was this always the case?).
It may be used in a statement or a negative form: I've always lived in London; I haven't always lived in London.
In negative statements always can also mean that the action has not been regularly performed as/when it should have been: He hasn't always done his homework (he sometimes forgot, or neglected it), this does not imply that there was a continuous period when he did not do his homework.

Ever and **Never** are used for remembered experience; *ever* is used only in question forms: *Have you ever lived in London?* (I know you don't live there now, but did you once?) The answer, if positive, is usually given in the past simple: *Yes, I lived there for ten years when I was a child* (a period of time now over) or with *used to*: *Yes, I used to live there when I was a child* (past habit, now over). **Never** is used chiefly in statement forms, to deny experience: *No, I've never lived in England.*

F **Future uses:**

a · Like all present tenses, the present perfect follows *when* to create a future time marker: *I'll come when I've written this letter.* (I will write this letter first, and when that is complete, I will come.). *After* and *as soon as* can be substituted for *when* in this usage, but these are not used with the negative.

b **Before:** *He'll come before I've written the letter* (The letter will not be complete before he comes. He will arrive while I am writing it or before I begin it, but the letter (result) will not be finished). It is never used with the negative.

Suggested Contexts

Note: Contexts must show the present relevance of the tense. It is helpful to show this schematically, in contrast to the past simple. The past simple is represented as a single block of time, of any duration, any distance from 'now', but unconnected.

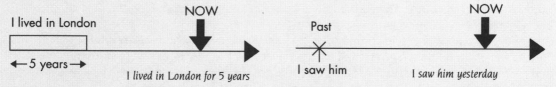

I lived in London for 5 years   *I saw him yesterday*

The present perfect covers a period of time, of any length, begun in the past but attached or related to 'now'. A piece of elastic, with a drawing pin attaching it to a 'now' marker provides a visual demonstration. Once the pin is withdrawn (the relevance to 'now'), the tense required is the past simple. (This also assists with teaching *for* and *since*; *for* is represented by the elastic, which can stretch to any length; *since* becomes a second drawing pin from which it is stretched to 'now')

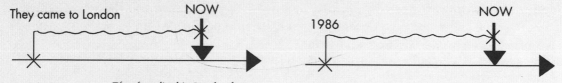

They have lived in London for years   *I have lived in London since 1986*

A **For uncompleted action where both actor and results remain:**

* Geographical or currently relevant historical information from fact sheets. (This forms a useful contrast with the past simple.) *The building was a school, but it has been a hotel for three years* etc.
* An anniversary; golden wedding/retirement): *We have been married for …*
* Protest against new rules, a new road, or other changes: *We've always played tennis here.*

B **Where the identified time span is not yet over:**

* The diary entries of a day's events, some of which are done, others changed: *What has he done today?* (Useful to contrast with: *What did he do this morning?*)
* A list of the week's necessary tasks. The students are told that it is now Wednesday night, and asked to produce a timetable for Thursday, by finding out from each other which tasks are already complete and what remains to be done. The activity works well as an information gap exercise, or small group work, and is most effective if some activities are repeated.

C *Where the action was in the past but the results are still present*:

- A picture series, showing expressions (horror/surprise/exhaustion/delight etc.) The students explain why: *What has happened? He's seen a ghost/won the pools* etc.
- A picture story leads to an elicited narrative. Begin in the present continuous (*What's he doing?*), then introduce a new picture showing a strong clue (e.g. a hospital) and ask *What's happened?*
- Make a check list of activities to be done before going on holiday (for example). Then use an information gap technique to establish – *Which tasks have we done? What have we forgotten?* The same context can be used, with groups of students creating their own lists and cross-checking with other groups: Group A: *Have you turned off the electricity?* Group B: *Yes. Have you emptied the freezer?* Marks may be given for each point which the opponents missed. (Any kind of preparation, wall-papering, methods of money-raising, may be used for this exercise).
- Using a video, one group is shown part of a story, then the video is stopped. The group must explain the scene on the screen to others who have not seen the film. (The past action should be chosen for its present consequences: *The man has hidden in the cupboard because ...*)
- Use a simple scientific or visual experiment, where changes take place. (e.g. litmus paper etc.) *What has happened?*
- Students work in pairs to examine something (e.g. each other's appearance). Each secretly makes changes, each partner must say what the other has done.

D *Where the memory of past events is present and relevant*:

- Interviews, explaining past (relevant) experience.
- Students are given comparative biographies from which they try to choose the best candidate for a job.
- Students compile or interpret comparative graphs: *Which company has made the greatest profit?*
- "Guess who?" Students are given the life experience of a mystery personality (who must be alive), and try to guess their identity. Students can produce their own data for others to guess.
- "Guess my secret". Each student chooses an unusual event from his past life, and submits it to the teacher, (*I've ridden an elephant*), others attempt to guess. They may ask questions in any tense; *Can anyone do it? Did you do it in France? Have you done it many times?*
- Questionnaires on the students' own lives, especially their hobbies and spare-time activities.

E *With time markers*:

Just:

- Give the diary entries for a day's events for several people, nominating times: *Where is x now? He's just gone to the dentist* etc. (to stress imminence).
- Dialogue or role-play set in an office, where a secretary is making excuses: *He's just gone out. But I've just seen him* etc.
- Using either pictures or photographs elicit descriptions from the students in terms of the actions shown; *He's just kicked the ball and it's broken the window.*

Yet/Already: (usually taught together)

- Give or elicit a list of tasks or visits to be completed. Groups choose six priorities and cross-check.
  Group A: *Have you seen Notre Dame yet? They haven't done it yet. We've done it already.*
- Compare the photographs or sketches of an unfinished project against a plan of the completed project, (drawn or written): *What have they done already? What haven't they done yet?*
- Role-play in which a customer is asking for his car, for example, on which repairs are incomplete.

Still: (usually taught after *yet* and *already*)

- The contexts suggested for *yet* and *already* are also suitable for *still*, but *still* is used here to express even greater surprise: *They still haven't seen Notre Dame/planted trees/painted it.*
- A reunion in which old friends ask about old possessions, habits, or ambitions: *Have you still got that car? I still haven't seen it.* The exercise may be based on fact sheets, or run as a role-play or for dialogue-building.

F **Future uses:**

- Students are given instructions out of sequence, and asked to record them, (*You do A when/after/ before you have done B.*), then give reasons; '*If you haven't got X, you can't do Y.*'
- A video or story is interrupted. Students predict the outcome; *He'll arrive before she's hidden it* etc.

Learner Error: Form, Spelling and Pronunciation

1 Past participle irregularity leads to false patterning: I *think* may become *I have thunk* etc.

2 Contracted forms create phonic problems:

a /aɪ hæf/, /aɪ haːf/, /aɪf/ for I *have*
b Contracted s understood as *is*: *He is broken it.* This leads to confusions with the passive.
c Contracted forms are sometimes lost altogether: I *felt* for I've *felt*; he *stopped* for He's *stopped*.

Learner Error: Meaning and Function

Conceptually this is a very difficult tense. Here are some common reasons for error.

1 Students use *gone* for *been* and vice versa; *I've gone to London today.* *He's not here. He's been out.* They may also create other incorrect forms of *be* on the pattern of the present perfect; *I've been to London today.* I *was to London yesterday.*

2 Students fail to understand the concept of the tense. They may avoid it altogether except in set expressions (*Have you got/ever ...?*), usually substituting the past simple. This is closer to American usage, but does not cover all meanings; *Have you eaten?* enquires about present hunger, rather than past activity.

3 Most Western European languages have a form which appears similar, and students from these language groups often use the present perfect incorrectly as a direct equivalent: *After I have visited my aunt I have gone to the shop*; *I have eaten my dinner yesterday.*

4 In some other languages there are ways to indicate incomplete action. The present perfect may be used incorrectly for this: *I have eaten my dinner when he came* for I *was eating my dinner*; other students may think that it can never be used for incomplete action and produce: *London stood by the Thames for 1000 years* for *London has stood ...*

5 Where the action is not yet complete, students may use the present simple or present continuous, especially with *since* (French/Spanish/Indian languages); *I am knowing him since I was small.*

6 The similarity of the mother tongue form may lead to the use of *be* as an auxiliary with some verbs, creating an apparent passive, I *was left.*

PRESENT PERFECT CONTINUOUS: analysis

Full Form (Spoken Form)			Negative Form (Spoken Form)		
I you we they	have ('ve)	been eating	I you we they	have not (haven't) ('ve not, *rare*)	been eating
he she it	has ('s)		he she it	has not (hasn't) ('s not)	

Question Form	
Have you been eating? (*neutral, but may express challenge*)	Haven't you been eating? (*expects answer 'yes'*)

Tag Questions	
You've been eating, haven't you? (*expects answer 'yes', often a challenge*)	You haven't been eating, have you? (*expects answer 'no' or expresses surprise/challenge*)

Questions to draw the target

What have you been doing? ——————————⟶ (draws the target, but is often not neutral, requiring explanation or excuse)

Why are you (so) (+ adjective)?
Why are you so thirsty? ——————————⟶ *I've been running.*

What's the matter with (+ object under repair)?
What's the matter with the car? ——————————⟶ *It's been leaking oil.*

When do you (+ physical symptoms)?
When do you feel giddy? ——————————⟶ *When I've been bending down.*
(may also draw: *When I bend down.*)

This tense is often used as an explanation or excuse and elicited by comment rather than question:

I'm sorry I'm late. ——————————⟶ *That's all right, we haven't been waiting long.*
You've lost weight. *Yes, I've been dieting.*

Notes

1 Stress on the auxiliary *have/has*, or on *not* in the negative, produces an emphatic form.

2 Spelling:

a Verbs ending in a short vowel followed by a single consonant often double the consonant before adding *-ing*.

b Verbs ending vowel-consonant-*e* commonly drop *e* before adding *-ing*: Compare: I *hope*, I *have been hoping*; I *hop*, I *have been hopping*.

c Verbs ending in *y* conform to the rule adding *-ing*, but verbs ending *ie* commonly change to *y*. Compare: I *cry*, I *have been crying*; I *lie*, I *have been lying*.

3 Stative uses:

a Verbs describing a state (e.g. to be) rarely take a continuous form, as this often suggests pretence, like mime or acting: *What have the children been doing all afternoon? They've been being aeroplanes.*

b Verbs of involuntary sensation (*smell/hear/see*) take the present perfect continuous only to suggest a developing symptom: I *have been seeing double*; or state of affairs: I've *been seeing a lot of him lately*.

c The verb *to have* for possession (stative use) can also be used for progressive physical symptoms: I *have been having headaches lately*; or for repeated acquisition: I've *been having a lot of letters from viewers recently*. In either case, British often substitutes *to get* for *to have*.

4 The present perfect form I *have been to London* has no continuous variant; there is no form *I *have been being to London** for example. Forms such as I *have been swimming* are probably best considered as the present perfect of a base verb I *go swimming*.

5 Phonetics:

a The contracted form of *has* is identical to the contracted form of *is*, even in spelling, and are often confused.

b Where the participle begins with the sound /n/ the word *been* is sometimes heard and understood as *be*, producing forms such as *I *have be knitting.**

6 The form I've *not been eating* (compare I *haven't been eating*) is unusual, but still encountered (especially about health) I've *not been feeling well lately*.

Meaning and Function

The tense chiefly focuses on continuous or repeated activity, engaged in before the present, but relevant to it, and on the continuous duration of that action. The action is seen as temporary (i.e. not a permanent truth or usual habit) and may or may not have been completed at the time of speaking.

A **Used as an explanation for the present situation or the appearance of the speaker**, caused by the recent and ongoing nature of the activity, which may or may not be completed :
I *won't shake hands, I've been baking* (my hands are covered in flour, I don't usually look like this).
I *must sit down, I've been running* (and now I'm exhausted, I am not usually breathless).

B **To account for a period of time now finishing**. The tense indicates that the action filled the time.

a As an excuse for failure to be somewhere, or do something, which was expected by the listener.
I'm *sorry I'm late, I've been seeing the headmaster* (so I have just arrived).
I *didn't iron your shirt, I've been cooking all morning* (this morning is fully accounted for).

b With a time marker, the tense draws attention to the uninterrupted nature of the activity, and by implication, the length of the period itself. This is a common conversational usage, and is often a complaint. In this usage the action is usually incomplete, or ceases at the moment of speaking: *I've been waiting for you for two hours* (I'm still here, and I have done nothing else. You've come). *They've been promising to build it for years* (the promise is continually renewed, but no building).

(C) **It is used to draw attention to the repeated or continuous nature of an action or habit resulting in present expertise or knowledge**. This usage usually includes a time marker: *I've been learning French for ten years* (I know some)/*I've been living here since 1970* (I know the area).

(D) **It is used for new, temporary habits** which have become constant or continuous (often with a time marker): *He's been seeing a lot of her lately. He's been doing a lot of wood-carving.*

(E) **It is often used in talking about health, to describe new and developing symptoms**: *I've been getting/having headaches. I've been putting on a lot of weight.*

(F) **With verbs of wishing/hoping** etc. The tense is a polite device, suggesting that the wish or thought was constantly in the speaker's mind; *I've been looking forward to meeting you / hoping to meet you.* With mean/intend etc., the tense shows a recognition that the speaker has failed in his/her duty; *I've been meaning to visit her* (I know I should have visited her, but I haven't).

Suggested Contexts

(A) *Explaining the present situation or appearance:*

- Students are shown pictures of physical mess, and are asked to suggest reasons; *Why are his hands dirty? He's been changing a tyre.* (**See photocopiable page 5a.**)
- Students are given photos or drawings showing unusual clothing etc. and asked to suggest reasons; *Why is he wearing large gloves? He's been gardening.*
- Alibi; students are given a list of suspicious circumstances, and asked to invent excuses for these.

(B) *Accounting for a period of time now finishing:*

Complaints and excuses especially for delay, practiced in dialogue building or role-play exercises:

- A company explains its failure to provide services; *We've been waiting for the parts* etc.
- A husband waiting for his wife; *I've been sitting here for an hour.* This context can be useful for underlining the context of 'time just finished', *I'm sorry, I met my mother and had my hair done, and I've been driving around looking for a parking place* (this implies: I've only just found a place now).
- Students are given a list of jobs, some of which are completed, others not begun; *Have you washed the car? Yes. Have you weeded the garden? Yes. Have you done the shopping? No. I've been washing the car and weeding the garden.* (This is useful for short practice, and contrast with the present perfect.)
- As a challenging question, especially in tag form, and in the negative; *You haven't been cutting Mother's best roses, have you?* This is possibly best approached as a reading or listening exercise especially for intonation practice.

(C) *Explaining present expertise:*

- Several occupations are outlined, each requiring more than one area of expertise (e.g. tour guide on a trip to Spain). Students are given cue cards showing 'experience up to now', and must decide which occupations best suit them, and why they are the best candidates; *I've been driving buses for ten years; I've been giving guided tours for a year; I've been living in Spain for 6 months* etc.

Note: This exercise can be extended to include a contrast with the present perfect, by additional dates; I've *done this job before*, etc.

- Questionnaires on 'time up to now' basis. Students fill them in as an information gap exercise; *How long have you been learning English?/living in this city?* etc. (Note: This can be usefully extended with some checkback to the present situation; *Do you drive a car? How long have you been driving?* etc.)
- Reading a bar chart, showing the duration of different activities. The subjects can be chosen to suit student needs; X *has been exporting cars/playing football/learning German longer than* Y etc.

Ⓓ New, temporary habits:

- Students are given a list of examples of odd behaviour, and asked to find a reason; *He's been washing his hair every day, catching a different bus, staring out of the window. Why? He's in love.* Then the situation is reversed. They are given the statement and asked to compile the clues; *How do you know he's got a new job? He's been wearing a suit.* Or Group A gives the 'clues', and group B guesses the reason.
- A discussion or prediction of commercial or political outcomes, based on authentic reading material, in which trends are visible; *Who'll win the election? Mr X has been getting a lot of support*, etc. (Note: Sport can be used, but often leads to the simple past, *They beat Real Madrid last week*.)
- Writing a police report on an individual who has been behaving suspiciously over a period of time.

Ⓔ Describing developing symptoms:

- Role-play or dialogue building exercises based on doctor-patient interview.
- Role-play or dialogue building exercises in which a customer with malfunctioning machinery, describes developing faults to a mechanic.
- The advice page. Students write a letter explaining their emotional symptoms, another student gives advice. Then students switch roles. Alternatively, provide one group with a list of problems and a second group with possible solutions, asking students to select the best solution for every problem.

Ⓕ Verbs of wishing/hoping etc. These are best practiced functionally in role-play.

- The effusive hostess and polite guest: *We've been (so) looking forward to meeting you* etc.
- For expressing intentions (for advanced students): *I've been meaning to ask you* ...

Learner Error: Form, Spelling and Pronunciation

1 Spelling variations in the participle can cause problems, but this is a fairly advanced tense.

2 Phonetics:

a In English-speaking countries elementary students may hear the tense used before it is formally taught, but not hear the auxiliary, producing **I been reading.**

b Students may understand the contracted s as *is* and produce forms accordingly: **He is been writing a letter.**

c *Been* is phonetically similar to *being*, and this may combine with confusion over the contracted s form to create forms modelled on other continuous tense: **He is being writing a letter.**

d The contracted *ve* is sometimes pronounced (or written) as *of* or *half*: **I of been writing/I half been writing.**

3 Confusion may arise with the passive form, producing patterns such as, **I have been walked.**

Learner Error: Meaning and Function

1 This tense is fairly common in colloquial British English, less common in American usage, and rarely appropriate in formal writing. Many students avoid it altogether. They may substitute:

a the present perfect (all nationalities do this). With some verbs this can be very close in meaning, although the continuous form suggests action in the more immediate past, and action capable of development. Advanced learners should ideally be able to differentiate between, I *have been painting the walls* (they are wet/ I am sticky), and I *have painted the walls* (and they are a different colour), or I *have been reading* Keats (but have not exhausted the study) and I *have read* Keats (and now I know his works).

b the present continuous, where the action is uncompleted at the time of speaking: *I am studying English for 5 years** (e.g. French speakers). In English this implies a plan to study for 5 years commencing from the time of speaking.

c the past continuous (especially Spanish and Slav speakers). In practice this is often a fairly satisfactory substitution for actions which were complete at the time of speaking: My *hands are dirty. I was changing the oil*. Clearly, it cannot be substituted on all occasions;* *He was growing his own beans for years.**

d the past simple (especially Arabic speakers); *I *waited since six o'clock.** This, again, fails to express the relationship of the tense to the present.

2 Students with a mother tongue which differentiates between complete and incomplete action may perceive the present perfect continuous as a tense referring only to incomplete action; I *have been waiting for four hours but the bus has not arrived* will therefore be produced correctly.

However I*'ve been waiting for you for four hours* which is used to express complete action, will be more difficult for students.

Past Section

Points to ponder

• For trainee teachers

The regular form of the past simple is created by adding *ed* to the root verb, (except for a few spelling variations.) However, many of the most common verbs have irregular past tense forms, (I *went*, I *bought* etc.). Do you think it is better to teach the regular pattern first, or irregular verbs, because they are the most widely used verbs?

Why is I *walked to school yesterday* less than satisfactory as a model sentence?

Why do students have difficulty with sentences like I *didn't do it*?

• For teachers' workshops

What exactly is the difference between the past perfect and the past perfect continuous?

Is it true that some verbs do not often occur in continuous perfect forms, and if so, why?

Is the past simple a reasonable substitute for the past perfect in most sentences?

Tenses relating to a point or period in time which is now over

In this section you will find the past simple and past continuous, the past perfect and its continuous form; the forms 'was going to' (future in the past) and 'used to' have also been included because they denote a particular relationship between an action and past time, because they are commonly taught and widely used and because they constitute tenses in other languages. The emphatic form of the past simple is included in a special section at the end of the book (see page 160, Emphatic Tenses). You will notice that the present perfect and present perfect continuous are not contained in this section. This is because these tenses, although referring to past action, relate those actions to the present time, as the name suggests, and it may assist students to conceptualise these tenses if they are perceived as present rather than past.

Diagrammatic representations of many of the tenses have been included because many students find this useful, and it serves to distinguish between different meanings of the same tense. However, it is important to be aware that the nature of time is perceived in different ways according to culture. This does not mean that it is impossible to use 'time-line' diagrams but it does argue caution. One cannot assume that the diagram represents time as all students conceptualise it.

PAST SIMPLE: analysis

Full Form	(Spoken Form)	Negative Form		(Spoken Form)
I you he she it we they	walked (regular) ran (irregular)	I you he she it we they	did not (didn't)	walk run
Question Forms				
Did you walk/run? *(neutral unless stressed)*		Didn't you walk/run? *(seeks confirmation)*		
Tag Questions				
You walked/ran, didn't you? *(expects answer 'yes')*		You didn't walk/run, did you? *(expects answer 'no' or expresses amazement)*		

Questions to draw the target

What did you do? (especially with expressions of time or order)

What did you do last night?
           - then? ————————————⟶ *I watched a film.*

What happened? (with expressions of time or order)

What happened afterwards? .   *He drove into a lamp post.*

How did you (+ verb)?

How did you get here? ————————⟶ *I ran all the way.*

Why did you (+ verb)? (often invites other tenses)

                                                I wanted to get home.
Why did you leave early? ————————⟶ *I was feeling sick.*
                                                I'd arranged to meet Sue.

When did you (+ verb)? (invites short answers)

When did you arrive? ————————————⟶ *The plane landed at three o'clock.*

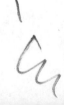

Notes

1 a Be, *have*, and *do* exist as auxiliary verbs but are also verbs in their own right:

He wasn't being very helpful. (past continuous)
I had a lovely day at the seaside. (past simple)
I didn't do a lot of gardening last weekend. (past simple)

With other verbs they help to create tenses as auxiliaries:

I was watching the T.V. when he rang. (past continuous).
I hadn't seen her for ages. (past perfect)
I didn't go to the theatre after all. (past simple)

b Although *be, have* and *do* are real verbs, they do not always behave like real verbs:

Be doesn't have the *do* auxiliary in the past:
I was late; I wasn't late; Were you late?

Have can drop the *do* auxiliary (archaic):
Had you a dog when you were young?
I hadn't a dog when I was young.

Modern conversational English however prefers the form with the auxiliary:
Did you have a dog when you were young?
I didn't have a dog when I was young.

Do is and behaves like a real verb:
I did my homework; I didn't do my homework; Did you do your homework?

2 Irregular verbs:

Many common English verbs change form, rather than add *ed*. There is little pattern to be found in these changes, and verbs of similar spelling in the infinitive may take quite different forms in the past simple (*think/thought, drink/drank; make/made, take/took*).

Some general patterns emerge:

a A vowel change in the body of the verb: *drive/drove, sing/sang, know/knew*, (even *take/took, eat/ate*, where the spelling may disguise the rule).

b This may be accompanied or replaced by consonant changes at the end of the verb; *buy/bought, think/thought, make/made*.

c Some changes are of spelling rather than sound (*pay/paid; lay/laid*), other verbs have variants based upon this (*learn/learned/learnt, burn/burned/burnt*).

d A few verbs obey none of these; *is/was, go/went* and *put/put* are the most common.

3 Spelling:

a Regular verbs ending in *y* commonly change to *i* before *ed* (*bury/buried, carry/carried*).
b Regular verbs ending in *e* add *d* (*breathe/breathed; love/loved*).

4 Phonetics:

In irregular past tenses similar spellings may have different pronunciations and some with the same pronunciation may be spelt differently: said /sɛd/; paid /peɪd/; read /rɛd/led/lɛd.
In regular verbs:

a After ./k/,/f/,/p/,/tʃ/,/tʃ/ *ed* is usually pronounced /t/ (*walked, sniffed, hopped, washed, watched*).

b After *t* or *d; ed* is usually pronounced /id/ (*wanted, prodded, added, hated*).

c After other consonants and vowel endings *ed* is usually pronounced /d/ (*rubbed, hugged, pulled, hummed, purred, closed, loved, glued, tied*).

d The sound of the past tense ending is sometimes masked by the sound of the words that immediately follow it. Compare, for example:

I *walk to school*/I *walked to school* with I *close down the shop*/I *closed down the shop*.

Learners will sometimes find it difficult to detect the *ed* ending and care is needed in selecting examples, especially at an elementary level.

Meaning and Function

(A) ***For an action in the past with time marker***. The past simple may be used for historical or narrative truth.

a   For single events:
I *saw him yesterday*. (time span specifically excludes the present)
A *man went into the forest*. (no time claimed). This is a 'narrative truth', and may be a piece of fiction.

b   For continuous or repeated events, now over:
Dinosaurs lived on the earth, (but they don't now). I *rode a bicycle when* I *was young*. (but I don't now)

Note: This usage is very close to *used to*, and is preferred to that tense in written English.

c   With *once*. Sentences using the simple past and *once* are often ambiguous:
I *rode a bicycle once*. (I rode it on a single occasion or I rode it often during one period of time. The latter, despite appearances, is the more likely meaning.)

(B) ***Polite conversation marker, with verbs of thinking, wishing,*** etc. introducing a request or suggestion.
It is often followed by modal verbs in the past form (*could/would* etc, (See page 118, Modal Auxiliaries). Advanced learners only:
I *wondered if you might give me a lift*. (Note: This may refer to a time still in the future.)
Compare also: I *was wondering if* … (more tentative), and I *wonder if* … (less tentative)

(C) **As a time marker in 'when' or 'while' clauses:**

a   Past time, for background actions taking place repeatedly:
He *whistled when he worked*.

b   Past time, for background actions taking place continuously:
He *whistled while he worked*.
(N.B. This use is very close to the past continuous in similar constructions.)

c   Indeterminate time, with modal verbs in the past form, particularly in clauses with *thought*. This creates an 'unspecified background time span'.
I *thought he might like one when he came*. (which may be past or future, equivalent to *on his arrival*)
(Compare to: I *thought he might like one when he comes* which has future reference.)
I *thought he would whistle while he worked*. (this may be present, or past)
(Note: I *thought I'd come when/while* I *had the car*– usually an informal explanation for present action.)

(D) **As a hypothetical future marker especially in 'if clauses:**
You'd *be glad if* I *sold it. Supposing that* I *sold it*. (future hypothesis)

Note: This is in fact a vestigial subjunctive, but it is identical in form to the past simple in all verbs but one. The exception is *to be*, which adopts the form *were* for all persons (*If he were here, Supposing* I *were late*.) especially in written or educated spoken English.

Suggested Contexts

A

a **Using a time marker to show single actions now over, clearly in the past:**
- Students are given an outline of a daily routine, presented in the present simple, using pictures. (He *does* this every day, so yesterday he …). Some routines lend themselves to regular *ed* forms more than others; *washed, brushed, cleaned, cooked*; *drove, went, wrote, left, bought, sold*, etc. (**See photocopiable page 1.**)
- Students are given a diary or diaries for given dates in the recent past. Make it clear that the actions actually happened. Entries in the diary will be in the infinitive (*4pm, see the doctor*). This affords simple transformational practice: *What did he do at four o'clock?* This may be used as an information-gap practice exercise.
- The day's activities (not routine) are given for a specified past date. Each student has some information, between them they have all the activities for the day. Ask and answer to build up the whole story. (Useful for practice of irregulars as the vocabulary is controlled.) (**See photocopiable page 2.**)
- Written practice, based on a historical or biographical date-list of persons or periods.
- Picture story. Many students will be accustomed to narrative passages in the present tense. This context cannot be used to introduce the past tense. (**See photocopiable page 6.**)

b **Repeated actions.** (post elementary levels) Teach as a past version of the present simple for habit:
- Old machinery or social history: *They made candles out of goose-fat* etc.
- From reading texts on social history etc. (Draw attention to the alternative *used to*.)

c **With 'once'.** Best introduced as a special lesson, and as a sequel to the repeated actions context.

B C D Best introduced as part of much later lessons on tentative suggestions, and conditionals.

Learner Error: Form, Spelling and Pronunciation

1 Irregular verbs are often treated as regular: *I runned* for I ran.

2 One irregular verb is sometimes falsely patterned on another: I *drink,* I *drunk*, I *think,* I *thunk*. This can be mystifying until the mismatch is recognised.

3 Students may produce full verb patterns by adding auxiliary verbs to modals or to the verb *to be* where they are inappropriate: *I didn't can* for I *couldn't* or *I did be*, or even *I didn't was.*

4 There may be an unwillingness to use *do* as an auxiliary with the main verb *do*; hence *I didn't it* for I *didn't do it*.

5 There is a strong tendency to omit the auxiliary and create negatives and questions from the full form: *He camen't* or *He not came*, usually caused by mother-tongue interference.

6 The auxiliary may be added to the past statement form *He did came*, or to the present statement form, creating the emphatic, He *did come*.

7 The *ed* ending may not be heard and therefore not produced: *Yesterday he walk to school.*

Learner Error: Meaning and Function

1   The past simple is perceived by some students as a literary tense (comparable to the past historic in some languages), usually used in writing but not speech.

2   It may be perceived by some students as the equivalent to a narrative tense used to describe recent events in their own language, (especially Asia Minor). They may use the past simple for recent events and prefer complex tenses (e.g. past perfect, or even the emphatic) for more distant events: *Dinosaurs had lived on the earth*; *I had left India when I had been small, but I came to England in 1985.*

3   The tense is sometimes assumed to be the equivalent to a mother tongue tense used for single, unrepeated acts, (e.g. passé composé). It may therefore be avoided for repeated actions, when the past continuous is often substituted: *My father was working in a shop, and many people were coming to him …*

4   The tense may be used where the verb has reference to the present in place of the present perfect: *I was in England since 1965.* (for I have been);*Did you finish your work yet?* (for Have you finished). (Note that this is standard American usage, but British English requires the present perfect.)

5   Students often find it difficult to accept that a past form has a future reference in some *if* clauses: *If it snowed tomorrow, I'd make a snowman.* (See page 106, Conditional Section.)

For hypothetical uses, students often use a modal auxiliary: *Supposing I will/would sell it* for *Supposing I sold it.*

PAST CONTINUOUS: analysis

Full Form (no contracted Spoken Form)			Negative Form (Spoken Form)		
I he she it	was	walking	I he she it	was not (wasn't)	walking
you we they	were		you we they	were not (weren't)	
Question Forms					
Were you walking? (*neutral*)			Weren't you walking? (*seeks confirmation*)		
Tag Questions					
You were walking, weren't you? (*expects answer 'yes, I was'*)			You weren't walking, were you? (*expects answer 'no, I wasn't'*)		

Questions to draw the target

What were you doing (+ time marker)? (may be challenging)

What was he doing when you arrived? ——————⟶ *He was gardening.*

Why didn't you (+ implied time marker)?

Why didn't you answer the door (when I rang)? ——⟶ *I was getting dressed.*

Why did you (+ implied time marker)?

Why did you miss the party (last night)? ——————⟶

I was expecting a phone call.

Why were you (+ place + implied time marker)?

Why were you in the kitchen (this morning)? ——————⟶ *I was washing the dishes.*

Where were you (+ time marker)? (where the activity suggests a place)

Where was he when you arrived? ——————⟶ *He was gardening.*

Notes

1 Stress on the auxiliary in the statement form (or on *not* in the negative) will produce an emphatic version of the tense.

2 Was is contracted to /wəz/ in the unstressed form. The stressed form gives /wɒz/.

3 Spelling: (as present continuous)

a Verbs ending in a short vowel followed by a single consonant, often double the consonant before adding *ing*.

b Verbs ending in vowel-consonant-*e* commonly drop *e* before adding *ing*:
I *hope*/I *was hoping*; (compare I *hop*/I *was hopping*).

c Verbs ending in *y* conform to the rule, but verbs ending *ie* commonly change to *y* before adding *ing*:
I *cry*/ I *was crying*; I *lie*/I *was lying*.

4 Verbs describing a state (e.g. *be*) or an involuntary sensation (*smell, see, hear*) do not usually take a continuous form as this suggests pretence or deliberate 'acting': He *was being an aeroplane.*

Meaning and Function

With time marker

The past continuous usually places an action in relation to a point or period of time in the past.

a **The point in past time is specifically mentioned; the past continuous action crosses it.**
I *was having a bath at ten o'clock.*
The action began before the point in time, was in progress at the point in time, was not completed by that time, and probably continued after it.

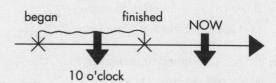

I was having a bath at 10 o'clock

b The point in time is replaced by an action in the past, which 'interrupted' the continuous action.
I *was having a bath when the telephone rang.*
The action began before the telephone rang, was in progress while the telephone rang, was not completed when the telephone rang, but may or may not have continued afterwards.

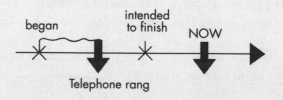

I was having a bath when the telephone rang

a **A period in the past is specified. The past continuous action fills it.**
I *was watching television from eight o'clock to midnight.* The action began at the start of the

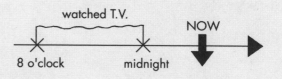

specified period and finished at the end of it.
This usage is often imprecise; it does not,
without strong additional evidence suggest
exactly 8–12, and is often used with loose
expressions of time:

I was watching television most of the afternoon.

b   The period in the past is defined by another
action also in the past continuous.

*I was buttering the bread while my mother was slicing
the tomatoes.*

I was having a bath when my mother was shopping.
Note that *while* suggests more totally
contemporaneous or collaborative actions.

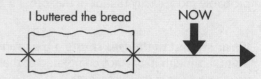

I was buttering bread while my mother was slicing tomatoes

c   **An action in the past continuous creates a
time period within which other actions, in the
past simple, take place.** With *while* or *when* this
suggests that the past continuous action
provided an opportunity or occasion for the
past simple actions. In this case the past
continuous becomes a kind of time marker
itself:

*He stole the money when/while she was getting on the
bus.I found the coin when/while I was digging the
garden.*

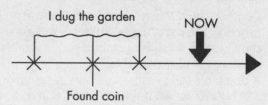

I found the coin when/while I was digging the garden

This usage also occurs with *as*, especially in written English: *As the sun was setting the old man walked
up the hill* or *The sun was setting as the old man walked up the hill.*

Other Uses:

1   Accounting (or demanding an account) for an activity, especially when the activity is not usually
permitted. The time is not specified, but understood, *What were you doing with my bicycle?* (The
answer may be, *I was riding it* but also *Don't be cross, I was only borrowing it.*)

2   Used in colloquial conversation, especially with verbs of motion, as a contracted form of *was
going to* (see page. 60, 'Was Going' Form) for abandoned plans. (Note: The plan is over (past) but
the time alluded to may still be future: e.g. *I was taking her to the cinema tonight* –but now I can't.)

3   As a polite conversation marker – usually with verbs of hoping, wishing etc. It is used to
introduce a new idea, request or proposal more politely and tentatively than the present or past
simple. This usage often has future reference:

I was wondering if you could give me a lift (compare – *I wonder(ed) if you could give me a lift*).

I was thinking I might go to the cinema (compare – *I think/thought I might go to the cinema*).

4   As a 'forceful disclaimer'. As above, except that the verb or auxiliary is stressed. It suggests that
the idea / proposal/request has been abandoned. It may appear as a rebuke:

I was hoping to do some work. (but now you've interrupted me)

I was planning to go to London. (but if you want me to do something else I won't go)

Suggested Contexts

The past continuous carries the context of an action which occupied a continuous time in the past. The action is usually relatively transitory: He *was standing on the river-bank* but not *The city was standing on the river bank*. The action **A crosses some identified time-point**, **B fills an identified period** or **C is itself a point in time crossed by another action**. The uses of the tense are probably most easily taught in this order with conversational uses at a more advanced level.

A

a **When the past continuous crosses a time point**; the action may or may not continue after that point, although it was not completed at that time, and the intention was to complete it, (*I was having a bath when the telephone rang*).

Did I begin my bath before the phone rang? Yes.
Did I finish my bath before the phone rang. No.
Did I finish my bath when the phone rang? Don't know.

Contexts must therefore make all these aspects clear, and be set up in a different tense, probably the past simple. Students will also have to be familiar with past time markers. Since the question *What were you doing at … o'clock?* is often a challenge, a context which permits challenge is also desirable.

- A timetable for a visiting celebrity is set up in the past simple – perhaps elicited: *What did he do at 3 o'clock?* He got into the car. 3:15 *Arrived at town hall* etc. The new tense is introduced with a time-line. Times are identified during the activities: *What was he doing at 3:10* Students can be encouraged to invent sentences in the new tense, based on known vocabulary.

- A crime was committed at a given time. The residents of the building were engaged in different activities (begun at different times, and set up in the past simple). The new tense accounts for actions happening at the time of the crime (*What was X doing at 10 o'clock?*). This can be a useful activity for oral practice, if each student has information on one inhabitant, and all but one has a corroborated alibi. The group must discover who is unaccounted for.

b Students are given an account, or a picture of, for example, passengers on the Titanic a moment before the disaster (or any similar cataclysm). The scene is set up in the past simple: *What happened next?* The new tense is introduced: *What was X doing when the ship hit the iceberg?* (This cataclysm context is favoured in many books, but requires a time-line to teach concept, and does not teach the use of the tense for uninterrupted activity but it can be an excellent follow-up.)

- A pictorial setting, in which the characters are engaged in different activities. This context can be enlivened by supplementary questions; *Who was nearest to the…?* *The person who was …* (etc.) (**See photocopiable page 4.**)

B

a **Where the past continuous fills a period of time:**
- A police enquiry: *Where were you/what were you doing between four o'clock and seven o'clock?* etc. Good oral practice, and an opportunity for distinguishing between actions which filled time (*I was wearing …*) and actions which took place within it (*I went to …*).

- Past history of members of the class: *What were you doing a year ago? This time yesterday?* (The same questions can be applied to pop stars, famous people etc.) Answers can be mimed, the group guess.

- Guessing mimes. The class guess after the mime: *Were you fishing? No I was playing tennis.* (Quick practice.)

b   Where the past continuous is itself a point in time filled by another action.

•   A comparison of historic events or people, or the early lives of members of pop groups, teams etc; *While Team A were warming up for the match, Team B were discussing tactics.*

•   A description of group work seen in action (e.g. video of a bank robbery, or village fete).

C *An action creates a time period within which other actions take place:*
     Best taught as a way of expressing a time marker. The context may be practised by using mime, based on cue cards: *I found a coin while I was digging the garden.* One student can act this out while others guess.

Other Uses:

1   Accounting (or demanding an account) for an activity.
     Best taught as a 'challenging context', such as a police interrogation role play. One student is chosen as the 'suspect' and draws a card showing an object. When he is challenged by the police (the rest of the class/group) must offer an excuse for possessing the object:
     What were you doing with the bicycle?

•   As part of a lesson on apologies:
     How did you break the plate? I'm sorry I was only putting the plate away.

2 and 3 should be taught as variations on *was going to*, after that tense is fully understood.

4   Could be taught as part of a series of lessons on polite requests at more advanced levels.

Learner Error: Form, Spelling and Pronunciation

1 Stative verbs may be used inappropriately, on the pattern of dynamic verbs:

a where the transitory nature of the past continuous is inappropriate: *I was being a schoolmaster* (implies pretence) whereas what is intended is *I was a schoolmaster*, or, *I used to be a schoolmaster.*

b for verbs of involuntary sensation: *I was smelling roses* suggests deliberate action, whereas what is intended is, *I could smell roses*, or, *I smelt roses.*

2 Some elementary learners produce *You was* for *You were* in the singular, in line with the rest of the singular form of *To be.*

3 Spelling: Many students have difficulty with the spelling variations, especially doubled consonants.

4 Pronunciation problems: Germanic speakers have difficulties with *w* (*was/were*). Other learners may precede /w/ by aspirated *h* /hw/. Far Eastern speakers may not produce unstressed *ing* especially before *in*, *I was shop in London.*

5 Unstressed *was/were* is sometimes difficult to distinguish from *is/are* for elementary learners.

6 Unstressed *was/were* is sometimes not included at all by elementary learners, especially when the past tense is already elsewhere in the sentence: *I met him when I shopping in London.*

Learner Error: Meaning and Function

1 The past continuous appears similar to the imperfect in several continental languages. It may be used as a direct equivalent:

a For repeated action in the past:
My father was taking me for walks when I was young. (English requires *took me* or *used to take*.)

b To denote action of extended duration:
I *walked to school every day.* *I was walking a long way.*

2 Students whose mother tongue has more developed systems for denoting incomplete action (e.g. Eastern European Students) may:

a Avoid past continuous when the action clearly continued after the time marker/verb:
I read when you phoned him for I *was reading when you phoned him.*

b Use the present continuous to indicate that the interrupted action continues to the present time:
I am gardening when the postman came.

c Attempt to mark incomplete interrupted actions by another tense, often the perfect;
I have gardened when the postman came.

3 Students with fewer past tenses than English (e.g. speakers of Arabic) may use the past simple for all past actions. As a result students may create a grammatically correct sentence, but convey the wrong meaning in terms of sequence or causality: I *made the tea when he came* (compare – I *was making the tea when he came*). I *cleaned the floor because he came* (compare – I *cleaned the floor because he was coming*).

PAST PERFECT: analysis

Full Form	(Spoken Form)			Negative Form	(Spoken Form)		
I you he she it we they	had ('d)	a) walked b) run		I you he she it we they	had not (hadn't)	a) walked b) run	

a) Regular verbs: use a past participle identical in form to the past simple.
b) Irregular verbs: use a past participle which usually differs in form from the past simple.

Question Forms

Had you walked/run? (*neutral unless stressed*)	Hadn't you walked? (*expects answer 'yes'*)

Tag Questions

You'd walked, hadn't you? (*expects answer 'yes'*)	You hadn't worked, had you? (*expects answer 'no' or expresses surprise*)

Questions to draw the target

When did you (+ verb) (of a sequence)?
When did you leave? ────────────⟶ After the film had finished.

Why did you (+ verb) (of causality)?
Why did you leave the exam early? ────⟶ Because I'd finished.

What had happened?
What had happened? ──────────⟶ He'd driven the car into a wall.

Why were you (+ adjective)?
Why were you late? ──────────⟶ I'd overslept.
Why were you so happy? I'd just got married.

Note: Adjectives of physical state often require the past perfect continuous.

Notes

1 Form: **Regular verbs** form a past participle with *ed*, similar to the simple past form.

2 **Irregular verbs:**

a Some form a past participle which is similar to the (irregular) past simple:
I *make*/I *made*/I *had made*; I *think*/I *thought*/I *had thought*.

b Many form a past participle which adds an *en*. This may be added to the basic verb form:
I *eat*/I *ate*/I *had eaten*; I *fall*/I *fell*/I *had fallen*; I *am*/I *was*/I *had been* (root form *be*).
This ending may be modified to:

• *n* especially where the base verb ends with *e* or *ow*: I *take*/I *took*/I *had taken*; I *know*/I *knew*/I *had known*.

• *ne* where the base verb ends in *o*: I *do*/I *did*/I *had done*; I *go*/I *went*/I *had gone* (the pronunciation is not standard).

c The *en* ending may be added to a past version of the base verb:
I *choose*/I *chose*/I *had chosen*; I *forget*/I *forgot*/I *had forgotten*; I *break*/I *broke*/I *had broken*.

d The past participle may be identical to the present or base form of the verb:
I *run*/I *ran*/I *had run*; I *come*/I *came*/I *had come*/; I *put*/I *put*/I *had put*.

e The past participle may be formed by interior vowel change and be different from either base or past forms: I *drink*/I *drank*/I *had drunk*; I *sing*/I *sang*/I *had sung*; I *sink*/I *sank*/I *had sunk*. There are no easily discernible rules to guide learners, and apparently similar verbs may produce past participles on different patterns: I *forget*/I *forgot*/I *had forgotten*; I *get*/I *got*/I *had got*. (N.B. American usage: I *had gotten*.)

3 Phonetics:

a Contracted form *it'd* pronounced /Itəd/

b All contracted statement forms sound (and look) identical to the contracted form of I *would* – I'*d*.

c Stress is on the past participle, not on the auxiliary *had* except in the emphatic form.

d The contracted auxiliary *d* is elided into a palatal stop in the example *he'd gone*, and is often not heard .

4 Note: The form I *had been* (deriving from *to be*) can be used incorrectly and perceived as the past perfect of *to go* in some circumstances:
He *had been* to London the day before (he went to London and returned the day before).
He *had gone* to London the day before (and was still there at the time I'm talking about).

5 The past perfect form *had had* is often contracted to a single *had*, especially in informal English. Hence:
He *told me he had had a good time*, may become, He *told me he had a good time*.

Meaning and Function

A **Used for actions previous to and affecting a nominated time in the past:**

a When the past moment is expressed as specific time, especially following *by*. The action in the past perfect occurred previous to the time, and the result of that action was still in force at that time.
By one o'clock he had cooked lunch (at one o'clock it was prepared, but not eaten).

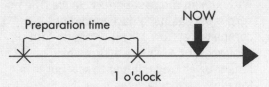

By 1 o'clock he had cooked lunch

b When the past moment is expressed as an action, usually in the simple past. This is often introduced with *when*:
He had cooked lunch when she arrived (she arrived to find the lunch prepared).

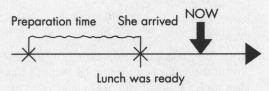

When she arrived he had cooked lunch

B **Used to express sequence and relationship of past actions with the past perfect clause used as a time marker:**
In this function the past perfect is not used in the negative.

a With *before* in the past perfect clause; to show that the main verb took place against a background of non-completed action. It often implies that the intention was to complete it earlier, or that this was likely:
The post arrived before he'd got dressed (the state of being dressed was not yet arrived at, probably not even begun; i.e. he was still in pyjamas; either the post was early, or he was late).
It was Thursday before I'd read it (I did not finish it until Thursday. I may have begun it before then, and I expected/intended to finish it earlier).

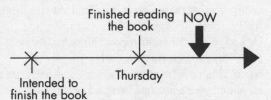

It was Thursday before I'd read the book

b With *after* in the past perfect clause to show the main verb against a background of completed action. It may indicate a preferred sequence or a state of affairs which could no longer be altered:
After she had done the washing, she had a cup of tea (she had a cup of tea, but waited until the washing was completed).

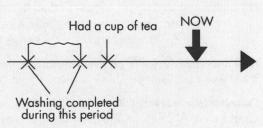

After she had done the washing, she had a cup of tea

After I'd bought the car, I found the rust (it was too late, I was already the owner of the car).
Note: A parallel construction exists, employing the past simple. The meaning is similar, although not identical in British English (see below). American usage prefers the past simple construction.

Compare:
The taxi arrived before he got dressed (the taxi arrived, then he got dressed; expresses sequence).
It was Thursday before I read it (I did not begin it until Thursday, I meant to begin it earlier).
After she did the washing she had a cup of tea (simple sequence, no suggestion of waiting).

c   With *when* in the past perfect clause. The main verb is set against a background of completed action. May indicate preferred sequence, or a state of affairs which could no longer be altered (similar to *after* but less forceful): *He put the music on loudly when she had left the house* (he waited for her to leave before he put the music up).

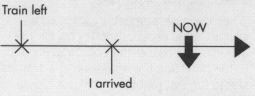

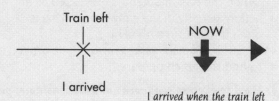

I arrived when the train had left (the platform was empty).

Note: The past simple construction suggests simultaneous action: *He put the music on loudly when she left. I arrived when the train left.*

C **To show the sequence and relationship of past actions with no time marker in the past perfect clause:**

a   With *before* in the time clause. Indicates that the main verb took place against a background of completed action. Often implies that the intention was to complete it later, or that this was likely.
He had got dressed before the post arrived. (The post arrived when he was already dressed. Either the post was late, or he was early.)
Note: this construction may be used with the negative to express strong unfulfilled expectations:
He hadn't gone a hundred yards before she called him (she called him surprisingly quickly).
He hadn't got dressed before the post arrived (it arrived surprisingly early).

b   With *when* in the time clause; used exactly as *before* above, but less forcefully:
He had got dressed when the taxi arrived.

D **Showing causal relationship between past actions** especially with *because, although* etc. A state of affairs existed as a result of past perfect action, which led to or explains the subsequent action:
I ran home because/since/as I'd missed my train. I wasn't tired although I'd run home.
Note: In uses A–D the sentences can be inverted, which changes only the emphasis.

E **As a narrative device to give background**, especially in written English;
It had been a good year for Martin … etc. (scene-setting for a story in the past simple).

F **Conversation marker, with verbs of thinking, hoping** etc., to convey a request or suggestion now abandoned. With emphatic use (stress on *had*) it is often disapproving, or expresses disappointment:
I had wondered if you could give me a lift (but now I realise that you can't).
I had hoped you would be on time (but you were late).

G **In reported speech**, and after *if*, when direct speech is in the present perfect : *"Have you seen her?" I wondered; I wondered if you'd seen her.*
"I've seen her," he said; He said that he had seen her.

Suggested Contexts

Ⓐ – Ⓒ *To express the sequence and relationship of action, the teacher needs to establish the order in time of past actions:*

- A situation built in the past simple where the order of events is important:
(e.g. A flat full of valuables – elicited in the past simple as an introduction; A *fire breaks out: What did the owner do first* etc. Establish the order of priorities. Then introduce the tense with *after/when;* After/when *he had called the fire brigade he rescued the baby.*)

- Reordering a picture sequence after hearing or reading a narrative, and justifying the new order:
No. *He bought the bike after he'd been on holiday,* etc.
Almost any series of past events where sequence is important lends itself to this treatment.

Ⓓ *To express the causal relationship between past actions:*

- Cumulative disaster. One wrong step leads to another; *He did/had to do …, because he'd done …* (some T.V. comedies etc. lend themselves to this treatment).

- Problem-solving. The narrative is interrupted, and the class is asked to deduce/guess the reasons for the action; *Why did he go in? Because he'd hidden the jewels there.* This is a useful exercise for practice rather than for introducing the tense.

Ⓔ *Used as a narrative device:* as part of a series of lessons on writing/reading etc. usually at an advanced level.

Ⓕ *With verbs of thinking, hoping* etc: part of a series of lessons on making suggestions, expressing irritation etc.

Ⓖ *In reported speech*: part of a formal series of lessons on transformations in reported speech.

Learner Error: Form, Spelling and Pronunciation

1 Difficulties occur with irregular past participles, but as this tense is almost always encountered after the present perfect, these difficulties are not usually identified as particular to this tense.

2 Phonetics:

a I'd may be interpreted as I *would* and this form may occur in written work; *He asked me if I would had a good time.*

b Students may fail to hear the difference between I *have done* and I *had done* for example, and confuse the two tenses.

c Students may fail to hear the contracted *d* and use the participle as a tense. This is not always obvious where a regular *ed* participle is involved, I *walked/I'd walked*, but can produce variants such as *I gone*, *I done* etc.

3 The contraction of I *had had* to I *had*, may lead to confusion in identifying the tense, especially as American usage often prefers the simple past to the past perfect; *He told me he saw her.*

Learner Error: Meaning and Function

1 The past perfect suggests some relationship between two events in English, thus *After he'd eaten breakfast he went to work*, describes two proximate actions. Some Eastern European languages have a tense which suggests just prior completion so that they might say: *After he'd had breakfast he went to bed*, because the second action followed the first, though it was much later.

2 Students whose mother tongue marks the distant past as distinct from the recent past may use the past perfect as a 'distant past' tense (Indian sub-continent):
Dinosaurs had lived on the earth, and cave men had lived in caves.

3 Many students perceive the past perfect as a difficult tense and avoid using it altogether; substituting the past simple. In many cases this creates a grammatical sentence, although often with a slightly different meaning.

4 Past perfect constructions with *when* may cause problems because:

a It may be used as an alternative for either *after* or *before* depending on the context;
He rescued the body when (after) he'd called the fire brigade.
He hadn't gone far when (before) she called him.

b Substituting the past simple for the past perfect may be satisfactory with other time markers, but creates the idea of simultaneous action with *when*: *He came after I left. He came after I'd left.* Compare: *He came when I'd left; He came when I left.*

5 *Before* and *after* used with the past perfect cause problems of sequence for some students; *He left before I had done my homework.* Students see *done my homework* as belonging to *before*.

PAST PERFECT CONTINUOUS: analysis

Full Form	(Spoken Form)		Negative Form	(Spoken Form)	
I you he she it we they	had ('d)	been eating	I you he she it we they	had not (hadn't) ('d not, *rare*)	been eating

Question Forms	
Had you been eating? (*fairly neutral*)	Hadn't you been eating? (*expects answer 'yes'*)

Tag Questions	
You'd been eating, hadn't you? (*expects answer 'yes', often a challenge*)	You hadn't been eating, had you? (*expects answer 'no', or expresses surprise/challenge*)

Questions to draw the target

Why were you so (+ adjective and time in the past)?

Why were you so tired (when we met)? ⟶ *I'd been running.*

Why did you have … done?

Why did you have the tap mended? ⟶ *It had been dripping* (may also invite: *It was dripping*).

When did you (and action in the past)?

When did you notice the crack? ⟶ *After/Not until I'd been living there for three weeks.*

This tense is often used as an explanation or excuse and is more realistically elicited by comment rather than question:

I'm sorry I was late yesterday. ⟶ *That's all right, we hadn't been waiting long.*

I was surprised to see you there. ⟶ *Yes, I'd been taking my radio in to be mended.*

Notes

1 Form. Stress on the auxiliary, *had*, or on the *not* in the negative, will produce an emphatic form of this tense.

2 Spelling. There are variations in the spelling of the present participle:

a verbs ending in a short vowel followed by a single consonant usually double the consonant before adding -*ing*: I *hop*, I *had been hopping*

b verbs ending vowel-consonant-*e* commonly drop the final *e* before adding -*ing*: I *hope*, I *had been hoping*.

c verbs ending in *y* conform to the rule adding -*ing*, but verbs ending *ie* commonly change to *y*: compare I *cry*, I *had been crying* with I *lie*, I *had been lying*.

3 Verbs describing a state (e.g. *be*) or an involuntary sensation (see, hear, smell) do not usually take a continuous form, as this suggests pretence, or deliberate action:
He *had been being an aeroplane* (pretended to be one); I *had been smelling the roses* (deliberately sniffed them).

4 Note that the past perfect form I *had been to London* has no continuous variant, (i.e. there is no form *I *had been being to London.*) Forms such as I *had been swimming*, are probably best considered as the past perfect of the base verb I *go swimming*.

5 Phonetics:

a the contracted form '*d* of *had* is identical to the contracted form of *would*, and is often heard and written as such.

b where the participle begins with the sound /n/ the word *been* is sometimes heard and understood as *be*, producing forms such as *I had be knitting* or even *I had becoming* (especially where the verb *become* is already known).

6 The form I'*d not been eating* is unusual, but still encountered especially in Scottish and Irish English, and in older written dialogue.

Meaning and Function

(A) Relative to another past time, and used with a real or implied time marker. The action took place in the time leading up to the identified moment, and was temporary, or expected to be temporary.

a **To explain the action of the main verb**, by giving background information about the activity which led up to it, whose results were still evident at the time of the main verb, and which was either continuous, repeated, or habitual over a limited period of time:
He *could understand the film because he'd been studying French at school* (continuous previous action, with results at the time).
She *came to see me because I'd been writing to her for years* (repeated action over a given period)
I *wasn't feeling well because I hadn't been taking my tablets* (habitual action over a short period)

b **To convey the ongoing, continuous nature of an action** which led up to the past moment in time. Often used to draw attention to the length of the action:
He *had been cleaning the car for over an hour before/when he realised it was the wrong one.*
Compare: He *had cleaned the car inside and out before/when he realised it was the wrong one*; the use of the past perfect here draws attention to the completed as opposed to the ongoing action.

(The use of the present perfect continuous is used especially in complaints because of the emphasis placed on the ongoing action, e.g. I *had been waiting for an hour before the bus came.*)

c **To convey an action which was ongoing** but over, or virtually over, when interrupted by the main verb but whose results were still evident at that moment;
When he came I had been baking (the cakes were on the table, and the smell of baking in the air).
I'd been wallpapering all morning but I still accepted his invitation to lunch (although I was sticky and tired).

d **In reported speech**, or past questions, where the direct speech form uses the present perfect continuous;
He said he had been thinking about it ('I've been thinking about it,' he said).
He asked if you'd been taking her to school (he said to me, 'Has x been taking her to school?').

B **With verbs of thinking/feeling** etc. A conversational marker, used to introduce an idea now abandoned. It suggests that the idea was repeatedly in the mind;
I'd been meaning to visit her (I thought actively many times about a visit but now its too late).
Compare: I *meant to visit her* (I intended to do it).

Suggested Contexts

A

a **To explain a state of affairs in the past.** With the narrative set in the past, this tense deals with activities which led to the situation, and which happened before it.

• The police find a room full of evidence of strange activities, (may be set up with pictures, cartoons, or objects in a bag). *What had the occupant been doing before the police arrived?* (imprint in soap – *he'd been making keys* etc.)

b **To convey the ongoing nature of an action. Part of a series on complaints.** 'I'd been wearing my new *shoes for ten minutes when the heel broke.* This context is limited, but is useful for practice if each student has a 'complaint' and has to match the complaint to the faulty item. (**See photocopiable page 56**)

c **To convey an ongoing action which was interrupted. Problem solving:** students are given statements in the past perfect continuous, and asked to predict the "results", e.g. *He lent on the wall but I'd been painting it.* Students may predict: *He got paint on his clothes.* They are then given the results and asked to produce the activity which caused them. (*I had oil on my hands. I'd been changing a tyre* etc.) This may be done competitively, in groups, with bonus marks for imaginative solutions.

d **Reported speech**. *Part of series of lessons on direct and reported speech.*

B **With verbs of thinking and feeling**. Part of series of lessons on expressing mild regret, missed opportunities etc.

Learner Error: Form, Spelling and Pronunciation

1 Spelling: this tense includes the present participle which creates spelling difficulties, but as it is usually taught much later than other continuous tenses, these problems are not regarded as related to the tense.

2 Phonetics:

a Students may understand the contracted '*d* as *would* and produce forms accordingly: **I would been writing a letter.** (This may be perceived by the teacher as an attempt to produce I *would have been writing a letter* and the two forms, indeed, are often confused by students.)

b Students may fail to distinguish *had* from *have*, and continue to use the present perfect continuous form, especially as some of the force of /d/ is lost before /b/ in *been*: *I have been waiting for an hour when the bus came.*

c Elementary students living in English-speaking countries may hear the tense in use and attempt to reproduce it in a form which appears to echo what they already know: *I happy knitting*; *I happy in reading .*

3 Confusion may arise with the passive form. This may produce sentences on the pattern of *I have been walked.*

Learner Error: Meaning and Function

1 This tense is not common in English, and many students avoid it altogether. They may:

a substitute the past perfect. This is often very close in meaning; the difference lies in the attitude of the speaker. Advanced learners should ideally be able to differentiate between e.g. I *had been painting the walls* (and they were wet) and I *had painted the walls* (and they were a different colour).

b substitute the past simple. This is less satisfactory especially in sentences with *when*: I *read for an hour when he came in* (I started reading when he came in); I *had been reading for an hour when he came in* (I had read for an hour uninterruptedly before he came in).

2 Eastern European students may perceive the tense as denoting only incomplete action and use it as a more distant version of the past continuous, perhaps on a mother tongue pattern. They may use I *had been painting the walls when he arrived* for I *was painting the walls when he arrived*.

3 This tense may be perceived as a version of the mother-tongue 'anterior tense', because of the apparently 'double' past *had been*; it may be used to describe very remote actions (Indian languages), *Dinosaurs had been living for millions of years.*

USED to: analysis

Full Form (no contracted Spoken Form)			Negative Form (Spoken Form)		
I you he she it we they	used to	dance	I you he she it we they	used not to (didn't use to) (usedn't to, *rare*)	dance

Question Forms	
Used you to dance? Did you use to dance? (*neutral unless stressed*)	Usedn't you to dance? Didn't you use to dance? (*seeks confirmation*)

Tag Questions	
You used to dance, didn't you? (*expects answer 'yes'*) *Very rarely*: You used to dance, usedn't you?	You didn't use to dance, did you? (*expects answer 'no'*) You usedn't to dance, used you?

Questions to draw the target

What/Where/When/how did you use to (+ verb and time marker?)

(Note: The full sentence form in the answer is unrealistic in conversation.)

What did you use to play at school? ⟶ *I used to play (tennis).*
Where did you use to live? *I used to live (in the country).*
When did you use to go to bed? *I used to go to bed at (nine o'clock).*
How did you use to get to school? *I used to catch the bus. (By bus.)*

What did you do (+ habit time marker)?

What did you do at the weekend when you were at college? ⟶ *I used to go to the cinema and play sport.*

Have you ever (+ verb)?
(requires present perfect for question and usually draws an amplified answer)

Have you ever been riding? ⟶ *I used to ride but I don't have much spare time now.*

Can you (+ verb)?

Can you play the piano? ⟶ *I used to play quite well when I was young.*

Notes

1 Form: The tense is used normally in spoken or informal written communication.

a In formal written communication it is usually avoided altogether: I *used to be* becomes I *was*; I *didn't use to ride* becomes I *didn't ride*.

b Two versions of the negative and question form exist:
The full form I *used not to ride* and the question *Used you to ride?* are still found in formal educated speech and writing. The contracted spoken form I *usedn't to ride* is now very rare. I *didn't use to ride/Didn't you use to ride?* is common in spoken English. The full form I *did not use to ride* is rare except as an emphatic.
Note: The negative tag I *ride now but I used not to* is slightly more common than other forms of the negative without *did*; nevertheless, I *ride now but I didn't use to* is the most common form of the tag.

c Short answer forms cause problems. With most constructions the base form is correct: *Do you ride a bicycle? No, but I used to. Are you a cyclist? No, but I used to be.* The verb is required to complete the construction where it is seen as a discontinued state not a discontinued habit: *Have you got a bicycle? No, but I used to have/have one* (seen as state of possession); *Do you play tennis on Thursdays? No, but I used to* (habit).

2 Spelling: (see phonetics) *used to* and *use to* are pronounced identically leading many native speakers to produce the variant spelling *Did you used to*, *I didn't used to* This is particularly widespread as the form is rarely formally written.

3 Phonetics: *Use to* and *used to* are both pronounced identically, /ju:stʊ/.

a Learners often write/understand *I use to swim.*

b Some learners hear *he is to swim* (unstressed sound of *used*).

c Some learners produce *used* (zd) confusing the /zd/ pronunciation of *It is used to pump up tyres* with the /st/ pronunciation of I *am used to riding a bike to work.*

d *To* (except in tag forms) is unstressed and may be unheard or misheard by learners:
I used ride a bike, *I used a ride a bike.*

Meaning and Function

A **Discontinued or presumed discontinued habit**:
I *used to ride a bike* (but I don't ride one any more).
I *didn't use to wear glasses/I used not to wear glasses* (but I wear them now).

I rode a bike
NOW
I used to ride a bike

or

I didn't wear glasses
NOW   I wear glasses now
I didn't use to wear glasses

B **Discontinued (or presumed discontinued) state**:
There used to be a bank on the corner (but not now). This function (usually with *to be*)requires a different short answer tag: *He is tidy now, but he didn't use/used not/to be.* Some other verbs like *have* (*got*) for possession, and modal verbs (*may, can etc.*) are often seen in British English as describing a state (possession, ability, likelihood) and therefore attract the longer tag. Modal verbs like *may* and *can* (see page 118, Modal Auxiliaries) cannot follow *used to*: *He hasn't got a car now but he used to* (acceptable), *used to have one* (preferred). *He can't drive a car now but he used to* (*drive* is implied) or *He can't drive a car now but he used to be able to.*

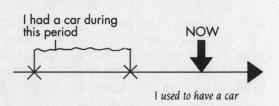

Note: Both **A** and **B** can be used in polite conversation to check if previous knowledge is still true: *I remember him. He used to play the piano. He used to be a handsome man.*
(These allow the responses, *He still does, He still is,* but it is presumed that this is not so.)

C **Modest disclaimer**: *Do you play tennis? I used to play a bit.*
A polite way of implying that the speaker previously had some degree of skill, and may therefore still have it. It does not necessarily mean the that activity has been discontinued.

Suggested Contexts

A **Discontinued habit**:

- Draw a sketch of a young man and elicit a list of lively hobbies/activities which he is involved in, (He *plays tennis* etc.). Draw a second sketch of the same man, but 50 years older and elicit the difference between past and present activities: *Does he play tennis now? No he used to play tennis.* (Use dates to emphasise the past and present division.)
- Using an historical picture with information on outmoded processes, compare past and present techniques. Use other tenses to draw the 'used to' construction: *'What are they doing in the picture? Do we do this now? We used to do it in a different way.*

B **Discontinued state**:

- Using a photograph of a town known to the class, at a given date, mark the differences between 'then' and 'now': *In 1902 there was no bank* leading to *used to, There used to be a market place there.*
- Using a photograph or plan of a building before and after renovation; elicit the differences: *The house used to have a gate. It used to be green* etc. (**See photocopiable page 8.**)
- Using a diagram of the management structure of a defunct company: *There used to be two directors.* etc.
  A and **B** Many contexts lend themselves to a combination of the two:
- School reunion. Identifying characters with known past habits, physical characteristics.
- Lottery winner, before and after win.

- Lifestyle in Britain and home country (where applicable).
- Childhood and adulthood.
- Historical social conditions, dress etc.
- Local history.

C **Modest disclaimer:** Part of notional/functional lesson on modestly claiming skills.

Learner Error: Form, Spelling and Punctuation

1 Many errors are caused by difficulties in hearing the tense (see phonetic notes above):
He is to ride for *he used to ride*, this can lead to errors in other persons, I *am to ride*, etc.
He used a ride for *he used to ride*, can lead to associated problems, (perceiving *ride* as a noun).
He used ride a bike (N.B. care should be taken not to produce stressed *to* in the correction.)
Advanced learners may produce the /zd/ form, by analogy with other known uses of *used to*.

2 Short forms: students produce the standard short tag form for state, producing *I'm not fat now, but I used to.*

3 with other known, or half-known constructions with *used*:

a with I *am used to riding a bike* (i.e. I am accustomed to it), producing *I am used to ride a bike* or *I used to riding a bike*

b with I *got used to riding a bike* (i.e. I became accustomed to it), producing *I got used to eat rice in my country* or *I used to eating rice.*

c with It *is used for pumping up tyres* (i.e. this is its purpose), producing *I used for ride a bike* or *I am used for ride/riding a bike.*

d with It *is used to ride a bike* (i.e. it is part of the equipment necessary), producing *I am used to ride a bike* or apparently correctly, I *used to ride a bike* (with /zd/ pronunciation).

Learner Error: Meaning and Function

1 Students outside of English-speaking communities may avoid the pattern altogether, and substitute a formal construction such as I *rode a bike*, or I *would ride a bike*.

2 The tense is sometimes perceived as the direct equivalent of an imperfect tense in the mother tongue, and used as such:

a for a single action, interrupted in the past, where English would use *was … ing*: I *used to lay the table when the postman came* (for I *was laying*).

b for an action not discontinued; I *used to have long hair* (when the person still has long hair).

c more commonly *used to* is avoided in favour of the past continuous, which is closer to an imperfect tense in the mother tongue; *My father was taking me for walks* (for *used to take me*).

3 The construction is sometimes avoided in favour of a translation nearer to the mother tongue equivalent especially on 'stylistic' grounds: *I had the use to ride a bicycle* (perhaps also derived from I *had the use of a bicycle*), *I had the habit to use a bicycle* or *I had the habit of using a bicycle.*

4 Occasionally, when the perfect tenses have been taught or if they feature in the mother tongue, students use a perfective form, perhaps because of an implied statement about the present; (this habit/state is not discontinued). *I have used to ride a bicycle* or *I had used to ride a bicycle.*

WAS GOING TO: analysis

(Sometimes referred to as 'Future in the past')

Full Form (no contracted Spoken Form)			Negative Form (Spoken Form)		
I he she it	was	going to eat	I he she it	was not (wasn't)	going to eat
you we they	were		you we they	were not (weren't)	
Question Forms					
Were you going to eat? (*neutral unless stressed*)			Weren't you going to eat? (*expects answer 'yes'*)		
Tag Questions					
You were going to eat, weren't you? (*expects answer 'yes'*)			You weren't going to eat, were you? (*expects answer 'no', may express surprise*)		

Questions to draw the target

What were you going to do?
(Note: this may invite short answer unless carefully contextualised.)

What were you going to do? ⟶ I *was going to play the piano.*
(Play the piano).

What were you going to do with it? ⟶ I *was going to mend it.*

What were your plans?
What were you planning to do? ⟶ *We were going to fly to Paris.*

Shall we (+ suggestion)?
Shall we go out for a meal? ⟶ I *was going to wash my hair tonight.*

Why don't you (+ suggestion)?
Why don't you write to them? ⟶ I *was going to go and see them.*

Why didn't you (+ verb)?
Why didn't you come to the party? ⟶ I *was going to (come), but I was ill.*

Notes

1 *Form*: Where the main verb is *to go* the tense is sometimes abbreviated to avoid repetition. Thus: I *was going to go* becomes I *was going* etc. This is sometimes also applied to *come* and other forms of motion. This looks like a past continuous, but the auxiliary verb is stressed: I **was** *coming (was going to come), but the car broke down.* We **were** *leaving tomorrow, but we had to postpone it.*
N.B. The full form I *was going to go* is perfectly correct, although less colloquial.

2 An emphatic form of the tense (for insistence or contradiction) is made by stressing the auxiliary *was/were* in the full (statement) or question form, and the *not* or *wasn't/weren't* in the negative.
Note: *Go/come* etc. usually take the full form in the emphatic. In informal colloquial speech only a contracted form of the emphatic may be used for future plans, usually with a double stress: I **was singing** *at the concert, but I've got a sore throat.*

3 Phonetics:

a *You were going* is often heard as *you are going*, and may be misinterpreted as such.

b Note that *was* is pronounced /wəz/ in unstressed positions, /wɒz/ when it is stressed.

4 This tense is chiefly used in speech and informal written form.

M eaning and Function

(A) **Used to indicate a plan formed in the past and later abandoned, or altered:**

a Where the activity was planned for a time now in the past:
I *was going to play football, but it rained* (so I didn't).
I *was going to catch the 4:30 train, but I missed it* (so I didn't).

b Where the activity was planned for a time still in the future:
I *was going to visit the museum this afternoon, but my car won't be ready* (so I can't go).
I *was going to play football, but it's raining* (so I won't).

(B) **Used to indicate a plan formed in the past and not yet carried out, but not necessarily abandoned:**

a Gently refusing a suggestion/invitation. Suggests a willingness to compromise:
Would you like to go to the disco? I *was going to do some work* (but I could be persuaded to go).

b Often used as an apology or an explanation (especially in the empathic form). In this usage, attention is drawn to the previous nature of the plan: I *was going to tell you about it* (I planned to tell you, but you have forestalled me by finding out).
Why don't you go to the fete this afternoon? I **was** *going* (I planned to but I've changed my mind).

(C) **Used to insist on a plan already formed**, often to invite the listener to take appropriate action:
I *was going to water the plants in the green house* (so either come with me, or go away, please);
I *was going to tell you something* (so please let me have your attention).
Note: The form I *was going to* exists also as a normal past continuous, and means I *was on my way to* (literally, I *was in transit*). In these circumstances the plan may well have been subsequently executed.
Compare: I *was going to answer the door* (i.e. on my way) *when I found the money in the hall* to:
I *was going to answer the door* (i.e. that was my intention) *when I realised who it was* (so I didn't answer it).

Suggested Contexts

 A

a **Abandoned or altered plans for past time:**
The context must give a) the original plan b) the cause of alteration, and often c) the altered plan. (**See photocopiable page 7.**)

- Choose a pop star or show business personality and invent a schedule: *Arrive at 9* etc; then the flight is delayed/diverted; find the differences; *He was going to arrive at 9, but he didn't arrive until 6.*
- Police arrests; suspects are found in a building containing gold. They were carrying different objects, (matches and paraffin, electric drill etc.). Students list probable plans; *B was going to use the drill to open the safe* etc.

b **Plans for the future:**
- Students choose a holiday/entertainments (from a brochure) in groups; they are then given 'last minute offers'; What changes would they make? *We were going to catch the train but now we're going by air* etc.
- Two people with overlapping/conflicting schedules. Ask the students to redraw the schedules in order to have a more sensible distribution of tasks: *She was going to mow the lawn, but he'll do that.* etc.
- Life plans: Ask students what their plans for the future are. Would their decisions change if they won £1 million? This is useful for contrast with plans which still exist: *He was going to buy a bicycle. He's still going to marry Mary.*

B

a **Past plans not yet carried out**. As part of lesson on suggestions/invitations. Politely not accepting, or offer to compromise. Set up two conflicting timetables; try to come to a compromise.

C **Insistance on past plans.** Part of lesson series on polite requests, inferences etc.

Learner Error: Form, Spelling and Pronunciation

1 Phonetic problems:

a *Was* is often eliminated (perhaps also because of the past/future combination): **I going to water the plants in the greenhouse, but …**

b *You were* may be perceived as *You are* (phonetically similar in the unstressed form), and consequently the tense is seen as having a present form; **I is going to …** from the unstressed *was*).

Learner Error: Meaning and Function

1 Students tend to avoid this tense, and may substitute colloquial expressions: e.g. *I meant to go to the shops.* This creates a fair substitute, but is not appropriate in all contexts.

2 Students are particularly unwilling to use the tense when the plan is for future time. In this context they may prefer to substitute verbs of wishing or wanting with *that*: **I wanted that I go to the fete** or substitute a near-translation based on a mother tongue pattern: **I had the intention to go to the fete*/wanted to go to the fete.*

3 Typically, students do not respond to question-forms appropriately, when the plan is for future time. *What were you going to do this afternoon?* (suggests half-invitation). A typical answer might be: *I am going to study* (which suggests a lack of compromise.) English usage however suggests I *was going to study* (but you could persuade me) or I've *got to study*, (and you can't persuade me).

4 The similarity of the past continuous I *was going to* (for 'in transit') can cause problems of understanding.

5 Contracted forms such as I *was coming*, I *was going* are often not perceived as belonging to the tense, or other verbs are treated as though they conformed to this irregular pattern.
Compare: I *was coming to the party but the car broke down* (this was my intention, abandoned) to
I *was driving to the party but the car broke down* (the breakdown occurred on the way).

6 Students may attempt to create a past simple form of this tense and produce I *went to* … . This occurs in colloquial British speech, but has a different force: I *went to hit him but* I *stumbled*. (The speaker was about to begin the action, but was prevented.)

*F*uture *S*ection

Points to Ponder

- *For trainee teachers*

  I'm going to London.
  I'm going to catch the train.
  The construction of these two sentences is very similar, but it is not identical. Can you see why not? There are several common ways of expressing a future in English. Which of the following suggests that a) you are making up your mind as you speak b) you already have an appointment c) this is a general plan:
  I'm seeing the dentist tomorrow.
  I'm going to see the dentist tomorrow.
  I'll see the dentist tomorrow.

- *For teachers' workshops*

  We shall pick you up at the airport. We will (or we'll) pick you up at the airport.
  Shall I arrive early or shan't I? Will I arrive early or won't I?
  What do you see as the essential difference between *will* and *shall* in these sentences.

Introduction

In this section you will find most of the verb patterns used to refer to events or plans which have not yet occurred. Contrary to convention the label "future simple" has not been used. This is because the verb used with future reference is not "simple" in the literal sense since it does not consist of a single word based on the verb stem as the past and present simple do. *Will* and *Shall* which in other texts come under the "Future Simple" label are treated specifically in a separate section (page 73, Will/Shall Future).

EFL teachers will be faced with the task of differentiating between types of future, a task that can be problematic, especially if the native language of the student uses fewer constructions to express future time than English. In fact four English future forms may translate the "simple future" in other languages and all four use present constructions. One important distinguishing feature is the moment of decision in relation to 'now' and the certainty of arrangements and the attitudes held at the moment of speaking. In this section these are treated individually under the following headings:

1 **Timetable Future**: (present simple with future time marker)
   This form is used to indicate:
   a Scheduled or regular timetabled events: *The bus leaves at three.*
   b Personal plans which rely on scheduled services: *We leave on the four o'clock bus.*
   c Personal plans which form part of a schedule: *We visit Vienna on Tuesday, go on to Paris on Wednesday* etc. This usage of the present simple is very restricted and as the form involves few problems not already posed by the present simple itself, its treatment will be confined to this introduction.

2 **Diary Future**: (present continuous and future time marker)
   I'm seeing him tomorrow;
   denoting a plan or intention already fully entered into.

3 **'Going to' Future:** (present continuous of *to go*)
I'*m going to see him tomorrow*;
which often denotes a plan previously decided upon.

4 **Will/Shall Future**: (present form of a modal, usually *will* or *shall*)
I'*ll see him tomorrow*.
(*Will* has some functions and meanings which are not future in intent. A common usage is to express instant decision.)

Also included in this section are:

5 **The Future Continuous.**

6 **The Future Perfect.**

7 **The Future Perfect Continuous.**

'DIARY' FUTURE: analysis

(Present Continuous + future time marker)

Full Form	(Spoken Form)		Negative Form	(Spoken Form)	
I	am ('m)		I	am ('m) not	
he she it	is ('s)	walking	he she it	is ('s) not (isn't)	walking
you we they	are ('re)		you we they	are ('re) not (aren't)	

With a future time marker: I'm walking to school **tomorrow.**

Question Forms

Are you walking tomorrow?	Aren't you walking tomorrow?
(*neutral question*)	(*suggests surprise or disappointment*)

Tag Questions

You're walking, aren't you?	You're not walking, are you?
(*expects answer 'yes'*)	(*expects answer 'no'*)
I'm walking, aren't I?	I'm not walking tomorrow, am I?
(*no form *amn't I*?*)	(*expects answer 'no'*)

Also: I'm walking tomorrow, am I not? (*this is very formal; expects answer 'yes'*)

Questions to draw the target

What are you doing tomorrow? (often an invitation)

What are you doing tomorrow? ⟶ *I'm entertaining the boss (all day).*

What am I doing tomorrow? (often a request for instructions or a reminder about engagements)

What am I doing tomorrow? ⟶ *You're meeting the chairman at 10 a.m., addressing a meeting at 12 a.m. etc.*

Would you like to (+ verb)? Shall we (+ verb)? (where the invitation is not possible because of previous arrangements)

Would you like to go to the cinema tonight? ⟶ *I can't, I'm babysitting.*

Why don't you/can't you (+ verb + implied future time)?

Why don't you speak to the headmaster about it? ⟶ *I'm seeing him in the morning.*
Why can't you come to the play? ⟶ *I'm working late next week.*

What are your plans?

What are your plans for tomorrow? ⟶ *I'm having lunch with Sue at one o'clock.*

When can you/Will you be able to (+ verb)? (fitting something into a schedule)

When can you mend the washing machine? ⟶ *I'm coming to your area tomorrow. I'll do it then.*

Notes

1   The spoken negative has two possible forms, like the present continuous; He *isn't coming tomorrow* tends to be more neutral; He's *not coming tomorrow*, more emphatic. Note that there is only one form of the spoken negative in the first person singular. This leads to the extraordinary form of the first person tag question, I'm *coming, aren't I?*

2   Verbs describing a state or involuntary sensation (stative verbs), do not usually make a future in this way. Where it does occur it suggests a deliberate act or pretence:

a   To *be*: Very rare in this tense, except to describe role-playing; I'm *being Father Christmas in the play tonight.*

b   To *have*:

•   For possession, is almost always future, with or without the time marker: I'm *having a new coat.*

•   For health, it is regarded as stative: I'm *having a cold* is future, and suggests pretence.

•   For enjoyment or experience: I'm *having a bath tonight*; the verb is dynamic, and so is regular and requires a time-marker.
    Colloquial British and American English prefers I'm *getting* to I'm *having* for possession.

c   Verbs describing involuntary sensation, (*smell, see, hear*), almost never form a future in this way. However, some stative verbs also have dynamic uses, where the action is under voluntary control and is therefore susceptible to future planning. These uses commonly constitute a 'diary' future:
    I'm *seeing him in the morning*; The *judge is hearing the case this afternoon.*

3   Future markers used for this tense:

a   All dates and times future to the time of speaking; (*tomorrow, on Monday, this afternoon, next week, in January, on the 10th, at 3 o'clock* etc.).

b   Generalised future markers; (*soon, later on, in a little while, sometime* etc.).

c   *Now* and *today* with this construction may be genuinely present actions: Now I'm *adding the butter, today we are filming in Kew Gardens*, but are more often future markers indicating imminent action: I'm *seeing the headmaster now* and I'm *ringing Susan today* (later on today). The difference is often marked by the position of the time marker, as shown in the examples.

d   *Just* also occurs in this construction, for imminent action, but is usually associated with the contracted form of *going to*, see Note 4.

4   The 'Going to' future, may contract with verbs of *coming/going* and motion generally, to avoid constructions such as, I'm *going to go*, I'm *going to come*. This contracted form appears identical to the diary future, but does not suggest the element of prior arrangement. The contracted form does not require a future marker, but *just* often occurs colloquially in this construction, between the auxiliary and the rest of the verb, making the construction exactly that of the diary future, I'm *just leaving*. This usage does not imply prior arrangement (compare: I'm *just going to leave*). In the same way, many native speakers will contract constructions like I'm *going to go swimming* to I'm *going swimming*.

5   Spelling:

a   Verbs ending in vowel-consonant-*e* commonly drop *e* before *ing*: I *come*, I'm *coming*.

b   Verbs ending in a short vowel followed by a single consonant commonly double the consonant before *ing*: I *run*, I'm *running*.

c   Verbs ending in *y* obey the rule adding *ing*, but verbs ending *ie* commonly change to *y* before *ing*: I *carry*, I'm *carrying*; I *tie*, I'm *tying*.

6   Stress on the auxiliary, or on the negative will produce an emphatic form of this tense.

7   Pronunciation: These problems are associated with the present continuous, but very occasionally reappear when the tense appears with a new meaning:

a The contracted form *he's is* sometimes heard as *his*, *it's* as *is*.
b The last sound of the contracted auxiliary is lost when the following verb begins with the same consonant, which may cause problems for beginners: I'm *mending/I'm ending*; I'm *meeting/I'm eating*; He's *sleeping/He's leaping*; You're *riding/You're hiding*. etc.
c In verbs ending with *o*, a distinct /w/ sound is pronounced before *ing*: *going*.

Meaning and Function

A **For pre-arranged plans:**
I'm *picking her up at six* (she is expecting me).
We're leaving tomorrow (we have packed, bought our tickets etc.).

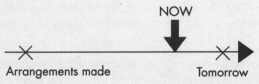

We're leaving tomorrow

B **For refusing invitations** or deferring them, but suggesting a previous arrangement: I'm *sorry I can't come, I'm going to the theatre on Tuesday*.

Suggested Contexts

A **Prearranged plans.** Any clearly defined plans, where arrangements are already made:

• Pair work or as a dialogue building exercise: A secretary, trying to make an appointment for someone to see her employer; both consult their diaries and they try to find a mutually possible time. This requires structures such as, *What about Wednesday?* (No, I'm *sorry I can't manage Wednesday, I'm attending a conference.*) (**See photocopiable page 3**.)

• Information gap activity: the arrangements for a pop-star or for a journey. Different members of the group are given different pieces of information, and asked to put together the whole itinerary. (**See photocopiable page 10**.)

• Each student is given a schedule of a holiday (a bus-tour for example), and asked to compare information with other students. Which is the better value? Which is more interesting and why? *We're visiting six art galleries. We're staying in better hotels* etc.

B **Refusing and deferring invitations:**

• Pair work. One student is given a list of commitments, the other offers an invitation. Find a suitable date, or make it clear that no date is suitable. If cue cards are used, there is scope for work on intonation. I'm **babysitting** *tonight* (I can't come); I'm *babysitting* **tonight** (but ask me again).

C Prepare a general contrastive lesson with other futures, showing that this tense denotes plans less easily changed than other tenses.

Learner Error: Form, Spelling and Pronunciation

1 Students attempt to make diary future forms of stative verbs when these are not appropriate, especially with verbs of sensation: *We're knowing his decision tomorrow.*

2 Students may use the stative Have in the present continuous, and so make an involuntary 'diary future'. I'm having a red coat; I'm having a cold (both of which are future, implying prior arrangement).

3 Contracted forms may continue to create difficulties for beginners.

4 Spelling (*comeing, runing* etc.) may be a persistent problem.

5 The two variant forms of the spoken negative may cause problems if teachers are unaware of this. Beginners may be taught one version, and find that the teacher is inadvertantly using the other in classroom interaction.

6 The tag/question form, I am driving tomorrow, aren't I? Aren't I coming? etc. appears grammatically confusing. Am I not is a possible written form but is not normally used in conversation.

Learner Error: Meaning and Function

1 There is often confusion with other future constructions. For example the diary future may be used:

a where going to would be more appropriate: What are you going to do now? I'm watching television.

b where will for volunteering would be more appropriate: The kettle's boiling. I'm switching it off in a moment. These errors are often disguised because the resultant sentence is possible; the error is in the mismatch of future tenses.

c where will for prediction would be more appropriate; *By 2040 the oil is running out*.

2 Speakers of Arabic who mark future time in the mother tongue by using only a time marker often use the present simple + time marker for any future tense; *I shop tomorrow*.

3 Many languages have a separate simple future tense based on the stem of the verb. Speakers of these languages are often unwilling to use the diary future, and substitute the will form, which is often seen (and taught) as the primary future tense in English; What are you doing tomorrow? I will go to the dentist. An appointment at the dentist is more likely to form part of a prearranged plan – so the "will" form is unsuitable although grammatically correct.

4 Learners make diary futures from stative verbs inappropriately:

a Verbs of sensation; We're eating at the new restaurant tonight *We are liking it*.
We're knowing his decision tomorrow.

b As any continuous form of have for possession appears future, learners often produce inappropriate future tenses by accident; I'm having a sore throat (for pretence) for, I'm getting a sore throat (progressive condition).

5 Markers may create problems:

a Now is interpreted literally, I'm taking it back now. This leads to an unwillingness to use this in future constructions, and loss of comprehension.

b In British English presently means in a moment, not at present and is therefore a future marker. In some American English contexts it means at present, and is equivalent to the English currently.

c Actually means in fact, and is not a time marker. This causes problems for Romance language speakers who assume it to be equivalent to now (actuellement).

GOING TO FUTURE: analysis

Full Form	(Spoken Form)			Negative Form	(Spoken Form)	
I	am ('m)			I	am ('m) not	
he she it	is ('s)		going to walk	he she it	is ('s) not (isn't)	going to walk
you we they	are ('re)			you we they	are ('re) not (aren't)	

Question Forms	
Are you going to walk? (*often a challenge or invitation*)	Aren't you going to walk? (*expects answer 'yes'*)
Tag Questions	
You are going to walk, aren't you? (*expects answer 'yes', may be an invitation*)	You aren't going to walk, are you? (*expects answer 'no', may express disapproval*)

Questions to draw the target

What are you going to do?

What are you going to do? ——————————————⟶ *I'm going to take the dog for a walk.*

What are your plans? or What are you planning to do?

What are your plans? ——————————————⟶ *We're going to fly to Paris.*

What's going to happen next? (with picture/reading clues)

What's going to happen? ——————————————⟶ *He's going to fall into the water.*

Why don't you (+ suggestion)?

Why don't you write to them? ——————————⟶ *I going to go and see them.*

Notes

1 Form: Where the main verb is *to go* the tense is sometimes abbreviated to avoid repetition. Thus *I am going to go*, becomes, *I am going*, especially when followed by *to*: *I'm going to bed*. This is sometimes also applied to *come* and other verbs of motion. This looks like a 'Diary future' (often without the time marker), but conveys no notion of previous firm plan or arrangements, and may cause serious confusion to students (and teachers) attempting to differentiate usages.

Note: The full form, *I am going to go* is perfectly correct, although less colloquial.

The form *I am going (to)* exists also a normal present continuous, and means *I am on my way(to)*.

2   An emphatic form of the tense (for insistence or contradiction) is made by stressing the auxiliary (*am/are*) in the full (statement) or question forms, and the *not* or *isn't/aren't* in the negative.
Note: *Go* and *come* and other verbs of motion usually take the full form in the emphatic.

3   Note that the form *I amn't* does not exist. Conversational English produces the unusual negative tag I *am, aren't* I; the more formal I *am, am* I *not* is now becoming rare in colloquial speech.

4   There are two forms of the spoken negative, except in the first person singular. *You're not* tends to be more emphatic than *You aren't*, but the forms are largely interchangeable. This may lead to problems if one form is taught and the other is inadvertantly used by the teacher especially with elementary classes.

5 Phonetics:

a   The final *g* of *going* is usually not sounded, except in the emphatic form, and the *to* is unstressed, producing /t ə/ or /tʊ/ in British English. In American English this is so marked that the form is sometimes written as *gonna* in informal dialogue.

b   *You're going* is phonetically close to *you were going* (unstressed), and may be misinterpreted as such.

M eaning and Function

This tense is based on the present continuous of *going to*, and in some ways it continues to carry a present continuous connotation. It describes present intentions, held before the time of speaking and expected to continue after it.

A **It is used to indicate a general plan or intention.** It does not, of itself, indicate that arrangements have already been made (compare the Diary Future), although this is possible.
Compare: *Are you going to buy that car (tomorrow)?* (Have you decided to buy it?)
Are you buying that car (tomorrow)? (Have you arranged/agreed to buy it?)

B **It is used to predict future events, based on present concrete evidence.** (It is sometimes called the 'evident now' future for this reason.) The predicted events are often, though not always, imminent:
It is going to rain. (I can see the clouds.) Compare: *It'll rain.* (I base this prediction on previous knowledge.)
I'm going to be sick. (I feel ill.) Compare: *I'll be sick.* (I warn you, based on previous experience.)

Note: Many fortune tellers use the construction *You are going to (meet a tall dark stranger)*, since the predictions are supposedly based on evidence. T.V. meteorologists also use the 'Going to' future, when working with a weather map, *The cold front is going to come in from the Atlantic*.

C **It is used to express intention**, arguably a form of A, but where the plan/intention is formed in the immediate past and is now insisted upon. In comparison to *will*, *going to* often sounds more conversational and less determined but a lot depends on intonation and stress.

a   In conditional sentences: *If he comes in, I'm going to leave* expresses neutral prediction, and determination. Compare *If he comes in, I shall leave* for instant decision.

b   Insistence on plans, often because the listener is likely to disapprove: *I am going to wear that hat*; Compare *I will wear that hat. I shall wear that hat* for instant decision.

c   Especially with *have to*, it expresses regrettable necessity of future action: *I'm going to have to report this.* Compare: *I'll have to report this.* (no regret); *I will have to report this.* (This is a decision I have come to after deliberating.)

Suggested Contexts

The tense can be introduced in this way to elementary students. Give a command: *"Open the door please, Wu"*. Wu walks to door and reaches for the handle. *"Stop. He's going to open the door. Open the door. Good. Close the door."* Before it is shut, interrupt again; *"Stop! He's going to close the door."*

(Note: it is important that Wu is no longer walking when you interrupt, to overcome the base meaning of *going to*. Reinforce this with the same activity but using sedentary actions. It is hard to determine whether *going to* has the function of 'plans', or an 'evident now' function in this context, but to introduce the form this kind of exercise can be useful, since the construction can be used correctly with either meaning, and the distinction is not essential for learners at elementary level.)

(A) *For general plans:*

- Holiday plans. Students are given a destination, guide book, map and budget. The class decides how best to spend the money/time. The exercise can be set up with suggestions such as, *Why don't we …?: Let's …* etc. Then the new tense is used to reiterate; *We're going to see the Louvre* etc. Then give a similar task, with a different destination for group work and elicit discussion and feedback. (Note: This can be contrasted with the 'diary' future, *We're visiting Versailles on Tuesday*, (the trip is already booked). Note also that planning a journey easily leads to the *going to go to/ going to* contraction.)

- Personal plans. *What are you going to do at Christmas/when you leave school*. This can be set as a questionnaire; where appropriate the teacher can check whether the diary future is a possible alternative, (are arrangements already made? etc.).

- Interrupted video film. Guess the next action; *What's he going to do next?* Check the answers against the film.

- Photographs/pictures of people dressed in particular ways; *What is he going to do? He's going to fly a space craft.*

(B) *To predict future events, based on present evidence:*

- Use contexts (pictures, video etc.) in which settings provide clear evidence of the outcome, for example, a man in football kit, *He's going to play football.* (**See photocopiable page 9a.**)

- Select a picture series in which the outcome is self-evident. (Cartoon series/films sometimes lend themselves to this.) *He's going to fall down the hole. He's going to meet his wife.*

- At post elementary levels. A contrastive lesson with predictive *will*. *Its going to rain/It will rain. He's going to be tall/He'll be good at sport.*

(C) *To express intention:*

This is probably best introduced after students are familiar with *will* for instant decision, determination, and conditional prediction. The necessity for teaching the distinction often arises from student enquiry at an upper intermediate/advanced level.

Learner Error: Form, Spelling and Pronunciation

1 Students may produce deviant forms of the first person singular with negative forms and tag questions: *I amn't* *I aren't*.

2 Students may produce or understand *are going to* for *were going to* and vice versa.

3 Students may hear *I'm gun a/I'm gone a*, especially in a native speaker environment, and spell the form accordingly. They may also interpret *you're* as *your*, *they're* as *their*, and *he's* as *his*. This may produce apparently meaningless written forms such as *your gun a fish*, *he's gone a eat*, *he's going a fish* and (especially Far Eastern students), *he's gone eat*.

4 Students are often unwilling to produce the forms *I'm going to go* and especially *I'm going to come*. The full form is correct in English, although native speakers often prefer the contracted form *I'm going/I'm coming*.

Learner Error: Meaning and Function

1 Many students fail to differentiate the contracted form of *going to* from the 'diary' form, and use them indiscriminately. Hence: *What's he going to do? He's going swimming* is the acceptable contracted form for *He's going to go swimming*, because the main verb is *to go*. *He's diving* for *He's going to dive* is unacceptable. The substitution of *going to* for the diary future, is more common, and more idiomatically acceptable, since *going to* does not negate the idea of previous arrangements: *What are you doing tomorrow? I'm going to see the dentist* (for *I'm seeing the dentist*). However, this may mask an inability to distinguish the forms.

2 Many students prefer the *will* future because it is closer to their mother tongue and use this at all times, often inappropriately: *What are you going to do this summer? I will go home*.

3 Students may perceive *going to* as indicating:

a present action, unless there is a time marker (on the pattern of the diary future) Hence: *I am going to read it tomorrow* is seen as future. *I am going to read it*, is seen as meaning *I am on my way to read it*. This is especially true of learners whose mother tongue marks future time only with markers (e.g. Arabic speakers and some Indian languages).

b imminent activity only (often on a mother tongue pattern), hence: *I am going to see the film tonight* but not *I'm going to see it sometime* (Romance language speakers).

4 The sentence *What am I going to do?* is often an expression of despair, and a request for advice. Hence the answer is not for example, *You're going to be late* but *Why don't you take a taxi* or *I'll give you a lift*.

WILL/SHALL FUTURE: analysis

Full Form	(Spoken Form)			Negative Form	(Spoken Form)	
I you he she it we they	will shall	('ll)	go	I you he she it we they	will not (won't) shall not (shan't)	go

Question Forms

Will you go? (*neutral*)	Won't you go? (*can express invitation*)
Shall I go? (*expresses willingness to undertake an obligation; makes a suggestion; asks for advice*)	
Shall you go? (*a possible form, but rare*)	Shan't I go? (*a possible form, but rare*)

Tag Questions

You'll go, won't you? (*expects answer 'yes'*)	You won't go, will you? (*expects answer 'no'*)
I shall go, shan't I?	I shan't go, shall I?

(*Requests the agreement of a person in authority for a desired course of action*: (I shall be in the team, shan't I?; *invites the listener to recognise the logical consequence of an action*: What if you miss the bus? Well then I shan't go, shall I?)

	You shan't go, shall you? (*a possible form, but rare.*)

Questions to draw the target

Volunteering and instant decision.

Often the natural response to a comment or suggestion.

I'm thirsty. ⟶ *Shall I put the kettle on?*

How can you (+ verb)?

How can you find out? ⟶ *I'll ring my brother.*

How will you (+ verb)?

How will you get there? ⟶ *I'll walk.*

What will you/he do to help? ⟶ *He'll bring a cake. Shall I bring the sandwiches?*

Prediction.

Prediction (especially with *if* or *when*)

What will happen/you do?

What will you do when/if it rains? ⟶ *We'll move indoors.*

What will happen if the oil runs out? ⟶ *We'll start using nuclear power.*

Expressing determination.

Usually a response to a statement:

She doesn't think you'll pass the exam. ⟶ *Well she's wrong. I will pass.*

Will/shall forms occur in response to a command or challenge:

Go to bed! ⟶ *I won't /shan't.*

Expressing commitment (in a formal situation).

What do you intend to do?
How will you tackle this? ⟶ *We shall reduce unemployment and cut taxes.*

What about ...?
What about the bill? ⟶ *I'll/shall pay by credit card.*

Logical deduction.

Who's that? ⟶ *It'll be the postman.*

Capacity/potential.

What will it do?
Why do you want it? ⟶ *It'll do 10 km to the litre.*

Persistence.

What annoys you?
Why does he annoy you? ⟶ *He **will** interrupt me.*

Notes

1 Some functions can only be expressed with *shall*, others only with *will*.

2 With other functions the *will/shall* forms are interchangeable for the first person pronouns. In written form however, in some cases *shall* is still considered the correct form.

3 In spoken English *will* is more common and is reduced to *'ll*. Arguably *shall* has no separate form but *'ll* is usually accepted as being the contracted form.

4 *Shall*
The use of *shall* suggests that the speaker is expressing his authority over the listener who is in turn bound by that authority. Hence, especially in legal, biblical and archaic texts we find:
You shall not go, I *forbid it.* (feudal authority, for example)
The vendor shall be liable for tax. (legal authority)
Heaven and earth shall pass away. (divine authority)

The speaker may also use *shall* where he takes on the responsibility for an action and expects the listener to be bound by the action:
I *shall be there at 3 o'clock* (this is my decision and I expect you to meet me there).
Compare:
I *will be there at 3 o'clock* (as a matter of course; if you're there at that time we can go and have a drink together).

5 Will

a In the negative *won't* is used to express unwillingness but doesn't always refer to the future:
He *won't listen to a word I'm saying*.

b With *you* for:

- making requests: *Will you follow me, please*.
- giving orders: *Will you be quiet!*
- giving formal invitations: *Will you have some more tea?*
                                   Won't you have some more tea? (an alternative and more pressing invitation).

6 *Won't* and *Shan't* are used for refusing, usually in response to a command or challenge:
I *won't give you your money back*.
(Here the refusal is an expression of the speaker's volition.)
Go to bed! I shan't!
(Here the refusal is an expression of the listener's volition in response to a person in authority to whom he feels bound, but in this case, unwilling, to obey.)
Won't is also used for inaminate objects:
The *car won't start*.

7 Pronunciation: *Will* is reduced to /wəl/ in the unstressed form. For strong determination and persistence it is not reduced.

8 *Will* and *Shall* cannot be used with other modal verbs (see page. 118, Modal Auxilaries).

9 An emphatic form of the tense (used for contradicting) is formed by stressing the *will/shall*.

Meaning and Function

A *Volunteering and instant decision:*
When an action is decided on at the moment of speech and where there is no previous plan.
(Compare other future forms e.g: I'm *seeing the dentist tomorrow* (I have an appointment) I'*ll see the dentist tomorrow* (If I can make an appointment.)
Volunteering is an example of instant decision. The offer may be introduced with *Shall I?*

a   *Shall I do the washing up for you?*
b   *Shall we go to the cinema tonight*.
    Note also the use of *shall* for asking advice and instructions:
c   *Shall I wear the flowery dress or the plain one?*
d   *Shall I open the door?*
    With will: *There's someone at the door. Don't worry. I'll go.*
    Which shoes do you want to take? I'll take the brown ones.
    The question form with *will* becomes a request: *Will you open the door, please?*
    Other people's services can be volunteered: *My husband will drive you*.

B *Prediction:*
Will/shall forms may be used when a prediction is made based on judgement, knowledge or guesswork.

a   With a future meaning: I *wonder where I will/shall (I'll) be in 10 years time.*
    They'll be here soon.
b   With a conditional form, in the main clause: *If you ask, I'm sure he'll offer to help.*
c   With a present meaning: *I'm sure she'll be home by now.*
    When the speaker feels that circumstance rather than volition dictates his course of action, *shall*
    may be used: *I shall have to go instead of her.* (I have no other choice.)

C   Expressing determination:
Note the varying degrees of determination in the following:
I *will pass this exam* (against all odds).
I'*ll pass this exam* (with a suggestion of confidence). The contracted form is intrinsically less
forceful.
I *shall pass this exam.* The use of *shall* implies a commitment on the part of the speaker to pass the
exam as part of an undertaking that he has made to the listener.

D   Expressing commitment:
a   Public declarations of policy: *We will/shall cut taxes.*
b   Threats: *I will/shall tell your mother.*
c   Promises: *will* is used to express the voluntary nature of the undertaking: *I will ('ll) buy you a*
    new toy.

Note: The following are not future in meaning. *Shall* forms are not appropriate:

E   Logical deduction:
Where the speaker makes deductions on logical grounds:
That'll be the postman. He'll have my letter.

F   Capability/Potential:
Will is used as a common variant of *can* to describe the potential of an inanimate object.
The crane will lift half a ton.
Compare: *The weightlifter can lift half a ton.*

G   Persistence (especially habits):
*He **will** slam the door.*
Compare also:
He's always slamming the door.
*He **will** keep slamming the door.*

S uggested Contexts

A   Volunteering

* Role play: Organising a party etc. Students volunteer contributions, I'*ll bring the cups* etc. (with *will*
  you/shall I?) Can be combined with cue-cards suggesting likes and dislikes, (*You like cooking/.music.*
  You don't like cooking).

* Students are given a list of tasks which are normally done by another member of staff who is
  temporarily absent. They volunteer to help.
  This exercise works better if students are given timetables with their own commitments and if
  tasks cannot always be carried out by a volunteer: Thus: *Take the post. I'll take the post. Go to the*
  dentist.I'll phone the surgery to cancel the appointment, (not *I'll go to the dentist*).(**See photocopiable page 3.**)

- Role play. Students must find excuses for not doing a given activity: I *can't wash up now, I've got to go shopping. I'll wash the dishes.*
  Instant decision: This is probably best taught by contrasting other futures, concentrating on the time of the decision. (Volunteering is, of course, a kind of instant decision).

B *Predicting*

- The teacher introduces a narrative (preferably in the present simple) but stops at points where two or three possibilities arise: *What will happen next?* This works well in conjunction with a map or diagram. Follow the route: *Which way will he turn? Where will he be? What do you think he will do next?*
- The same exercise may be used with video or film (especially of someone engaging in strange behaviour, in order to avoid *going to*).
- Essay work/discussion: *What the world will be like in the year 2100.*

C *Expressing determination*

This is possibly best taught in conjunction with stress and intonation, as part of a series on challenges/determination etc.

D *Expressing commitment*

- Class or group discussion, drawing up a political manifesto with election promises, for example.
- Role-play. A dismissed employee or suitor promises to reform. This works well with *have*: *You have broken all the plates. I'll be more careful in future.*

E *Logical deduction*

- *That'll be the postman.* Taught as part of a series on logical deduction, with *can't be/must be.*
- *That'll be £2,* taught functionally as part of topic on shopping.

F *Capability/potential*

Students prepare a sales talk promoting a car for example: *It will do 10 Km to the litre.*

G *Persistence*: best taught as part of a series on expressing irritation.

Learner Error: Form, Spelling and Pronunciation

1 *Will* and *shall* used before other modal verbs: *I will can* etc.

2 Some learners (e.g. Germanic speakers) have difficulty with the *w*, and pronounce it /v/.

3 Many learners have difficulty with the short *i* sound, and produce /wi:l/.

4 Learners new to this tense have difficulty with the reduced form of *will*. They may stress *will*, thus producing an inappropriate meaning.

5 *Will* is sometimes perceived as the future of *To be*, and some false beginners are reluctant to add *be* in the same sentence. Hence *I will late* etc.

Learner Error: Meaning and Function

1 Many students regard this as the 'real' future and use it at all times: *I'll see the doctor tomorrow* for *I'm seeing/ going to see the doctor.*

2 There is widespread confusion about the use of *will* and *shall*, especially at higher levels. Students may use *shall* inappropriately, for prediction or deduction: *I *think he shall be* Prime Minister*. *That *shall be the postman.* *
Students may use *shall* in the first person at all times: I *shall make the tea* for I'*ll make the tea.*
They may use *shall* in all volunteering contexts, *Shall *you make the tea*?*

3 Usages which are not future in reference create confusion, especially where students believe they have understood the concept of *will*.

4 Students may substitute *can* for *will* in usages for logical deduction and capability. This may be because of seemingly parallel uses: *That *can be the postman** derived from That *can't be the postman.*

FUTURE CONTINUOUS: analysis

Full Form	(Spoken Form)		Negative Form		(Spoken Form)	
I we	will ('ll) shall	be walking	I we	will shall	not	(won't) (shan't)	be walking
you he she it they	will ('ll)		you he she it they	will not (won't)		

Question Forms	
Will you be walking? (*neutral*)	You won't be walking, will you? (*seeks confirmation*)
Tag Questions	
You will be walking, won't you? (*expects answer 'yes, I shall/will'*)	Won't you be walking? (*expects answer 'no, I won't'*)

Questions to draw the target

What will you be doing (+ time marker)?

What will he be doing this time tomorrow? ⟶ *He'll be sunbathing.*

Why aren't you (+ diary future)?

Why aren't you coming to the party ⟶ *I will be taking my driving test.*
(*on Wednesday*)?

Why must I/should I …? (questioning advice)

Why must I take a book? ⟶ *You'll be sitting on the train for hours.*

Where will you be (+ time marker)?(where the activity suggests a place)

Where will you be when I arrive? ⟶ *I'll be working in the library.*

Notes

1 The *shall* form exists as an alternative form of the first person in formal British usage.

a Where the speaker has previously undertaken to perform an action which now constitutes an obligation:
   I *shall be picking mother up at ten* (so I can't meet you until afterwards).

b Where the speaker makes a decision to act at the time of speaking, and formally undertakes/threatens/ promises to fulfil that decision:
I shall be reporting this to the police. I shall be recommending you for a medal.

2 The *will* form indicates prediction of neutral events: *We will be having a party on the 20th. I will be seeing him tomorrow.* In speech, the *will* form is always contracted.
(See also page 73, Will/Shall)

(Note that Scottish, Irish and American usage prefers *will* in all circumstances.)

3 Stress on the auxiliary in the statement form (or on *not* in the negative) will produce an emphatic version of the tense.

4 Spelling. The variations of the present participle are the same as in all other continuous forms.

a Verbs ending in vowel-consonant-*e* commonly drop *e* before *ing*: *I come/ I'm coming.*

b Verbs ending in a short vowel followed by a single consonant commonly double the consonant before *ing*: *I run/ I'm running.*

c Verbs ending in *y* obey the rule and add *ing*, but verbs ending *ie* commonly change to *y* before *ing*: *I carry/ I'm carrying. I tie/I'm tying.*

5 Stative verbs do not usually take a continuous form (see page 12, Present Continuous). However, since this tense is used for logical deduction and prediction, stative verbs may occasionally take a continuous form. Hence *You'll be feeling hungry; I expect I shall be hearing bells next!*

Meaning and Function

A **Denotes an action which is expected to cross a point or fill a period of future time:**
Chiefly used to account for a person's unavailability, or to discuss timetables and schedules.

a **When a point in future time is specified and the action is protracted.** Used to predict actions expected to begin before the point in time, continue across it, and continue after it: *This time tomorrow he'll be lying on the beach.*

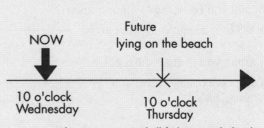

This time tomorrow he'll be lying on the beach

b **When a point in future time is defined by another action** (usually in the present simple, in a time clause with *when*). In this case, the action may not necessarily continue after the specified time:
I'll be working when you arrive (but I may stop then).

c **When a future action fills a specific period of time:**
I will be watching television from eight o'clock to midnight.
The action is expected to fill a specified time period. Note: This usage can be imprecise; it does not necessarily suggest exactly 8–12. It

stresses the unbroken nature and ongoing process of the action, and implies that this is somehow relevant to the listener:

I *will be watching television tonight* (that is where you will find me).

Compare: I'*m watching television tonight* (this is my plan).

d **When a period in the future is defined by another action**. This action may be in the present simple or present continuous but not in a future tense:

I *will be buttering the bread while my mother is slicing the tomatoes.*

I *will be buttering the bread while my mother slices the tomatoes.*

I *will be buttering the bread when my mother is slicing the tomatoes.*

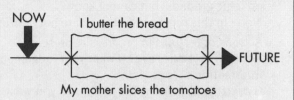

I *will be buttering the bread while my mother is slicing/slices the tomatoes*

Also: I *will be buttering the bread when my mother slices the tomatoes.* This suggests that my mother's action is shorter than mine.

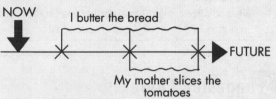

I *will be buttering the bread when my mother starts slicing the tomatoes*

B **Reassuring/reasserting arrangements**. The tense is used when an action is expected to begin at a specified time. Perhaps most helpfully seen as a combination of *will* for prediction and the 'diary' future (and often instead of 'diary' or Going to futures). It is used when the listener/reader is expected to be affected by, or involved in, the action. It stresses the process of the future action, as well as the fact of it:

a With a time marker, when the action is momentary, in which case it begins and ends at the specified time:

We'*ll be arriving at Heathrow at 6 o'clock* (and you are either a passenger or you are meeting a passenger).

Compare: *We are arriving at Heathrow at 6 o'clock* (this is an arrangement of which I am informing you).

or *We arrive at Heathrow at 6 o'clock* (and this is part of a timetable of activities which we have made).

b With a time marker and protracted action. The action is expected to begin at the specified time.

We'*ll be eating at 8* (so be ready at that time/don't arrive until later).

c The point in future time is marked by another action (usually in the present simple or present perfect, in a time clause.), where it is predicted that the action will take place immediately. Often used to reassure:

He'*ll be leaving as soon as the taxi has come* (and we are expecting a taxi, so don't worry).

He'*ll be leaving as soon as the taxi comes* (whenever that is, but don't worry).

Compare: He'*s leaving as soon as the taxi comes* (that is what he has arranged to do).

C **Threatening or promising future action.** The decision is taken at the time of speaking, and the listener is expected to be affected by the action or threat. It is often used with *shall*. It invites the listener to contemplate the process, not merely the fact of the projected action.

a With a time marker or where there is an implication that the action or threat will be carried out soon: *I shall be writing to your mother.*

b With *now* as time marker for imminent future, used especially with verbs of departing in colloquial conversation: *I'll be getting along now; I'll be going now* (i.e. immediately).

D **Logical deduction/speculation.** The speaker makes a judgement about an action which he deduces on logic grounds, but cannot know.
Note: In this function *shall/shan't* are not appropriate (see Notes).

a Actions or feelings in progress at present:
What will he be doing now? (I want your judgement); compare *What is he doing now?* (I want information).
(I expect) you'll be feeling hungry (i.e. do you want something to eat?).

b With a future time marker, the future continuous may indicate a similarly deduced future action (especially with verbs of thinking/hoping etc.) The action is expected to account for all the time available:
What will he be doing tomorrow (do you think)?; compare *What will he do/is he doing tomorrow?*

Suggested Contexts

A

a **When a point in future time is specified and the action is protracted:**

- A timetable of future events is set up using the *shall/will* or 'diary' future (present continuous + time marker). Arbitrary times are then taken which fall during activities. This is useful for contrast: *At 2:30 we are leaving. At 3 o'clock we'll be sitting in the bus/travelling to Paris* etc. (**See photocopiable page 10.**)

- Students in pairs are given conflicting timetables from which they try to work out a convenient meeting time. This needs 'diary' future, and comparison between tenses: *At 3 o'clock he's meeting the mayor, so at ten to 3 he'll be driving to the town hall* etc. (**See photocopiable page 3.**)

- Plans for Christmas, for example: *What will you be doing on Christmas day?* This could be used as a class questionnaire.

b **When the point in time is defined by another action:**

- Pair or group work. Students are given timetables of future events so that X is partway through an activity when Y begins, or completes an action, and vice versa: X *will be having lunch when Y arrives at the station*, etc. They are asked to compare timetables in this way.

- A 'family group' is imagined, and a list of programmed activities for each member is built up. Then the teacher adds a list of tasks and which should be done at given times: *Who can meet Grandma from the train? When Grandma arrives, X will be working. Y will be playing tennis. Z will be shopping.* Find family members who are able to undertake the tasks, and elicit explanations if they cannot. Ensure that the tasks are organised so that most can be undertaken by someone.

- Compare holiday/weekend plans within groups. Draw up a table of comparative plans and read it back: *Paul will be arriving home when Annette's train leaves the station.*

c **When the action fills a period of time:**

- Information gap exercise. Give students a list of proposed activities for 3 or 4 individuals, with times for commencing and finishing. Fill in the timetable: *Paul will be working from lunchtime till six o'clock*, etc.

- Role-play. Making excuses for one's inability to undertake an action at a given time.

d **When a period in the future is defined by another simultaneous action:**

- Comparing life-plans: *What will Wu be doing when Emil is studying in America?*

- Elicit from each student a list of jobs (e.g. party preparation) with allotted times for each activity. Distribute it among the groups/pairs.
  Compare times and activities: *What will you be doing while Alain is preparing the food?*
  (Note: This is really reaffirming arrangements, but it fits both categories.)

B **Reassuring and reasserting arrangements:**

- Role play or dialogue building exercises based on a hospital or similar institution. A nurse outlines the routine: *At eight o'clock we'll be bringing your breakfast.*

- Travel arrangements: *We'll be waiting at the airport. I'll be carrying two red suitcases* etc.

- Comparative exercise with other futures to underline the 'reassurance/personal involvement' element. (advanced). *The coach will be leaving in 10 minutes* (this includes listener and therefore becomes a warning). *The coach leaves in ten minutes* (this is an objective announcement).

C **As part of series on threats, warnings and promises.**

D **Logical deduction/speculation:**

- One group of students choose a famous personality. Another group try to guess his identity by inviting speculation about his present activities: *What do you think he'll be doing now? What will he be wearing?* etc.

- Guessing game. The class is told that an imaginary personality left on holiday yesterday: *What do you expect he will be doing now? This afternoon?*

- Speculate on your own life – 20 years into the future. (Ask the students to form groups and compare notes on their predictions.)

Learner Error: Form, Spelling and Pronunciation

1 Students may make a continuous form of stative verbs where this is inappropriate: *I'll be being a teacher.*

2 Learners may use *shall* in the second and third person: *He shall be catching the 4 o'clock train.*

3 Learners may use *shall* in the first person where obligation/pre-arranged plan is not implied. This is rarely serious, but may create a slightly pompous tone: I *expect I shall be studying Russian.*

4 Learners may omit the unstressed *'ll* sound, when first learning the tense: *I be leaving at eight.*

5 Learners occasionally misinterpret *be* as a prefix (as in *become*). Hence I *will be coming*, may be interpreted as *I will becoming.*

6 Variations in the spelling of the present participle may create continuing problems: I *will be *shoping** etc.

Learner Error: Meaning and Function

1 Many learners try to avoid the tense altogether, usually substituting another future form (often *will*).
   This may produce a sentence which is apparently correct, but which implies a different sequence.
   I'll work when you come for *I'll be working when you come.*
   I'm working/going to work at 10 o'clock for *I'll be working at 10 o'clock.*

2 Often learners attempt to use this tense for simultaneous action in both clauses:
   I will be buttering the bread while my mother will be slicing the tomatoes.

3 Learners fail to appreciate the element of reassurance/relevance to the listener carried by this tense.
   They are therefore unable to distinguish between this and other future forms, and use it
   inappropriately.

FUTURE PERFECT : analysis

Full Form	(Spoken Form)			Negative	(Spoken Negative)	
Regular verbs: use a past participle identical in form to the past simple.						
I we	will shall	('ll)	have finished	I we	will not (won't) shall not (shan't)	have finished
you he she it they	will	('ll)		you he she it they	will not (won't)	
Irregular verbs: use a past participle which usually differs in form from the past simple.						
I will have eaten		I'll have eaten		I will not have eaten		I won't have eaten

Question Forms

Will you have finished? (*usually expresses readiness to make arrangements*) Will you have finished? (*or will you need more time?*)	Won't you have finished (by then)? (*expects answer 'yes', usually expresses surprise or acts as a reminder*)

Tag Questions

You'll have finished, won't you? (*expects answer 'yes'*)	You won't have finished, will you? (*expects answer 'no' or expresses surprise*)

Questions to draw the target

How much will you have done (+ time marker, usually with *by*)?

How much will you have done by this afternoon?   →   I'll have finished the whole job by then.
What will have happened (by then)?   The icecaps will have melted.

Why will you be/do you think you will be/expect to be + verb/adjective?

Why do you think you'll be late?   ——————→   By the time I've finished, I'll have missed the bus.

Notes

1 Form: Past participles are formed exactly as the past perfect, (see page 45, Past Perfect).

Shall/shan't may occur for *will/won't* in the first person, in both singular and plural, where the speaker undertakes or promises that the action shall be performed (e.g. because he expects the listener to be personally affected by the outcome or timing of the action): We *shall have finished your car by then*. or where the speaker himself feels obliged by circumstances or commitments: I *shall have left by the time you arrive*.

2 Pronunciation:

a The pronunciation of the *ed* ending varies, depending on the last letter(s) of the verb: *stopped, walked* /t/; *opened, carried* /d/; *wanted, landed* /ɪd/.

b H*ave* is commonly reduced to *ve* in speech, although not written in this form: ◄ I *won't've arrived by then*. This is sometimes mistaken for *of* even by native speakers.

c Stress on the *will/won't* produces an emphatic form of the tense.

3 Note especially: I *will have been* (from To Be) is used and perceived as the future perfect of *To Go* in some circumstances; I *will have been to London* (I will go to London and return before that time), but I *will have gone to London* (and that is where I will be at the time).

4 Note that American usage prefers to avoid this tense, usually substituting a future passive, or a construction with *through* and the present participle: When *will you be finished*? When *will you be through reading it*? (Compare to British English: When *will you have finished it*?)

M eaning and Function

(A) **A point in future time is indicated in the sentence usually with 'by'.** (By Tuesday, by 4 o'clock, by then). It is predicted that the action will be completed by that time, and have a direct effect upon it.

a With single actions; the action is wholly in the future He *will/won't have arrived by then*; (so he will/won't be here at that time).

b With protracted actions; these may or may not have been begun before the time of speaking: I'll *have painted the room by then* (so we can use it then). These usages occur with *just*, *already* or with *still* (but not usually with *yet*). I'll *just have finished work by then* (so I can come with you then, but no earlier). I'll *already have finished work* (so I can come with you then, or even earlier). I *still won't have finished work* (*by then*) (so I won't be able to come with you/you'll have to wait).

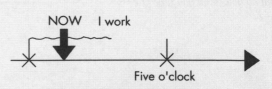

I will have finished work by five o'clock

B **A *period of future time* (often 'a lifetime') is *implied or stated*.** The action in the future perfect may be past, in progress or planned at the time of speaking, but will be completed before the end of the time, and directly affect the remainder of that time. It is often found in conditional sentences, or with expressions such as *at least*.

Whatever happens, at least he will have had a good education. (his education may be over, in progress, or planned, but whatever the case, once completed he will benefit from it).

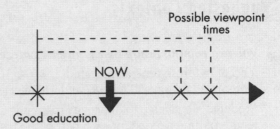

Whatever happens, at least he will have had a good education

C **Logical deduction.** The speaker predicts/deduces that actions have already taken place, which have a direct result upon a present situation. This usage does not need a time marker, but may take *by now, by this time*. (*Shall/shan't* are not appropriate in this function.)

He has left. (present perfect, certainty)

He will have left by now (future perfect, prediction, based on probabilities)

It also suggests that some other (implied) action can or cannot take place as a result;

He'll have arrived home by now (I predict he is now at home. You can contact him there).

This usage is found with:

- *Just*: *He will have just left* (if you hurry you might catch up with him).
- *Already*: *He will already have left* (You are too late).

  and in the negative and question forms with:

- *Yet*: *He won't have left yet* (I think he is still at home, so you're not too late).
  Will they have left yet? (Do you think I am too late?).

  and in the negative only with:

- *Still*: *They still won't have arrived* (so you won't be able to contact them until later).
  (For further notes on *just/already/yet/still*, see page 24, Present perfect).
  Note that these time markers can occur in a variety of positions:

a   Before the auxiliaries (*already, still*): *They already will have left.*
b   Between the auxiliaries: *They will just have left.*
c   Between *have* and the verb (*already, just, yet*). *They will have already left.*
d   At the end of the sentence or clause: *They'll have left already.*
   Note that in other positions these words carry a different force and may alter the meaning of the sentence: *Yet they won't have arrived. They just won't have arrived. They won't still have gone.*

Suggested Contexts

(A) *Where a point in future time is given.* Contexts must make clear that:

a   a point in future time is indicated;

b   a predicted action will be over and will affect the situation at that time.

- Students are given a joint activity (planning a newspaper, a trip, a party). They estimate the length of time needed for each part of the task. Then dates are given for future meetings and deadlines. Groups or individuals predict what steps will be completed by then, from the estimates: *We'll have written the editorial by then, but we won't have finished the illustrations.* This can be a role play or a real activity. (**See photocopiable page 3**)

- Students are given a number of bookings (e.g. for hotel rooms, restaurant tables or similar). Some bookings overlap. Groups are asked to maximise the use of rooms/tables. *A is arriving at 5, but B won't have left by then* etc. This exercises uses limited vocabulary, but offers a useful demonstration of the context, especially in relation to other future tenses.

- Members of the group predict their own futures and describe what they will have done by a given date: *I'll have left school/started university/got a job* etc. This can be made more communicative by getting each student to predict three items for himself, and one for each of the other members of his group; they must try to match/compare predictions.

- Ecology debate. e.g. "The state of the world in 2050." This will require other future tenses, but is useful as a revision exercise. This may be done as a written exercise if preferred.

(B) *Where a period in future time is implied or stated,* (More advanced usage.) The context must make clear that the perfect form implies that the "doer" of the action is expected to act in that period.

- Counting your blessings. Students outline the experiences which they have had/are having which they believe will be valuable throughout their lives, or those which they hope/expect to escape altogether: *At least I'll have heard Yehudi Menuhin/won't have fought in a war.*

(C) *Logical deduction.* Few situations call for sustained use of this tense. The context must make clear that a   the speaker is talking about now;

            b   the speaker is making a deduction, not speaking from knowledge.

- Students are given a series of pictures, or other cues, from which one certain fact can be deduced (present perfect); and others guessed at (future perfect). E.g. You call at a friend's house in the evening, (give students a picture of a darkened house, with an open garage. An outline of his lifestyle/interests are written on the back):
  He's gone out. Where is he? He'll have gone to the pictures. He'll have taken Lisa. etc. This is more interesting if different groups have differing (not contradictory) information: *He won't have gone to the pictures. He's broke.*

- Predicting disaster. Give students a picture (or other cue) of someone cooking for example. Set the scene: *It is 3 o'clock. The telephone rings.* Introduce other time-checks: *It's ten past three. What is the situation? The dinner will have burnt.* This can make a useful cross-check with the future continuous: *It will be cooking nicely.*

Learner Error: Form, Spelling and Pronunciation

1 The past participle may be formed on an incorrect pattern. This tense is usually introduced at an advanced level, so this error tends to occur with less common verbs: *I will have shaven* etc.

2 Pronunciation:

a The reduced form *ve* may be interpreted, written or pronounced *of*. This occurs chiefly where students have heard non-standard native pronunciation or spelling (*I will of*).

b Unfamiliar *ed* forms may be mispronounced, often on a false pattern: I *will have learned*. /l3:nd/ (compare: My *learned friend* /l3:nid/).

3 The *shall* form may be mistakenly used with 2nd and 3rd persons.

4 Students often produce this form for the present perfect in time clauses after *when*, especially if the mother tongue contains a tense formed on a similar pattern (e.g. French) *I'll see him when he will have come.*

Learner Error: Meaning and Function

1 The presence of *will/shall* in the form, may lead learners to think of the action as necessarily future. The use for actions already begun (*We'll have written the editorial by then*) and for actions already completed (*At least I'll have heard Yehudi Menuhin*) may cause great confusion, especially to learners who previously believed they had understood the context of the tense. It is perhaps most useful to revise the tense, stressing that the future reference is the time of the result of the action, not the action itself.

2 There may be confusion because without a future time marker the tense usually has present reference (logical deduction: *He'll have left*). It may be helpful to present this as a perfect form of *will* for logical deduction, (i.e. a form which draws attention to the present situation rather than present action, using *will* simply to express the guess).

3 Students may avoid using the tense at all, except in exercises devised to require it.

4 *Yet* is sometimes inappropriately used:

a with future intention: *I won't have gone yet* (for I *won't have gone by then*).

b with the statement form: *I will have gone yet* (for I *will already have gone*).

5 *Yet*, *still*, *always* and *just* cause difficulties with word order.
This may lead to:

a ungrammatical sentences: *Just he will have gone.*

b unintentionally different meanings: *Yet they won't have arrived. They just won't have arrived. They won't still have left.*

FUTURE PERFECT CONTINUOUS: analysis

Full Form	(Spoken Form)		Negative Form		(Spoken Form)	
I we	will ('ll) shall	have been walking	I we	will shall	not (won't) (shan't)	have been walking
you he she it they	will ('ll)		you he she it they		will not (won't)	

Question Forms	
Will you have been walking? *(usually expresses concern for the possible consequences)*	Won't you have been walking? *(expects answer 'yes', expresses surprise or reminds the listener of the expected consequences)*
Will you have been walking? *(Will you need a rest?)*	Won't you have been walking? *(You will probably be tired. You seem to have forgotten this)*

Tag Questions	
You'll have been walking, won't you? *(expects answer 'yes')*	You won't have been walking, will you?) *(expects answer 'no', expresses surprise)*

Questions to draw the target

How long will you have been (+ verb + implied future time)?

How long will you have been studying English
(when you finish your course)? ⟶ *I'll have been studying for 2 months.*
(expect short answer: 2 months)

Why will you be/do you think you will be (+ adjective describing a physical state)?

Do you think you'll be tired? ⟶ *Yes, I'll have been running for 20 minutes.*

What (do you think) he will have been doing this morning? (for guessing unknown activities)

What do you think he'll have been doing? ⟶ *(I think) he'll have been playing football.*
(expect short answer: *Playing football*)

N.B. This tense is more realistically drawn by comment or statement:

You'll be tired when you arrive. ⟶ *No, I'll have been sitting all the way.*
There's Jim. He looks tired! *He'll have been playing football.*

Notes

1 Spelling: The spelling of the present participle may still create problems;

a Verbs ending in vowel-consonant-e commonly drop *e* before *ing*: I *come*/ I'm *coming*.

b Verbs ending in a short vowel followed by a single consonant commonly double consonant before *ing*: I *run*/ I'm *running*.

c Verbs ending in *y* obey the rule, but verbs ending *ie* commonly change to *y* before *ing*. I *carry*/I'm *carrying*. I *tie*/I'm *tying*.

2 Stative verbs rarely create continuous tenses. Stative verbs may occasionally occur in this tense for logical deduction of ongoing physical sensations, especially with verbs of thinking or expecting: *You'll have been having headaches, too, I expect?*

3 *Shall/shan't* may occur for *will/won't* in the first person only, where:

a the speaker expects the listener to be personally affected by the outcome or timing of the action: *I shall have been working for 10 hours, so I shan't want to go out.*

b the speaker feels constrained by circumstances or commitments: *Come by all means, but I shall have been painting.*

4 Pronunciation:

a H*ave* is commonly reduced to '*ve* in speech, although it is not written in this form: *I won't've been* … This may be mistaken for *of*, even by native speakers.

b B*een* is commonly reduced to /bɪn /in speech.

c Stress on *will* or *won't* produces an emphatic form of this tense.

Meaning and Function

A ***The tense is used to express the predicted duration of an event, viewed from a future time.*** A point in future time is identified, and the tense 'looks back' to an action which began before that point, or was continuous or continuously repeated up to that point. It may or may not continue after that time. The duration of the action is specified, usually with *for* (*for a month, a year, three hours*).

a The action begins in the future, continues to the viewpoint time, and may or may not continue after it.
By this time tomorrow, I'll have been travelling for twelve hours.
By the time you get here I'll have been working for an hour.

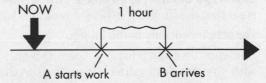

By the time you get here, I'll have been working for an hour

b The action began before the time of speaking, will continue to the 'viewpoint' time, and may or may not continue after it.
By Christmas, I'll have been working for this company for 20 years.
The action may be continuously repeated, rather than continuous.
By Christmas, he'll have been riding that bike for 20 years.

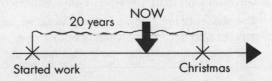

By Christmas, I'll have been working for this company for 20 years

c   With *already*, it suggests that the action is expected to continue after the viewpoint time.
By the time you come, I'll already have been working for an hour.

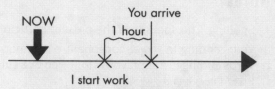

By the time you come I'll already have been working for an hour already

B **The tense is used to explain a predicted mental or physical state** caused by repeated or continuous activity which happened before the 'viewpoint' time:
He'll be tired when he gets home. He'll have been travelling all day.

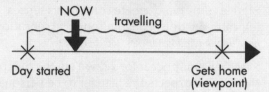

He'll be tired when he gets home. He'll have been travelling all day

C **The tense is used to express logical deduction** about the causes of a present physical or mental state, in terms of repeated or continuous action in the immediate past. The speaker guesses at the cause of the 'state' but cannot know for certain:
There's Jim. He looks tired. He'll have been playing football.
(*Shall/shan't* are not appropriate in this usage.)

Note: the tense in this usage can be used when discussing photographs, for instance, where the evidence is present but the event itself was in the distant past.
Why are you wearing that hat (in the photograph)? I'll have been collecting honey (I am only guessing, I don't remember the event).

Suggested Contexts

A **Expressing duration of an action, viewed from a point in future time.** The context must make it clear that the duration is being measured backwards from the given 'viewpoint time.'

a   For actions entirely in the future:

* Students are given a list of scheduled flights taking off 'today', plus a list of imaginary characters with different destinations. Then times in the day are identified, and the progress of the individuals is compared: *By 2 o'clock X will have been travelling for an hour.* Once the concept is clear, the teacher can add 'take-off' times (for example: *The plane took off at 6 this morning*) before the time of speaking, thus making it clear that the action may have begun in the past. This extension also allows for useful contrast with other tenses: *Y is travelling now. By 2 o'clock she will have arrived.* Other verbs and contexts (relatives waiting/pilots flying etc.) can be added.

* The students are given a future timetable, as an information gap exercise. They are to ask and answer and determine when people arrive, leave, and do different jobs: *When Jill arrives, John will have been working for three hours. When John arrives Peter will have been driving his lorry for an hour* etc.

b   For actions in the future and already begun:

• Base the exercise on the student's own experience. Identify points at which they expect to stop certain activities, and check the expected duration: *How long will you have been studying English/ going to school*, etc.). Then add information about other people's activities. This allows the teacher to cross-check the concept of continuous activity: *By Christmas I will have been studying English for a year, but Miho will have stopped studying.*

B **Explaining a future mental or physical state:**

• Quick oral practice. Making excuses, being difficult, and turning down an invitation:
I'll be too tired. I'll have been working late.
I'll need a shower. I'll have been gardening.
This can be useful, quick practice if the teacher (or another student) provides the 'state', and the student produces the reason: *I'll be stiff. I'll have been sitting down for too long.*

• Students are given a timetable of a VIP's visit, and asked *What will the VIP need and why?* *She'll need a shower. She'll have been travelling. She'll need a chair. She'll have been standing up all day.* This can be usefully linked with practice of other tenses: *She won't need a meal. She'll have eaten.*

C **Logical deduction:**
This is probably best taught as part of a series on logical deduction. It is difficult to build an entire lesson on this usage alone. Quick exercises are possible.

• Look out of the window and speculate about passers-by: *She'll have been visiting the dentist.*

• Look at photographs (or a video) and guess the reasons for the present scene. Ensure that the right answer cannot be known with certainty: *Why is she rubbing her feet? She'll have been standing up too long.*

Learner Error: Form, Spelling and Pronunciation

1 Since there are three auxiliaries in this tense, learners may confuse the order: *I have will be working/I will be having working.*

2 Students may omit one auxiliary altogether, *I will been working*. This error may not emerge until a writing stage, as the unstressed *ve* is almost lost in speech.

3 The contracted *ve* may be perceived as *of*, *I will of been working*.

4 Very occasionally students make errors with *will/shall*, *They shall have been walking*.

5 The spelling of the present participle may continue to create problems, I'll have been *shoping*.

6 Students sometimes confuse this form with a passive construction (perhaps because of the influence of *been*) *I will have been worked.*

7 Forms such as I *will have been shopping/swimming* may be regarded as the future perfect of a verb *to go shopping*, rather than a future perfect continuous of *To shop*.

Learner Error: Meaning and Function

1   This is not a common tense. The chief difficulties arise with the concept.
    Learners find it hard to accept that actions already begun may be framed in the future perfect continuous. They may substitute other tenses:

a   *By Christmas I am working there for 20 years* (because I am already working there).

b   *By Christmas I have worked there for 20 years* (because I have already worked there).
    (Note that informal native speech permits this construction with idioms using *come* or *this*: *I've worked there for 20 years come/this Christmas.*)

c   *By Christmas I will be working there for 20 years.*
    Note that substituting the future perfect often creates a satisfactory substitute:
    By Christmas I will have worked there for 20 years.

2   The function expressing logical deduction about a present state is rarely understood, even by advanced learners. *Can* is sometimes substituted.
    He can have been fishing. (Compare: *He can't have been fishing.*)

3   Learners may use a time construction with *since* instead of *for*:

a   *I will have been working since three years.* (This may be a mother tongue confusion.)

b   *I'll have been working since 1990.* This is not grammatically incorrect, but English rarely requires the future here (a present perfect continuous is normally used) unless the 'viewpoint time' is relevant: *I'll qualify for my pension at Christmas. I'll have been working since 1970.*

4   The tense may be confused with a passive, probably because it contains *been*.

5   Most students try to avoid this tense altogether.

Conditional Section

Points to Ponder

- ### For trainee teachers

  What seems to you to be the difference between the following sentences?
  If you heat it, it melts.
  If you heat it, it'll melt.
  Why do you think foreign speakers have difficulty with sentences like:
  If it rained tomorrow, I'd wear boots.
  What is the function of *rained* in that sentence?

- ### For teachers' workshops

  In the third condition, is it true to say that any statement in the negative happened and that any statement in the positive did not happen? What do you suppose causes most confusion with this verb pattern?
  How far do you feel that a sentence like *If you're going to be like that, I'm going*, is in fact a first conditional sentence?

Introduction

Conditionals are patterns expressing the relationship between two actions, where one action is the reason, or the occasion, for the other. There are four conditional verb patterns, usually known as:

1 **The General Condition** which expresses a general rule, where the condition is or could be repeatedly fulfilled: *If you heat ice, it melts.*

2 **The First Condition** which refers to the future, where the condition may or may not be fulfilled: *If it rains, I'll wear a hat.*

3 **The Second Condition** which refers to the future, where it is very unlikely that the condition will be fulfilled: *If I saw a lion, I'd run away*; or talking about the present or future, where the condition cannot possibly be fulfilled: *If I were you, I'd come more often.*

4 **The Third Condition** which refers to the past, and where the condition was not fulfilled: *If I'd woken up earlier I wouldn't have missed the train.* or where the speaker does not know if the condition was fulfilled: *If he had picked up the snake, it would have bitten him.*

In all conditional sentences the clause containing the condition (usually introduced by *if*), may be placed before or after the other clause, affecting emphasis but not intrinsic meaning. Hence, *If you heat ice, it melts*, can become *Ice melts if you heat it*. Note that where the *if* clause introduces the sentence, it requires a comma at the end of the clause.
The General Condition expresses a fact, or a rule; the other conditionals express hypothesis, opinion and probability, and therefore contain a modal verb in some form. This is not necessarily *will* or *would*. It is often said that the second condition requires *would* in the main clause. In fact, any past form modal may be substituted, according to meaning: *If I saw a lion, I might faint.* Each conditional verb form has a base form consisting of a combination of tenses which is characteristic. Other combinations may occur, but these are used for particular effect and are listed separately in the Notes section of each conditional verb form. Verbs follow their normal patterns according to tense, with the exception of the semi-subjunctive *were* for *was*.

GENERAL CONDITION: analysis

Base Form	
If you heat ice, it melts.	*(statement of general rule, objective statement)*
That cat scratches if you stroke it.	*(statement of general rule, often based on experience)*

Question Form	
Does ice melt if you heat it?	Doesn't ice melt if you heat it?
If you heat ice, does it melt? *(neutral question)*	If you heat ice, doesn't it melt? *(expects answer 'yes', checking or reminding)*

Tag Question	
Ice melts if you heat it, doesn't it? If you heat ice it melts, doesn't it?	*(seeks confirmation)*
That cat scratches if you stroke it, doesn't it?	*(seeks confirmation/or explains my actions, i.e. I never stroke it)*

Notes

1 The general condition is used to express truths or maxims and generally occurs with the full (positive) statement in both clauses: *If you heat ice, it melts.* Combinations including negatives are possible:

a In the if clause: *If it doesn't rain, the crops die.*
b In the other clause: *If it rains, the birds don't sing.*
c In both clauses: *If it doesn't rain, the crops don't grow.* (N.B. Putting a negative in both clauses often produces a sentence very close in meaning to a sentence with no negative in either clause. However, they are not necessarily interchangeable; *If you eat poison, you die* does not imply *If you don't eat poison, you don't die*, only that you don't die from that cause.)

2 As the general condition is used to express universal truths, the base form pattern often occurs with impersonal constructions such as *You* (in the sense of *anyone*); *They* (in the sense of 'those in authority' or 'people'); *It* (for weather or natural phenomena); *He* (for anyone previously nominated, such as 'the player'). etc. However, other constructions do occur:

a It is also used to express an observed pattern of behaviour: *If his master whistles, the dog comes at once.*
b For ironic effect: *If I get into the bath, the telephone rings.* (i.e. this has become a universal law).

3 **Base form:** present tense in the *if* clause, and in the main clause. This is almost always the present simple in both clauses, but present continuous (with present reference) present emphatic or present perfect may occur for particular effect:

Present continuous (with present or general reference only):

• In the If clause: *If the kettle is boiling, it whistles* (always).
• In the main clause: *If it whistles, the kettle is boiling.*
• In both clauses: *If bubbles are forming, the mixture is boiling.*

Present emphatic:

• In the If clause: *If he **does** come, he helps me with the cooking.* (stresses the infrequency of his coming)
• In the main clause: *If he comes, he **does** help me with the cooking,* (stresses that the 'helping' is intense)
• In both clauses: *If he **does** come, he **does** help me with the cooking.* (both of the above)

Present perfect:

- In the If clause: If *the train has left, he always walks.* (implies, when he finds out)
- In the main clause: If *the car is not in the garage, he's gone.* (this is a logical conclusion)
- In both clauses: If *he has taken the car, he has gone fishing.* (this is a logical conclusion)

4 With the general conditional construction *if* can be replaced by *when* or *whenever*, often without changing the sense.

5 There are also some specialised constructions which can cause problems, although they are not common:

a Using the imperative in the main clause: If *he comes, call me.*
This is arguably not a general condition at all, but a kind of first condition, based upon the present simple used for timetabling (i.e. as a future); certainly it has future reference. On the same pattern we find usages such as: If *he comes, I'm out!* This is ambiguous, but with future reference, it can be taught as a variant of *Tell him I'm out.* This does not, however, account for rare utterances like: If *he comes, I'm off!*

b Where the present continuous is used with future intention, the sentence is a first condition. This is unusual, but occurs especially with verbs of motion or with time markers, (diary future):
If *the bus comes, I'm getting on* (i.e. as a shortened form of *I'm going to get on*); If *I pass the exam, I'm buying myself a new hat* (tomorrow).

c Occasionally *going to* occurs as a normal present continuous (meaning *on the way to*), and as such may have general reference, and occur in general conditions: If *you're going to the bank, the bookshop is on your left.*

6 **The General Condition in the past form.**
There is also a past form of the general condition. It refers to habits, laws, patterns of behaviour and causal relationships in the past. The base form is in the past simple in both clauses:
If *primitive man wanted fire, he made it by striking two stones together.*

Note: The past form of the first condition (If *it snowed, we would wear boots*) (habitually) is so close in meaning to the general condition that it is often effectively interchangeable. (It is also identical in form to the second conditional but not in meaning.) The difference is one of emphasis. The general conditional in its past form is rather dogmatic, claiming universal and general truths, or offers a clinching point in an argument; the past form of the first conditional refers to individuals and specific truths. Variations occur, as outlined n Note 3 above, with the parallel past tenses:

Past Continuous: If *the kettle was boiling, it whistled.*

Past Emphatic: If *it did rain, it poured.*

Past Perfect: If *the car wasn't in the garage, he'd gone to London.*

Meaning and Function

With present forms

(A) **To express general, natural, universal or scientific laws:** If you heat ice, it melts.

(B) **To denote general truths about observed patterns of behaviour:** If his master whistles, he comes.

(C) **To express causal relationships**: If you push the button, the door opens.

(D) **To suggest an ironic causal relationship between two events**: If I wash the car, it rains.

(E) **To express the function of a person or device:** It lights up if an intruder gets in.

(F) **To express a logical necessity,** where the conclusion is always true given the data. It admits no argument, and is often used as a clinching argument: If it has three straight sides, it is a triangle. If his car isn't in the garage, he's in London.

(G) **To express a logical necessity,** but used where the conclusion is true at present: If he's standing at the bus stop (now), he's waiting for his sister to come home from school.

(H) **To give general instructions:** If he comes, tell him I'm out. (See note 5a above.)

With past forms

Exactly as A–G above, but where the condition is no longer met, the action no longer occurs, or the persons or thing doing the action is no longer encountered, at least by the speaker:

(A) If primitive life forms thrived, they multiplied.

(B) If a caveman needed a saw, he used a jawbone.

(C) If the trolley came off the wires, the tram stopped.

(D) If I got into the bath, the phone rang.

(E) If an intruder came in, the alarm lit up.

(F) If it had short legs, it wasn't a grasshopper.

(G) If he was standing at the bus stop on Tuesday, he was waiting for his sister.

The past tense refers to a specific time in the past, at which time the conclusion was necessarily true.

Suggested Contexts

With present forms

(A) **General and scientific truth:**

- Scientific laws: Students are given the names of common substances, and a list of questions; (What happens if you heat it/eat it? etc.) Others are to guess the substance from the properties listed: If you heat it, it melts. If you put it in water, it dissolves. If you boil it, you get steam.

- Expressing geographic position, and map-reading: If you go due east from the mountains, you come to the lake. This can be done as an information gap exercise. (**See photocopiable page 11**.)

- Compare the effects of common natural disasters, for example, too much and too little rain: *If it rains too much the river floods. If it rains too little the crops die.* Produce lists in pairs. Compare. Points may be awarded for interesting suggestions.

B *General truths about behaviour:*

- Behaviour of an animal species. This may be based on a video, film, visit or on class-room experience. The teacher sets a list of questions: *How does it behave if a light shines? if you touch it? if a bird flies overhead?* Students may then set their own questions, and form into groups for question-answer team games.

- Similarly, the behaviour of pets/plants etc. This makes a useful follow-up. Students argue the advantages of particular pets and their habitual behaviour.

- Questionnaire on the students' own habits; *How do you come to school if it is raining/fine?*

C *Causal relationships:*

- The class is given a number of *if* clauses, and main clauses, and asked to match the pairs (which causes which?)

- Students are given an *if* clause and asked to produce a list of 'results'. Work in groups, and compare the length and quality of the lists. Clauses can be lighthearted, *If I cook dinner …* or serious, *If rivers are polluted.* Note: It is useful to add variants; *If I'm cooking (at any time), I always wear an apron.*

D *Ironic causal relationships:*

Probably best taught as part of a series on expressing irritation.

E *Describing functions:*

- The class is given a diagram or a picture of a machine e.g. dog-exerciser, or whistling kettle and asked to explain how it works.

- Students are asked to invent a machine, and explain how it works.

- The class is given a description of duties of a particular job: *If the supervisor has signed the cheque, X posts it. If not, X takes it to the supervisor.* Students are asked to guess what job is described; then, individually or in pairs, they are asked to write their own description of duties for a job of their choice, and invite other students to guess.

F and **G** *Logical necessity:*

This is probably best taught as part of a series on logical deductions (probably taught after, and in comparison to: *it must be/ it can't be* etc.).

H *General instructions:*

In small groups, students work out general instructions on what to do in cases of emergency, fire drills etc.

With past forms

Exactly as A–G above, but using identified past connotations (e.g. dinosaurs, cavemen, ancient civilisations and machines, grandparents etc.).

Learner Error: Form, Spelling and Pronunciation

With the General Condition, it is often difficult to differentiate problems of form from problems of meaning and function. However, the following points should perhaps be noted:

1 Learners may experience any of the difficulties inherent in the verb forms employed. These are discussed fully under the separate sections for each tense.

2 **With present forms:** Learners may avoid using *if* or *when*, where the sentence is a universal truth; *You heat ice, it melts.*

3 **With past forms:** Learners may produce a general condition in the past form with a past tense in the *if* clause only; **If it rained the crops live.**

4 Learners may attempt to use the semi-subjunctive *were* where it is inappropriate; **If a dinosaur were hungry, he ate.* *If it weren't three-sided, it wasn't a triangle/weren't a triangle.**

Learner Error: Meaning and Function

1 In the present form the general condition causes few problems, because the meaning (universal or general truths) is close to the meaning of the present simple, which is the base form for the structure. Problems arise when variations occur. In particular, learners may use the present simple in both clauses in all contexts. Hence: **If the train leaves, he walks** (for *has left*) or **If he wears a hat, he goes to town** (for *If he is wearing a hat, he is going to town*).

2 With past forms: learners may substitute the general condition in its past form for the second condition: *If a lion came in, I ran* for *If a lion came in, I would run.*

3 Other variations may not be perceived as a general condition, but this is unimportant where it does not affect the ability to produce and understand the forms.

FIRST CONDITION: analysis

Base Form	
If it rains, I'll wear a hat. I'll wear a hat if it rains.	(*Prediction, promise or offer of future action, if the condition is fulfilled*)
Question Form	
Will he wear a hat if it rains? Won't he wear a hat if it rains?	(*neutral question*) (*expects answer 'yes' or reminds the listener of the likelihood of the activity occurring*)
Shall I get a taxi if I arrive late? Shall I bring in the washing if it rains?	(*asking for advice*) (*offering help or asking about obligation*)
Tag Questions	
He'll wear a hat if it rains, won't he? He won't go out if it rains, will he?	(*expects answer 'yes', invites the listener to agree*) (*expects answer 'no', expresses surprise or invites the listener to agree that this is self-evident*)

Notes

1 The first condition refers to future time.

2 It refers to conditions which seem (at least 50%) likely to be fulfilled at the time of speaking.

3 The base form has a present or future form in the *if* clause, and a future form in the main clause. The most common pattern is present simple in the *if* clause with a modal form in the main clause. Variations do occur:

In the 'if' clause

Present continuous:

- For actions currently in progress: *If you're watching television, I'll come back later.*
- For definite future plans: *If you're having lunch in town, I'll meet you afterwards.*

Present emphatic:

- For a condition which is currently unexpected but recognises or insists that this is still possible: *If it does rain, I won't go.*

Going to:

- For definite future plans, in the sense of *on your way to*: *If you're going to see mother, I'll come with you.*
- For expressing likelihood ('evident now future form'): *If it's going to rain, I'll take an umbrella.*
- For expressing insistence: *If you're going to talk like that, I'll leave.*

Modal verbs:

- *Will* for bartering: *If you'll bring the cakes, I'll bring the scones.*
- *Will* for persistence: *If you will eat too much, you'll get fat.*
- *Can* for ability: *If I can, I will.*

- Must for obligation: *I'll come if* I *must.*
- May *or* can *for permission: I'll have a cake, if* I *may. I'll borrow the car, if* I *can.*

Present perfect:

- For actions which may be over by the future time in question: *If you've left when* I *get there, I'll catch the bus.*

Future continuous:

- For actions which are predicted to be in progress at the relevant time: *If you'll be working, I'll catch the bus.*

Future perfect (rare):

- For actions which are predicted to be over by the relevant time: *If you'll have left when* I *get there, I'll catch the bus.*

In the main clause

Other modal verbs:

- All simple present forms: *If it rains,* I *can wear a hat/may wear a hat/must wear a hat/needn't wear a hat/daren't wear a hat.*
- Non time-specific simple past forms (Ought to/might/should): *If it rains* I *ought to/might/should wear a hat.*
  Also very occasionally:
  If it rains I *could wear a hat* (suggesting unlikely possibility).
  If it rains, I *should/would wear a hat* (giving advice; I *would* meaning *you should*).

Present continuous:

For expressing definite future plans, (often a threat): *If you do that, I'm leaving.*

Going to:

- To express insistence: *If you don't leave, I'm going to call the police.*
- To express future time ('evident now' future): *If he doesn't come in, he's going to catch cold.*

Future continuous:

- For predicted action in progress as a result of future action: *If you come at that time, we'll be eating.*
- For threats, warnings: *If he brings his friends, I'll be leaving early.*

Future perfect:

- For actions predicted to be completed by and affecting the future time: *If you come on Tuesday, he'll have left.*

4 The Imperative form, *Give it to him, if you see him,* should probably be regarded as a variation of the first conditional form since it clearly has a future and not a general connotation. This can be explained to students, as being a shortened form of *Will you ...?* (See also General Condition, Note 5a)

5 Requests with *Would.* The past modal form *would* is sometimes found in conditional requests. It is not past, it is merely more polite, (see page 122, Modal Auxiliaries) and should probably be regarded as a first condition, e.g. *If he comes in, would you make him a cup of tea, please.*

The first condition in its past form

This form refers to habitual, repeated actions in the past. The base form is in the past simple in the *if* clause, and *would* (past tense of *will*) in the main clause: *If it snowed, we would wear boots.* (habitually)
There is a close relationship between this and two other conditional patterns:

a it is identical to the form of the second condition, except that *used to* can be substituted for *would* in the past first conditional; compare *If it snowed, we would wear boots* (tomorrow) with *If it snowed, we used to wear boots* (past habit). The semi subjunctive form *were* is found instead of *was* in the *if* clause only, to show that the condition was rarely fulfilled: *If it were snowing, we would wear boots* (but it didn't often snow). Arguably this usage is a past form of the second condition, because it uses *were* and refers to unlikely conditions.

b The meaning of the general condition (*If it snowed, we wore boots*) is so close to the meaning of the first condition form that it is often effectively interchangeable (see General Condition, Note 6). Indeed, since the action is now past, *when* can often be substituted for *if*; *When it snowed, we would wear boots.* Variations occur:

In the 'if' clause

Past continuous: *If it was snowing, we'd wear boots.* (habitually)
Was going to: *If he was going to have a party, he would (always) invite us.*
Modals: *Could* for ability may occur in the *if* clause: *If he could come, he would.* (used to)
Past perfect: *If he had missed his train, he'd be late home.* (habitually)
Past perfect continuous: *If (when) he had been playing football, he would be tired.* (habitually)

In the main clause

Modal verbs: *Might* may be substituted for *would* when the action did not always follow from the condition: *If father came home early, we might sit by the fire and talk.*
Would and the continuous form: *If he came late, I would be eating.* (habitually)
Would and the perfect form: *If he came too late, I would have gone.* (habitually)

Meaning and Function

(A) **To predict what will happen if a likely future condition is fulfilled:** *If it rains, I'll get wet.*

(B) **To draw logical conclusions from a likely future event:** *If he is late, he'll miss the beginning of the film.*

(C) **To make offers, suggestions**: *If you come to my house, I'll give you a lift.*

(D) **To explain how things work, especially for warnings**: *If you push that button, it will blow up.*

(E) **To draw logical conclusions from probable present situations/events**: *If he's changing his shirt, he'll be late for the party.*

(F) **To barter services, or favours**: *If you'll cut my hair, I'll mend your TV.*

(G) **To make contingency plans:** *If they are out/have gone when we get there, we'll write them a note.*

(H) *Past tenses*
To describe repeated habitual action in the past: *If my brother had a sweet, I'd always want one too.* (Compare: *I used to always want one.*)

Suggested Contexts

With present forms

(A) **Predicting the outcome of a likely future condition.** It is important to set up a situation in which there are a limited number of possibilities, equally possible, of which one must occur. (This creates the context for likely condition.) Students are asked to predict, or suggest what will happen if each possibility occurs:

- Arranging a programme for an imaginary overseas visitor. It's not known in advance if the visitor is a man or a woman/old or young/Arab or Chinese etc: *If the visitor is a man, I'll take him to a football match. If he's young he won't want to visit museums.*

- An imaginary sister is expecting a baby. Will it be a girl or a boy? The couple have chosen names, schools etc; *What will they call it if it's a boy* etc. A list of possibilities can be built up, and used as an information gap exercise.

- There is a prize of a holiday, already won by an imaginary character. He can choose between a fortnight in the Swiss Alps, or two weeks on a Greek island; *What will he do/eat/see if he goes to Greece?* etc.

B **Drawing logical conclusions from a likely future event:**

- Map work. Students are told there is a robber in the bank, and are asked to position police to cover all possible escape routes, without having them directly outside the bank: *If he comes out of the front door, Car A will see him* etc.

- Students decide on the best route for an expected visit by an imaginary VIP, avoiding the unattractive parts of the city, taking in the beauty spots: *If she goes this way, she'll pass the gas works.* This is useful for introducing other modals: *If the goes this way she can see the fountains* etc. (**See photocopiable page 11**.)

C **Making offers and suggestions:**

- Making arrangements. Role play or dialogue building exercises in pairs: *If you phone me when you arrive, I'll pick you up.* (**See photocopiable page 3**.)

- Mini role plays, based on cue cards. Business or shopping, asking for items, services, appointments, not at present available: *If you leave your name and address, we'll send you a copy* etc.

D **Explaining how things work:**

Note: This usage is very close to the general condition, slightly less formal and dogmatic and therefore often used in conversation.

- Sales talk: *If you leave the hand-brake on, the warning light will come on.*

- Students in groups are given the context of a inexperienced cook/mechanic/childminder etc. about to undertake cooking/driving/bathing baby. They compile lists of warnings; *If you don't stir it, it'll stick* etc. Points may be awarded for the best lists.

E **Drawing logical conclusions from (present) situations:**

- Students are given a present situation; e.g. there is a thief somewhere in house, and they deduce the maximum number of likely conclusions; *If he's still here, he must be hiding upstairs, he'll have taken the jewellery, he'll be waiting behind the door,* etc. Other students may challenge, *He may have thrown the jewellery out of the window* etc. This is useful for practising the full range of possible variations.

F **Bartering:**

- Role play in which a dissatisfied customer is refusing to pay for services. The two sides try to reach a compromise; *I'll pay the hotel bill, if you'll deduct the price of the meal* etc. This works best if students can be persuaded to argue.

- Dialogue building exercise. Two people, each wanting the other to do something, barter services.

- The same context can be extended across a number of students, so that a chain of bartered services is set up.

G **Contingency plans:**
Students, in groups, set up plans to visit people or places. (Perhaps using *will* for instant decision.) Other groups then raise possible objections, using *might/may*. Answer these objections by creating contingency plans; *If the museum is shut, we'll go to the opera. If they've gone out, we'll leave them a note.*

With past forms

H **Describing repeated habitual action in the past:**

- Guided writing on the traditional past times of childhood (parties, games, school etc).

- Guided or classroom essay, based on reading/video/general knowledge about historic or literary figures: *If the empress had a bath, her servants would pour oils and perfumes into the water etc.*)

Learner Error: Form, Spelling and Pronunciation

1 Learners often attempt to introduce *will* with future reference into both clauses: **If it will rain tomorrow, I will wear a hat.**

2 Elementary students often attempt to use *will* with other modals, instead of replacing *will*: **If it rains, I will can come.**

3 More advanced students may attempt to use the past tense in *if* clauses, when *would* is used for requests, thus suggesting that the condition is unlikely, or hypothetical; *If he came, would you make him a cup of tea?* for *If he comes would you make him a cup of tea, please.*

4 Problems related to *will/shall* and other modals may occur.

Learner Error: Meaning and Function

1 More advanced learners may feel that they know the 'rule' and become confused by variations, especially those using *will/can* etc. in *if* clauses.

2 *If it snowed, we'd go skating*, may refer to past habit (likely) or future action (unlikely). Students often suppose that the reference is to past time only.

3 Students may use the semi-subjunctive *were* where it is not appropriate, for future reference, perhaps because of overlearning; **If you were early, I'll come** (often used instead of the present emphatic).

SECOND CONDITION: analysis

Base Form A	Base Form B
If I saw a lion, I'd run. I'd run if I saw a lion. *(prediction of future action following a very unlikely condition)*	If I were you, I'd go. I'd go if I were you. *(advice, or prediction of likely outcome of an impossible condition)*
Question Form	
Would you run if you saw a lion? (*neutral question*) Wouldn't you run if you saw a lion? (*expects 'yes', invites the listener to agree*)	
Tag Questions	
He'd run if he saw a lion, wouldn't he? (*expects answer 'yes', invites the listener to agree that this is self evident and explains the speaker's attitude*) You'd run if you saw a lion, wouldn't you? (*second person tag question may be a challenge or accusation or require the listener to agree*) You wouldn't run if you saw a lion, would you? (*expects answer 'no', expresses surprise, or seeks reassurance*)	

Notes

1 Base form A refers to future time and to conditions which are **unlikely** to be fulfilled.
The base form has a past form in the *if* clause and a past modal form in the main clause. The most common pattern is past simple in the *if* clause with *would* in the main clause.

2 Base form B refers to present, general or hypothetical time and to conditions which are **impossible** to fulfil. The base form is identical to Form A, except that this form calls for the semi-subjunctive form *were* instead of *was* in the *if* clause, for all persons. Hence: *If I were you, If you were me, If he were here.* etc. All other verbs use the regular past tense. The impossible condition often refers to present time or to a general state.

Variations do occur:

Form A Unlikely Condition

In the 'if' clause

Past emphatic: *If he did go, he wouldn't like it* (stresses the unlikeliness of his going).
Past continuous: *If it was snowing tomorrow, I'd make a snowman* (but it is unlikely to be snowing).
Was going to: (possible change in general plans; stress on *was*): *If he was going to walk, I'd like to go with him.*

(Note that many educated speakers still prefer to use the semi-subjunctive *were*, even when the condition could (possibly) be fulfilled, and this must be regarded as a correct alternative: *If he were taking his wife to the seaside, he'd go earlier.*)
Modal verbs: (simple past forms)
Could/would for polite requests: *If you could/would open the door, I'd be very grateful.*
Should for logical possibility, in formal English, in certain set patterns: *If he should come, I'd like to see him.*

In the main clause

Other modal verbs (simple past forms): *If it was raining, I could/might/should/ought to wear a hat* (but it is unlikely to be raining).

Would and the continuous forms: shows the continuous nature of the predicted action, if the condition was fulfilled, *If he missed his train, he'd be waiting for hours.*

Form B Impossible Condition

In the 'if' clause

Past continuous with were: *If it were snowing, we'd make a snowman* (but it isn't).

Was going to: (for plans) *If he were going to walk, I'd think he was crazy* (but he has no such intention).

Modal verbs: (*could* for ability) *If I could speak French, I'd talk to him. If I could, I would* (but I can't). (Often implies regret.)

In the main clause

Other modal verbs: (simple past form) *If it were raining, I might/could/should get wet* (but it isn't raining).

Would and the continuous form: (shows what predicted action would be in progress now, if the condition were fulfilled) *If he were here, I'd be wearing my uniform* (but he isn't and I'm not).

Would and the perfect form: (impossible condition only) *If he were lost, he'd have rung* (he can't possibly be lost, because he hasn't rung). (See also the Third Condition.)

The second condition in its past form

Base form A **Unlikely condition**: this conditional form has no past parallel.

Base form B **Impossible condition**: there is no formal past form but the third condition may be seen as a representation of it.

Informal English speech, especially non-standard speech, increasingly uses I *was* for I *were* when the condition is, in fact, impossible. (Hence *If I was you* etc.) Conversely, many people prefer the use of *were* in all uses of the conditional, especially written ones. Since the degree of likelihood is in the speaker's mind, it may be easier to teach students the *were* form first, for all uses, and clarify later.

A literary form of this conditional, which does not use *if*, exists, but is now rare:

A Unlikely future conditions: with *should* and the present form: *Should a lion come in, I'd run.*

B For impossible conditions: the *if* clause is inverted, like the interrogative form, using the semi-subjunctive where necessary: *Were I you/Had I the money, I would go on a luxury holiday.* (Note: This is not a question.)

M eaning and Function

Form A Unlikely Condition

(A) **To predict the results of unlikely future conditions**: I wouldn't recognise him if I saw him.

(B) **To make contingency plans for unlikely future events:** What would you do if you lost your job?

(C) **Suggesting improvements:** If you hung up your trousers, they wouldn't get creased.

Form B Impossible Condition

(D) **To express dreams and unfulfilled ambitions:** If had a million pounds, I'd buy a yacht.

(E)
a **To offer suggestions or advice:** If I were you, I'd clean them.
b **To express criticism**: If they were his, he'd clean them (so should you).

(F) **To imagine the results of changes in the status quo:** If he were prime minister, he'd make a few changes.

(G) **To draw logical conclusions from present or past events:** If he were going, he'd have rung.

S uggested Contexts

Form A Unlikely Condition

(A) **Predicting the outcome of unlikely future conditions;**

- Students are shown a lottery ticket: Will I win? (This establishes that the condition is unlikely, but possible.) The prize is one million pounds. What would you do if you won a million pounds? (Students must justify and amplify choices, as otherwise this easily becomes mechanical.)

- Elicit a list of future possibilities (any suitable topic from, What will happen to the earth? to What will the weather be like next Monday?; use will/won't for prediction). Classify these as likely/unlikely/very unlikely. (The won't column often provides good material for very unlikely conditions). Identify the outcome of likely events, practising the first condition. Then identify the very unlikely ones, introducing the second condition. The group decides about the unlikely events. How unlikely are they? Which is the appropriate conditional structure? This exercise helps to reinforce the concept.

- Each student is given two slips of paper. On one he is asked to write a question about an unlikely (or outrageous) future event, using What would you do? – What would you do if the roof fell in? On the second, he writes an answer, I would … The slips are redistributed so that each student has a question and answer that he did not write, and that do not match. They can then read them aloud and then attempt to match questions and answers.

- Questionnaire. (This may be done on an individual basis, in pairs, or groups.) Ask the students what they would do if they were confronted by a moral, social or cultural dilemma. If the topics are not too serious, students can score points for a 'personality profile' as in popular magazines: If you found a wallet would you take it to a police station, keep it, put it in a prominent place, leave it? What would you do if you found a pound coin? etc.(**See photocopiable page 12**.)

B **Contingency plans for unlikely events:**

- Discussion on safety. Look at the teaching environment: *What would you do if the roof fell in/the building caught fire/there was an earthquake* etc. (Other modals can be used for extended practice: *What would you do next? Whom should you contact? What ought you to do?* etc.)
- Discussion of future plans. Students are asked what they hope to do. (Use *going to* for general plans.) They are then asked for contingency plans: *What would you do if you couldn't … go to university* etc.)

C **Suggesting improvements:**

- Students are given an artistic task (e.g. items to arrange for a collage). Use discussion/role-play to achieve the best design: *If we put a green bit there, it would look better.* etc.
- Students are given a physical puzzle (e.g. rearranging matches to form three triangles etc.) to be solved by discussion only. (Conclusions can later be tested by experiment.) This exercise calls for the first and second condition, for likely and unlikely suggestions and requires monitoring.

Form B Impossible Condition

D **Expressing dreams and ambitions:**

- Students are asked about their ambitions. Then they give reasons for their choice; *If I were a pilot I could/would* etc. (Teachers should make sure that students are not expressing fulfilled ambitions.)
- Students are asked to debate or write on a theme such as, *If I had three wishes/If I could go anywhere in the world …*

E **Offering suggestions and advice:**
This is probably best taught as part of a series of lessons on giving advice. In British English the expressions *If I were you* and *I should …* (meaning *you should*) for advice are very common.

- Each student is given a problem, other members of the group offer advice. The 'problem holder' selects the best advice, and explains why. (This often practises other uses of the conditional: *If I did that, it would only complicate matters*.)
- Role-play: Shopping. A customer has faulty or non-functioning goods. A shopkeeper gives advice on the phone.

F **Imagining the effects that changes in the status quo would have:**

- Writing exercise. Identify a public figure (social, sporting or political). What changes would you make if you were Prime Minister/football manager/head of the school etc.?
- Election time. Selected students suggest what they would do as prime minister/head of school etc. The rest of group vote based on the strength of the arguments.
- A 'balloon debate', in which students are in an imaginary hot air balloon which is losing height. Students argue why they should not be the one to be sacrificed: What they would do for mankind if they lived? (Students may adopt roles.)
- A quiz. Students choose a famous person and can give up to twenty 'clues': *If I were this person, I'd live in England/wear a crown/open parliament* etc. (This can also be done with occupations/animals etc.)

G **Drawing logical conclusions from present or past events:**
Reading comprehension. Students are given a short text identifying the characteristics of a type of bird, insect or flower, for example. They are then shown a series of pictures, some of which fit the description exactly, some not quite. In pairs, they are asked to identify the species, then explain the reasons for their decisions: *If it were a grasshopper, it would have longer legs.*
(**See photocopiable page 15.**)

Learner Error: Form, Spelling and Pronunciation

1 Attempts are sometimes made to create a subjunctive form of all verbs, often with *might*: *If I might have a thousand pounds.* This may be explained by the fact that the subjunctive is often translated by *might* in many foreign text-books.

2 *Was/Were* for unlikely/impossible conditions causes much confusion:

a) Students are sometimes unwilling to create constructions with I *were*.

b) Occasionally, confusion occurs and learners interchange *were* and *was* in all persons, creating constructions such as, *If we was …*

3 Learners may experience difficulties inherent in the modals and tenses used in this construction.

Learner Error: Meaning and Function

1 Many learners find it difficult to believe that the past tense can actually refer to future time. They may substitute a future; *If I will be rich, I would buy a plane* (for unlikely condition) or a present tense for the impossible condition; *If I am rich I would buy a plane.*

2 When the verb in the main clause is *have*, the structure is sometimes mistakenly seen as a third condition: *If I'd had time, I would have a cup of tea.*

3 Most problems arise because learners fail to understand the difference between first and second conditions, a distinction which arises in the mind of the speaker (do I regard this condition as likely or unlikely?). This can lead to misunderstanding. (Compare, for example: *If you pass this exam, I'll take you out to dinner* and *If you passed this exam I'd take you out to dinner.*) Some learners resolve the difficulty by reserving the second condition for impossible conditions only and this can be difficult to detect, unless the teacher is alert to the possibility.

4 *I'd* for *I would* may be understood as *I had*, and vice versa. This is especially true when both forms occur in one sentence: *If I'd got a ticket, I'd go.*

THIRD CONDITION: analysis

There are two identical forms but each has a different meaning. They both refer to hypothetical actions in the past.

Base Form A
The speaker knows that the condition was not fulfilled and is therefore impossible, (as in the second condition): If I had known, I would have told you. (I'd have told you if I had known.) *(I didn't know so it was impossible for me to tell you.)*
Base Form B
The speaker does not know for certain whether the 'if condition' was fulfilled: If he had known, he would have told you. (He'd have told you, if he'd known.) *(I'm not sure whether he knew or not or whether he told you.)*
Question Form
If he'd known she was here, would he have come? *Two possible meanings:* a *He didn't know so he didn't come.* b *He came but it's not certain whether he knew or didn't know she'd be here.*
Negative Form
Wouldn't he have come if he'd known she was here? *Two possible answers:* a *expects answer 'yes'; he didn't know and so didn't come.* b *expects answer 'no'; he came but he didn't know;* *or can be a neutral question and therefore open to either interpretation.*
Tag Questions
He'd have come if he'd known, wouldn't he? *(I believe he didn't come because he didn't know.)* *(expects answer 'yes'; seeks confirmation)* He wouldn't have come if he'd known, would he? *(He came because he didn't know.)* *(expects answers 'no', seeks confirmation)*

Notes

Form A Unfulfilled Past Condition

1 This form refers to past time, and to conditions which were **not fulfilled.** Sometimes called the 'too late' condition.

2 It is usually formed with the past perfect in the *if* clause and *would have* (past modal perfect) in the main clause: *If I had got up earlier, I'd have caught the train.*

There are four common variations:

a A positive form in both clauses: *If I had known, I would have told you.* The action in the *if* clause did not happen, and this prevented the action in the main clause. (I didn't tell you, because I didn't know.)

b A negative in the *if* clause: *If I hadn't seen the pedestrian, I would have hit him.* The action in the *if* clause did happen, and this prevented the action in the main clause. (I didn't hit him, because I saw him.)

c A negative in the main clause: *If I'd seen him, I wouldn't have hit him.* The action in the *if* clause did not happen, and this caused the action in the main clause to happen. (I hit him, because I didn't see him.)

d A negative in both clauses: *If I hadn't braked, I wouldn't have skidded.* Both actions did happen, the action in the main clause was a result of the action in the *if* clause. (I skidded because I braked.)

In the 'if' clause

The past perfect may be replaced by the following forms:

Past perfect continuous: (where the outcome was caused or prevented by an action in progress)
If he hadn't been cycling in the middle of the road, I wouldn't have hit him (but he was, and I did).
If he'd been looking, I wouldn't have hit him (but he wasn't and I did).
If I'd been driving quickly, I would have killed him (but I wasn't so I didn't).

Modal past perfects: *Could have* (for past ability): *If I could have been there, I would have been there* (but I couldn't, so I wasn't).
The following are also possible, but rare: (*Might have* for past permission, is now old-fashioned)
Would have (for past willingness): *If he would have done it, I would have paid him* (but he wasn't willing).
Should have (known past obligation): *If I should have done it, I would have done* (but I didn't have to).
Past simple (for stative verbs especially where the state continues past the time of the action:
If I had a car, I'd have gone (but I haven't got a car, and didn't have one then, so I didn't go).
If he knew, he would have come. (Note: Some American usages prefer past simple to past perfect for all verbs, in this way.)
Semi-subjunctive: *Were* can replace *had been* for states which are impossible conditions at the time of the action.
If I were rich, I'd have bought one (but I am not rich and never have been, so I didn't buy one).

In the main clause

Would have may be replaced by the following forms:

a Any other past perfect modal except *ought to/should* for obligation;
*If I had known, I **could have/might have/should have** told you.*

b **Would and continuous** for actions resulting from or prevented by the *if* clause, which would be or are:

• In progress at the time of speaking:
If you had told me, I wouldn't be standing here now (but I am, because you didn't tell me).

• Planned at the time of speaking (diary future):
If I hadn't won that competition, I wouldn't be singing on television tonight.

Base Form B Unknown Past Condition

This form refers to past conditions which may or may not have been fulfilled. The speaker draws conclusions about likelihood from or about those conditions.

I   For past events whose logical results affect the time of speaking, formed with a past tense (usually the past simple) in the *if* clause, and with any modal perfect in the main clause:
If he came earlier, he'd have left a note/there would be a note. (there is no note here now, therefore I deduce that he didn't come earlier).

• *In the 'If' clause*

W*as going to* may be substituted for the past simple, for past plans, whose logical results have general or present significance. e.g. *If he was going to walk, he wouldn't have taken the car keys* (But the car-keys are not here, so I deduce that he probably took them, and therefore did not plan to walk).

• *In the main clause*

W*ould have* may be replaced by the following forms:
Any modal perfect (for probability or obligation): *If he went to the party, he will have/may have/must have/can't have/ might have taken the car* (I do not know if he went, or if the car has gone. These are my predictions about the likelihood of that).
Would be (or any other modal+be): *If he left the party at six, he would be (might be) home by now.*
Modal and continuous forms: *If he went to bed at 11, he may be sleeping now.*

II For past events whose logical results affected past time. The speaker has an open mind as to whether the condition was fulfilled or not. The form often has the past simple and a real or implied past time marker in the *if* clause and *would have* in the main clause:
If he picked up the snake it would have bitten him. (I do not know whether he picked up the snake. If we find out whether he was bitten, we shall know.)

• *In the 'If' clause*

Past continuous: may be used when the process (not the fact) of the action affects the logical deduction:
If he was mowing the lawn then, he wouldn't have heard the telephone.

• *In the main clause*

W*ould have* can be replaced by any past perfect or continuous modal .
When expressing uncertainty, modals other than *would have* are often more appropriate in the main clause:
If he went to London yesterday, he might have gone to the cinema (*might have gone* is really a guess).
Note: If we want to express disbelief we use the base form but *had* is stressed: *If he **had** been at the party, I would have seen him.*
In this usage the present perfect continuous is very common: *If he **had** been mowing the lawn, he couldn't have heard the telephone* (I don't believe that he was mowing the lawn).

Meaning and Function

Form A

(A) **Tracing cause and effect in past chains of actions:** If A hadn't happened, B wouldn't have happened.

(B) **Expressing fate and chance:** If I hadn't missed my train, I wouldn't have met you (But I did, so I did).

(C) **Justifying or explaining past actions:** If he hadn't turned it off, it would have boiled dry.

(D) **Blaming:** If you hadn't pushed me, I wouldn't have dropped it.

Form B

(E) **To deduce where persons or things are:** If he took it, he may have left it in his pocket.

(F) **To deduce where persons or things were:** If he took it, it may have been in that coat I took to the cleaners.

(G) **Saying 'it serves you right':** If he wanted it, he shouldn't have left it lying around.

Suggested Contexts

(A) **Tracing cause and effect:**

- Students are given a sequence of events in the past simple, each event causing the next. The teacher introduces the new structure, and students and teacher use it to retell the story. (*If I hadn't been in a hurry, I wouldn't have spilt the milk/needed the mop, opened the door/let the cat out. If the cat hadn't got out it wouldn't have met the cat next door/had kittens. So, if I hadn't been in a hurry the cat wouldn't have had kittens.*) Then students are given two unrelated events, and asked to create similar causal 'bridges'. (**See photocopiable page 13.**)

- Real life. Students are given an *if* clause (*If I hadn't come to this school*), and asked to finish it in the maximum number of true or likely ways.

- Historical or technological fact. Students are asked to predict what would have happened if some event had not happened, or had happened earlier. (It is best to keep away from recent political history.) This activity can be linked to reading, debate, etc.

(B) **Expressing fate and chance:**

- Students are given a biographical sketch of a famous person (an actor) in whose career chance played an important role: *If he hadn't broken his leg, he would have gone to Hollywood, and he wouldn't have met his wife.*

- The teacher shows a picture series, (cartoons etc.) where a situation was brought about by a series of chances. Students are invited to list the ways in which the predicament could have been avoided.

- As the previous activity but from a video extract of farce or situation comedy.

- As the previous activity but from literature, (e.g. Romeo and Juliet, tracing steps to tragedy).

(C) **Justifying past actions:**

- Dialogue building exercise/role-play. A customer is complaining of services (e.g. delivery), an employee justifies the companies actions: *If we'd left it on the doorstep, it would have defrosted.*

Complaints can be given by the teacher, or elicited from the students. (This can be combined with **D**.)

- Quiz. Students try to identify the names of people who averted or caused catastrophes from a series of clues: *If he hadn't put his finger in the hole, the dyke would have collapsed.* Then students write their own 'clues', others guess the identity of the mystery person.

D **To apportion blame:**

- A list of words is written on the board, and cards with the same words are distributed so that each student in the group has at least one card. (e.g. dog, milk, table. etc.) The teacher begins: *I saw you spill the milk.* Student with *milk* must then respond, blaming another person, *I wouldn't have spilt the milk, if you hadn't knocked the table* and so on round class. The same cards can be recycled, with different concepts.

- Role-play: A domestic crisis where one person blames another (e.g. lost cat): *It wouldn't have got out if you'd shut the window. I would have shut the window if you hadn't been smoking* etc.

E & **F** **To deduce where persons or things are:** Best taught as part of a series on logical deduction.

- Role-play: missing object (e.g. keys). *If they are not in your pockets, you must have left them somewhere.* etc.

- Students are told about an imaginary 'missing person'. They are given information, maps and timetables to help them deduce his possible whereabouts and movements: *If he caught the 10 o'clock train, he might be in London by now.*

- As for the previous activity, but in the past: *If she was here at 6, she couldn't have been there by 10.*

G **To say 'it serves you right' as part of a series on complaints.** There is probably not enough material for an entire lesson on this usage alone.

Learner Error: Form, Spelling and Pronunciation

1 I'd may represent I *had* or I *would*, sometimes in the same sentence. This leads to confusion: *If I would see/ seen him, I had told him.*

2 Students may wish to express events which did not happen by using a negative inappropriately: *If I had caught the bus I wouldn't have been here on time.*

3 Students may attempt to use *would have* in the *if* clause: *If he would have come, he would seen her.*

4 The non-standard native forms *would of* and *had of* may be heard and reproduced by learners: *If I had of seen you, I would of known.*

5 Other modals may be added to *would* rather than substituted for it: *I would can have come/I could would have come/I would have must come.*

6 Students may encounter the problems inherent in the verb tenses and modals used in this construction.

Learner Error: Meaning and Function

1 Students often confuse negative and positive meanings. This may lead them to produce sentences like: *If I hadn't been killed, I wouldn't be here.* (This is caused by a desire to express the negative idea: I *was not killed*). They may also misinterpret the construction when they hear it.

2 Many students attempt to avoid this construction altogether.

3 Variations in the base form may cause confusion to those students who feel they know the 'rule'.

4 The existence of the 'logical deduction' form causes confusion, as variations appear to break the third conditional 'rule.' Many students adopt the logical deduction form, even when past actions are known. *If he left, he would have seen her* rather than *If he had left, he would have seen her.* Intonation and expected answers of tag questions also cause problems.

Modal Auxiliaries

Points to ponder

• For trainee teachers

In England you must drive on the left.
In England you have to drive on the left.
These two sentences are similar in meaning. Write them both in the negative. Does this suggest any possible problems for EFL learners?

What, if any, is the difference between the following sentences:
Can you give me a hand, please?
Could you give me a hand, please?
Will you give me a hand, please?
Would you give me a hand please?
(The differences may exist in the circumstances under which you would say each of these sentences.)

• For teachers' workshops

Is it true to say that the present form of any modal auxiliary can be exchanged for will/shall in what we traditionally regard as the will future?
Do you feel that students experience more difficulty with the form or the function of modal verbs?

Introduction

There are a number of verbs which follow none of the usual patterns. Instead they follow a pattern of their own. They have only one present form, and one past form, in all persons. They are used only as auxiliaries, and form negatives and questions like the other auxiliaries (do/be/have), but are unlike them in many other respects. These 'modal' verbs usually indicate the speaker's attitude to the probability/necessity/advisability/desirability of the action in the main verb. Each modal has more than one meaning and the meanings of all modals are interrelated. They are best taught functionally, one meaning at a time, (rather than concentrating on the structure, except with very advanced students) and usually more than one modal will be appropriate to each function.

Although 'present' and 'past' forms can be identified, modal verbs are not time-specific. The present form can refer to present or future time, the 'past' form to past, present, or future. A 'perfect form' also exists, and this too may have past, present or future reference. Since the meanings of these forms are different from the 'simple' forms they are dealt with under a separate heading. Modal questions cause many problems, as each may have a variety of meanings, depending on context (function) and on stress and intonation in particular.

MODAL AUXILIARIES Simple Form: analysis

Present and Past forms:

Full Form	(Spoken Form)		Negative Form		(Spoken Form)	
I	will ('ll) would ('d) shall ('ll) should may might can could must — — —	eat	I	will would shall should may might cannot could must need dare ought	not not not not not not not not	(won't) (wouldn't) shan't (shouldn't) (mayn't) (mightn't) (can't) (couldn't) (mustn't) (needn't) (daren't) (oughtn't) to	eat

Question Forms

Will you walk?
(*invitation, request or neutral question asking for a prediction*)

Won't you walk?
(*pressing invitation, expresses surprise*)

Tag Questions

You will walk, won't you)
(*expects answer 'yes'*)

You won't walk, will you?
(*expects answer 'no'*)

Notes

1 These verbs exist only as auxiliaries. Unlike the other auxiliaries (*be/have/do*) they have no existence as full verbs.

a They have no infinitive with *to*. (There is no form *to must* for example.)
When an infinitive form exists, it is part of a different regular full verb. For example: *to can*: to put into tins.

b There is no present participle, and therefore there is no continuous form. I *am willing* exists, but is adjectival: I'm *very willing to give her a hand*.

c No passive form is possible.

d Question forms are made by inversion, as with other auxiliaries. (*Are you? Can I?* not **Do I can?**)

e Negative forms are made by adding *not* directly to the auxiliary, as with other auxiliaries: (*I wasn't/I mustn't*)
Note: *Will* and *shall* actually change form in the spoken negative (*won't/shan't* not **willn't/shalln't**). *Cannot* is commonly written as one word.

2 There is no *s* in the third person singular, even in the present form. (*I will/he will*; *I can/he can*. Compare: I *eat/he eats* etc.)

3 Present and past forms can be identified by turning present forms into reported speech: "*I will come,*" *he said*. *He said that he would come.*

a The present form may refer to present time, *I can speak French*, but frequently refers to future time, *You can go to the concert if you like*. Although *will/shall* are usually regarded as markers of the future tense, it is important to remember that both have functions which refer only to present or habitual time. (See pp. 00, will/shall)

b The past form refers to past actions, but may equally refer to present or future time: *I could drive when I was sixteen*, (past time); *I could drive if you're tired*, (imminent future or general future plan); *I could pick you up tomorrow*, (specific future time).

4 *Must* has no past form. *Ought To* and *Should* are past forms, but rarely refer to past time, except in reported thought or speech: *He thought he should/ought to leave early*.

5 *Needn't* is given as a modal verb in the negative only, as other uses of it are rare. They do, however, exist in question forms:

a In direct questions: *Need we go?* (direct inversion, with no auxiliary); *Need he go?* (direct inversion, no auxiliary, no third person s).

b In tag questions: *He needn't go, need he?* (The tag is made by inverting the auxiliary, no third person s.)

c In 'hidden' questions, after verbs of thinking etc; *Do you think he need go?*

Note: The verb *To need to* exists as a regular full verb, and behaves like every other verb, with an infinitive (*To need to*), 3rd person s (*He needs to*), and forms with auxiliaries (*Do you need to? I don't need to. He needs to, doesn't he?*). Continuous forms are rare, as this is a stative verb. *To need to* expresses a personal requirement to do something, *needn't* expresses a lack of outside obligation:
I need to go to the shops. I don't need to go to the shops. I needn't go to the shops.

6 *Daren't* is sometimes used as a modal, exactly like *needn't*. (*He daren't walk, Do you think he dare walk?*) However, the parallel regular verb is in very common use and the modal form is becoming more uncommon. The past form *durst/durstn't* is now obsolete. Perhaps because of the existence of the verb *To dare*, exceptional forms are sometimes encountered: *He doesn't dare walk*. Compare: *He daren't walk, he doesn't dare to walk*. Most English native speakers would accept this exceptional form. Meanings of *dare* are not significantly interrelated with other modals, and it has been omitted from the following functional analysis.

7 Similarly, *ought to* is given as a modal verb and conforms to modal patterns. However, non-standard usage often treats it as a regular verb in questions and negatives, using *did* as an auxiliary, especially in colloquial speech (**Did I ought to? You didn't ought to. I ought to, didn't I.**) Note that the form is treated as a past tense (taking *did*, not *do*). This form is common in non-standard speech, but is not produced by educated speakers.

8 In some functions (for example logical deduction) *can* exists only in the negative or question forms: *He can't be a dustman. He can't be, can he? Can he (possibly) be?*, but not *He can be a dustman* – which has a different meaning.

9 Although *will* is commonly regarded as a tense marker, it may be helpful to notice that almost any modal, in past or present form, can be substituted for *will/shall* in any tense made with these forms.

Hence: *I will/shall/can/may/might/could/should/ought to/needn't eat.*
I will/shall/may/might/could/should/would/ought to/needn't be eating.
I will/shall/may/might/could/should/would/needn't have been eating.

Note:

a The form *I would eat* exists, but is an incomplete sentence in modern English. *Can* is used with continuous sentences only in the negative: *He can't be eating*.

b Similarly in conditional sentences where *would* is regarded as the marker, any past modal form will substitute for *would*, changing the meaning but not the form:
If an elderly lady came in, I would give her my seat.
If an elderly lady came in, I could/should/might/ought to/give her my seat.

10 Pronunciation:

a *Will* is commonly reduced to *I'll* or sometimes to /wl/

b *Shall* is more commonly reduced to /ʃl/

c *Can* and *can't* are pronounced differently / kæn /,/ ka:nt /

d *Mustn't* is pronounced without the first *t*. As a result, many English native speakers write the form as *musn't* especially as the word occurs mostly in dialogue, and not formal written English.

11 Negatives:

a The forms *won't/shan't* are different from the statement form. *Cannot* exists as a separate word.

b The negative form does not necessarily negate the meaning of the statement form. The *not* may sometimes be seen as applying to the following verb, and not to the modal. Often the meaning is negated by another modal.

Must   I *must smoke* (there is an obligation to smoke). Compare: I *have to smoke*.
       I *must not smoke* (there is an obligation not to smoke). Obligation is negated by I *needn't smoke*.
       You *must be Mary* (I deduce that you are Mary).
       You *can't be Mary* (I deduce that you are not Mary).
       The form You *mustn't be Mary* means I *forbid you to be Mary* (impossible except in role-play contexts.)

May   I *may come* (it is possible that I will come but implies I may not come).
       I *may come* (I am allowed to come). I *mayn't come/*I *can't come*.

Can   I *can come* (negated by I *can't come*).
       You *can't be Mary* (negated by You *must be Mary*).
       The form You *can be Mary* means I *permit you to be Mary* (impossible except in role-play contexts).
       I *can not come* (not coming is a possibility).

Will   It *will rain* (certain prediction of a future event).
       It *won't rain* (certain prediction of a future event).
       Certainty is negated by It *might rain*, It *may rain*, It *could rain*.

Shall Usually negated by *shan't*, or *won't* for determination.

12 Modal verbs have a variety of interrelated meanings, and these are much influenced by stress and intonation, especially where meanings of one modal relate to the meanings of others.

M eaning and Function

(A) Physical Ability: *can, can't, could, couldn't*

a Actual present abilities:
   Can: Look, I *can touch my toes*.

b Hypothetical present or future abilities:
   Could: I *wish I could touch my toes*. (Compare: I *think I can touch my toes*. /I *think I could touch my toes*.)
            I *could touch my toes if I lost weight*.

c Past abilities:
   Could: I *could touch my toes when I was younger*.

(B) Learned Skill: *can, can't, could, couldn't*

a Actual present skills:
   Can: I *can drive*.

b Hypothetical present or future skills:
   Could: I *wish I could drive*; I'm *sure I could drive your car as well as he does*.

c Past skills:
   Could: I *could drive before I was ten*.

C **Potential:** (of machinery) *can, can't, will, won't, could, would, might, should, ought to.*

a Actual present potential:
Can: *The car can carry five passengers.*
Will (of machinery): *The car will do 45 miles to the gallon.*

b Hypothetical present or future potential:
Could: *My car could tow your caravan.* (easily)
Would: *My car would tow your caravan.* (it is tested to that capacity)
Might: *My car might tow your caravan.* (it appears to be strong enough)
Should: *My car should tow your caravan.* (I believe it has the potential)
Ought to: *My car ought to tow your caravan.*

c Past potential:
Could: *The first cars could do 20 miles an hour.*
Would: *My car would only do 60 miles an hour, so I got rid of it.*

D **Permission**
Giving Permission: *can, may, could, might*

a Present or future permission:
May: *You may go now/tomorrow.*
Can: *You can go too.* (more conversational and less polite)
Could: in expressions such as, I *suppose you could go.*

b Past (reported) permission:
Could: *She said I could go.*
Might: *She said I might come.* (now unusual, and slightly archaic)

Asking Permission: *can (I)? could? may? might? will you let me? would you let me? I wonder if I might?*

a Present or future permission (usually with *please*):
Might: *Might I make a suggestion?* (very formal, unusual)
May: *May I use your telephone?* (formal, polite)
Could: *Could I borrow your pen?* (less formal, polite)
Can: *Can I use your pen?* (conversational, less polite)
Also phrases such as: *Will/would you let me borrow the car? I wonder if I might interrupt the meeting?*

b Past (reported) events:
Could: *I asked if I could come.*
Might: *I asked if I might be allowed to speak.* (rare)
Would let: *I asked if she would let me.*

Begging Permission: *Can't I? Couldn't I? Won't you let me?*

a Present or future permission:
Can't: *Can't I watch the programme?*
Couldn't: *Couldn't I stay out late just this once?* (stronger)
Won't you let me: *Won't you let me go to the party, please?*

b Past (reported) events:
Couldn't: *I asked if I couldn't go to the dance.*

Refusing Permission: *can't, cannot, may not, won't, shan't, I won't let you, you mustn't.*

a Refusing present or future permission:
May not: *No, you may not go.* (very formal)
Cannot: *No, you cannot go.* (usually written)
Can't: *No, you can't watch television.*

Won't: *You won't go out until you've done your homework.* (more forceful)
Shan't: *You shan't go there again.* (very forceful)
Also: *I won't let you go out/I shan't allow you to go out/you mustn't go out.*

b Past (reported) events:
Couldn't: *She said I couldn't go.*
Wouldn't let: *She said she wouldn't let me go.*
Mustn't: *She said I mustn't go.*
(*Shouldn't* and *mightn't* are unusual in this function.)

E **Asking for things**: *can, could, may, might, would.*

a Present and future requests:
Can: *Can I have a sandwich please?* (conversational, less polite)
Could: *Could I have a sandwich, please?* (less formal, polite)
May: *May I have a sandwich please?* (formal, polite)
Might: *Might I have that in writing please* (very formal, unusual)
Also phrases such as: *I would like a sandwich, please? Would you/could you/will you/can you give me a sandwich please?*

b Past (reported) events:
Could: *I asked if I could have roast beef instead of chicken.*
Might: *I asked if I might have the day off.* (very formal)
Would: *I said I would like a cup of tea.*

F **Asking for Information:** *can, could, will, would.*

a Present requests:
Can: *Can you tell me the time please?* (conversational, polite)
Could: *Could you tell me the time please?* (formal, polite)
Will: *Will you give me your name, please?* (conversational, less polite)
Would: *I see you have a map. Would you direct me to the Post Office please?* (supposes that the person being asked has the information)

b Past (reported) requests:
Would/could: *I asked if she could/would tell me the time.*

G **Requesting action:** *can, could, can't, couldn't, will, won't, would.*

a Request for present or future action:
Can: *Can you get me some stamps, please?* (conversational, less polite)
Could: *Could you help me with this suitcase, please?* (formal, polite)
Will: *Will you post this letter for me, please?* (conversational, polite)
Would: *Would you hold the ladder for me please?* (formal, polite)
In the negative the request is strengthened, and may be more impatient. *Wouldn't* is not used in the negative form.
Also phrases such as: *Would you mind getting me some stamps, please.*

b Past (reported) requests:
Would/Could: *I asked if he could/would help me.*

H **Offering:** *can? could? may? shall I? would you like me to?*

a Offering present or future action:
Can: *Can I help you?* (conversational)
Could: *Could I do that for you?* (conversational, permits the answer *No thank you, I can manage*)
May: *May I do that for you?* (formal, polite)
Shall I: *Shall I carry that?* (conversational, polite. the commonest form in British English)
Also phrases such as: *Would you like me to carry that? May I be of any help?*

b   Past (reported) offers:
Could/Might: *I asked if I could/might help.* (*Should* is not used in this function.)
I asked if she would like me to help.

I   Invitations: *will, would, won't, wouldn't, can, could, shall we, I thought you might like to. Would you like to?*

a   Invitations to present or future events:
Will/Won't: *Will you come to the theatre with me tonight?* (polite)
Would/Wouldn't: *Would you come to the ball with me?* (formal)
Can: *I'm having a party on Friday. Can you come?* (conversational)
Could: *Could you come to dinner with me tonight?* (suggests that there may be difficulties)
Shall we: *Shall we go and see that film?* (suggests that willingness to go somewhere is automatic)
Also phrases like: *I'm going to Paris at the weekend. I thought you might like to come./Would you like to come with me?*

b   Past (reported) invitations:
Would: *The prince asked if she would come/would like to come to the ball.*
Could: *He asked if her friend could come to the disco.*

Accepting Invitations: *will, can, would love to, should love to.*

a   For invitations to present and future events:
Will: *Yes, we'll come to the party.* (informal, not very polite)
Can: *I can come to the disco after all.* (where there were previous difficulties)
Would: *I'd love to come to the party.* (both polite and conversational)
Should: *I should love to come to dinner.* (more formal)
(*Will* and *shall* are not used with *love to.*)

b   For past (reported) events:
Would: *I said I would go to dinner.*
I said I would/should love to go out to dinner.

Refusing Invitations: *can't, couldn't, won't/shan't be able to, would love to but …*

a   For invitations to present and future events:
Can't: *I'm sorry, I can't come tonight. I'm working.*
Couldn't: *I'm sorry, I couldn't come. Perhaps some other time?* (more formal)
Won't be able to: *I'm afraid I won't/shan't be able to come to the party.*
Would love to: *I'd love to come, but I'm babysitting tomorrow.* (conversational and polite)
(*Won't* alone is rarely used in this function, as it is impolite, *I won't come.*
It can be softened by using a continuous form; *I won't be coming.*)

b   For past (reported) events:
Could: *I said I couldn't come.*

J   Requests and commands
Agreeing to a request: *can, will.*

a   For present and future requests:
Can: *Yes, I can give Katy a lift.*
Will: *Yes, I'll post your letters. Where are they?*
(Also *could* in phrases like, *Of course I could help you.* Without a strengthener *could* often expresses reluctance.

b   For past (reported) agreements:
Would: *I said I would paint the gate this weekend.*

Refusing a Request: *can't, couldn't, won't, shan't.*

a   Refusing requests for present or future action:
Can't: I *can't do that today.*
Couldn't: I'*m afraid I couldn't babysit tomorrow.* (formal)
Won't/shan't be able to: I *shan't be able to help you.*

b   Rudely refusing:
Won't: No, *he won't make his own dinner.*
Shan't: No, I *shan't send it today.* (more forceful, first person only)

c   Past (reported) requests:
Couldn't: He *said he couldn't do it for us.* (polite refusal)
Wouldn't: He *said he wouldn't help to paint the gate.*

Apologetically refusing: I *would but* ...

a   Refusing requests for present or future action:
Would: I *would help you, but I'm working.*
(Past reported refusals require a complex form with *have*)

(L) **Expressing Reluctance:** *could (but), might, shouldn't, oughtn't to.*

a   Reluctance to perform present or future actions:
Could: I *could give you a lift, but you'll have to be ready on time.*
Might: I *might pick you up (but I won't promise).*
Shouldn't: I *shouldn't go shopping now, I'll be late.*

b   Reluctance (or pretended reluctance) to accept invitations:
Shouldn't: I *shouldn't eat any more cakes, but perhaps just one.*
Oughtn't to: I *oughtn't to have another slice, but perhaps I will.*
Might: I *might have just one chocolate.*

c   Reluctant refusal:
Mustn't: I *mustn't drink any more, I'm driving.*
Couldn't: I *couldn't eat another thing.*

(M) **Instant Decision:** *will, won't, might.*

a   For present or future events:
Will/won't: It'*s raining. I won't go to the shops today, I'll go tomorrow.*
Might: Oh, *is he going to the party? I might go, after all.*

b   For past (reported) events:
I *decided I would/might go after all.*

(N) **Volunteering:** *will, can, could, shall I?*

a   For present or future events:
Will: I'*ll fill in for him while he's away.*
Can: I *can take the dog for a walk if you like.* (conversational)
Could: I *could take Kate to town for you.* (formal)
Shall I?: Shall I *do that for you?* (but not I *shall do that for you.*)

b   For past (reported) events:
Would/could: I *said I would/could do his work while he was ill.*

(O) **Promising/threatening:** *will, shall*

a   For present or future events:
Will: My *husband will mend your car as soon as possible.*
Will: I'*ll stop your pocketmoney, if you are not careful.*

Shall: I *shall mend the pipe/tell your mother.* (more forceful)
Shall: *You shall have your bicycle.*

b For past (reported) events:
Would: I *promised I would look after the cat.*
Should: I *promised you should have it, and you shall.*

(P) Expressing determination: *will, shall, must*

a For present or future events (usually with stress on the modal):
Will: I *will pass my exams.* (I have made up my mind)
Shall: *They shall not pass.* (I take the responsibility)
Must: I *must lose weight.*
I *mustn't let him get the better of me.*

b For past (reported) events:
Would: I *made up my mind that I would pass my exams.*
Must: I *decided that I mustn't let him tell me what to do.*

(Q) Prediction

a For future events:
Certainty: *will, won't. She'll be late. He won't come to the party.*
Probability: *should, shouldn't. It shouldn't rain this afternoon. He should arrive at six.*
Possibility: *may, might, may not, might not, could:*
He may (not) come to the party. (more formal)
Paul might (not) come to the party.
Take your coat, it could rain. (conversational)
Faint possibility (stressed modal): I *suppose the plane could/might be delayed.*
(*Could* is never used in the negative statement in this construction.)

b For past (reported) events:
Would: I *thought she would be late, but she wasn't.*
Might: *He warned us that the plane might be late.*
(*Should* and *could* are rarely used in this function.)

(R) Expressing Logical Deduction

a For present states and general truths (usually with *be* or *have*):
Logical necessity: *can't, must*
Can't: *It can't be Susan, she's gone away for the weekend.*
Must: *You must be Dr Livingstone.*
(Note that *can* and *mustn't* are not used in this function.)

No logical necessity: *needn't*

Needn't: *That parcel needn't be ours at all. It might be Jim's.*

Logical certainty: *will, won't, couldn't, wouldn't*

Will, won't: *That won't be the postman, it's too early. It's six o'clock, they'll be leaving now.*
Couldn't: *That couldn't be Sam, he's got a moustache.*
Wouldn't: *It wouldn't be Sam, he hates shopping.*

Logical probability: *should, shouldn't, ought to, oughtn't to.*

Should, shouldn't: *That should be the postman. The dustman shouldn't be here yet. He should have some money, he's been to the bank.*
Ought to, oughtn't to: *He ought to be in London by now.* (conversational)

Logical possibility: *could, may, might, may not, might not.*

Could, might, mightn't: *It could be true. They might have some change in that shop.*

May, may not: *I think that's Sam, but it may not be.*

(Note that *can, can't* and *couldn't* are not used in this function.)

b With active verbs, in logical puzzles and argument. The degree of necessity or logical probability remains unchanged:

If all cats eat meat and Fido is a cat, then Fido must eat meat.

c For past (reported) deduction:

He realised that it must/might/could be a machine.

He realised that it couldn't/.needn't/wouldn't/mightn't be correct.

(Note that *will, won't, can't, should* and *shouldn't* do not occur in this function.)

S **Obligation and Compulsion**

Rules and Laws

a For present laws, with present and future reference:

Must: *You must drive on the right when you go to France.*

Mustn't: *You mustn't park on double yellow lines.*

Can't: *You can't smoke in the classroom.*

Should/Should not: *Guests should not smoke in the bedrooms.*

b Past laws:

Couldn't: *At one time drivers couldn't do more than 8mph on British roads.*

(Note that *must* and *mustn't* are not used in this function.)

Personal authority

a For present rules, with present and future reference:

Must: *You must finish your homework.*

Mustn't: *You mustn't smoke in the house.* (very forceful, general rule)

Can't: *You can't stay up tonight.*

Will/won't: *You will finish your food before you watch* TV. (very forceful)

Shall/shan't: *You shan't go out again for a week.* (Very forceful indeed, and now rare)

b Past (reported) authority.

Couldn't: *She said I couldn't go out.*

Must: *She said I must do my homework.*

Lack of Obligation: Rules and Laws

a For present laws, with present and future reference:

Needn't: *You needn't keep your headlights on during the day in the UK (although you have to in Sweden).*

Can: *You can park anywhere in the square.*

May: *Competitors may carry their bikes for a maximum of 20 metres.*

b Past laws:

Could: *At one time you could drive without a licence.*

c Past (reported) or hypothetical authority:

Could: *I thought you could park here.*

(Note that *needn't* and *may* are not used in this function. M*ight* is sometimes found, I *thought I might park here* but is very formal and rare.)

Lack of Obligation: Personal Authority

a   For present rules, with present and future reference:
Needn't: *You needn't make your bed.*
Can: *I can stay up if I like.*
May: *Guests may have a bath once a week.* (formal)

b   Past (reported) authority:
Needn't: *She said I needn't make the bed.*
Could: *She said I could have dinner at any time.*
(*Might* is possible, but very unusual and formal.)

🅣 Social and moral responsibility

a   For present responsibilities, with present and future reference:
Must: *You must go and see Sally, she's in hospital.* (forceful)
Mustn't: *We mustn't forget to send our Christmas cards early this year.*
Should/shouldn't: *They should resurface the road.*
Ought to: *She ought to look after her children better.*
(Note that reported past responsibilities usually require complex modal forms with *have*.)

🅤 Advice

a   For present advice, with present and future reference.
Strong Advice, where there are dangers if the advice is not followed:
Must: *You must see a doctor about your leg.* (forceful)
Mustn't: *You mustn't forget to water them, or they'll die.*
Should: *In the event of fire, you should ring the fire alarm and leave the hotel by the nearest exit.* (less urgent)
Ought: *You ought to see a dentist.* (conversational)

Strongly felt advice

Should/shouldn't: *You shouldn't carry a lot of money with you.*
Ought to: *You ought to ask for your money back.* (conversational)
I should: *Are you afraid of burglars? I should get a burglar alarm.* (meaning *you should*)

General advice

Could: *You could sent it by post.*
Might: *You might ask Peter if he knows. You might try at the Post Office.* (more formal)
Couldn't you: *Couldn't you post it?*
I would: *I would do it this way.* (meaning, *If I were you*)

Advice (with a negative form):

Shouldn't: *You shouldn't leave your bag unattended.*
Oughtn't to: *You oughtn't to smoke so much.*
I wouldn't/shouldn't: *I wouldn't tell him.*
Also phrases such as *I don't think you ought to/should go to the party.*
(Note that *must*, *could* and *might* are not used in this function.)

Advice to oneself

Must, mustn't: *I must lose weight.* (Does not mean I *will*)
Should/shouldn't: *I should stop smoking really.* (but I probably won't)
Ought to/oughtn't to: *I ought to do more exercise, but ...*

Advice for enjoyment

Must: *You must see that film, its terrific.* (forceful)
Should: *You should read this book, you'd like it.*
Ought to: *You ought to taste this!* (conversational)

Advice for enjoyment (with a negative form):

I shouldn't: *I shouldn't eat that. It tastes awful.* (forceful)
I wouldn't: *I wouldn't go to that restaurant, the other one is better.*
(Note *must* is not used in this function).
Phrases such as I *don't think you would like it* are often used.

b   Past (reported) advice uses the same structures:
The doctor said I must/should/ought to lose weight.
He said I should/ought to water them every day.
He said he would report it, in my place, etc.

V   Insistence on undesirable habits

a   For present habits with present and future reference:
Will: (stressed) *He **will** turn the volume up all the time.*
Especially with *will keep: He **will** keep losing his keys.*

b   Challenging habits or behaviour:
Must: *Must you make so much noise?*

c   Past habits:
Would (stressed): *He **would** lose his temper all the time.*

W   Past habits, customs and traditions

Would: *We would go skiing every year. The monks would gather for prayers.*
Might (for infrequent habits): *Sometimes we might spend Christmas with my aunt, but usually we would stay at home.*
(Note that this usage has no real present equivalent.)

X   Rebuke

For present action or inaction, with present and future reference.
Could: *You could do something, instead of just standing there.*
Can't /Couldn't: *Can't you turn the volume down.*
Might: *You might give me a hand.*
Needn't: *You needn't be so rude.*

Y   Rhetorical devices

a   In formal speech or writing. To introduce an argument:
Could: *It could be said that ... You could argue that ...*
May: *It may be true that ...*
Might: *It might seem that ...*
Must: *It must be admitted that...*

b   To introduce a statement:
Must: *I must say, that's a lovely dress. It must be said that ...*
May: *May I say how pleased I am to be here. We may note in passing...*
Ought to: *It ought to be stressed that ...*
Should: *We should note that ... I should explain that ...*
Could: *Could I just add ...*

To strengthen a statement or opinion (often in a set phrase)

a To strengthen a statement:
Must: It's very nice, I must say. Its very nice, you must agree.
May: That's a nice car, if I may say so.
Should/would: That was expensive, I should/would think.
Shouldn't: It'll rain tonight, I shouldn't wonder.

b To endorse an opinion expressed by others:
Should: I'm going to increase her salary. I should think so too! I should hope so! I should say she deserves it.
Shouldn't/wouldn't: I don't think it will rain. No, I shouldn't/wouldn't think so.

Differences between similar verbs:

1 Will and shall (see page 73 Will/Shall Future)

2 Should and ought to are very close in meaning:

a With neutral stress should suggests an obligation more moral and binding than ought to and therefore offers stronger advice, and conveys greater certainty in prediction. Ought to often suggests that the action is unlikely to be fulfilled; compare You should go (this is absolute) and You ought to go (but I know you don't want to).

b When the modals are stressed, this emphasises responsibility or obligation, but for logical deduction and advice the stressed form admits the possibility of something else occurring: I should go (but I probably won't) I ought to go (but I'm still hesitating).

3 May and might. Here are some guidelines, but they cannot hope to cover all uses:

a With neutral stress may suggests a rational possibility, arrived at after logical thought. Might suggests a possibility but carries no suggestion about previous consideration.

• For logical necessity may is a stronger suggestion than might, and usually more likely, or suggests something which might otherwise be overlooked: It may be her fault.

• For potential may suggests greater (rational) potential, and is therefore more likely: This may be used in baking (it is good for this purpose). This might be used in baking (for instance).

• For prediction of possibilities in conversation may is usually more formal, because it carries the suggestion of previous consideration: I may be late. I may come. Might is more casual, and therefore friendlier: I might be late. I might come. The difference is one of formality and attitude rather than likelihood, but as might is more neutral, it often suggests more likelihood in speech, but less in writing, where a position is naturally more thought-out.

b With stress on the modal. This emphasises the lack of certainty, so the form indicates much less likelihood. The greater the stress, the less likely the action. When stressed, the random nature of might makes it less likely. May still indicates a remote, but rational, possibility.
It might come today (anything is possible). It may come today (but I doubt it).

c With stress on the main verb the action is more likely than in the neutral form.

Suggested Contexts

It is not suggested that these are taught in this order. The best order will depend upon the needs of individual groups, but modals are probably best taught starting with the function at a basic level, and then expanding with other ways of expressing that function at a later stage. Many of the functions can be expressed in non-modal ways, and these may be taught alongside the modal forms (let's/shall we) or as a basis for them (perhaps it is/it might be; I have to/I must, I don't have to/I needn't).

Some useful contexts are:

(A) For physical ability

- Students are given physical tasks, (*touch toes, stand on one leg* etc.). All students are asked to attempt them. Then the teacher identifies who *can/can't*. The construction can be practised using other tasks.

- The class is shown a picture of a person with one leg in plaster for example, and a list of usual habits: He *plays football. Is he playing today?* No. He *can't.* He *plays the violin. Can he play today? Yes, he can* etc.

(B) Learned skill

- Based on class experiences compile a questionnaire: *Who can speak French? bake bread? drive? swim?*

- Set up a narrative (with pictures) in the present simple and continuous: A small boy wants to visit his grandmother. His mother is talking on the phone. He takes the car keys. All right? No, *he can't drive.* Then the class offers other solutions, He *can't ride a bike/horse/read bus signs* etc.

- 'What's my secret'. Class members identify, or are given an unusual skill. They must mime it. Other members guess: *Can you milk a goat?* No, I *can't. Yes, I can, but that isn't my secret.* This needs other structures, but is useful revision.
  Note: These meanings seem very close to an English native speaker but in many languages they require different verbs (e.g. French pouvoir/savoir). Both meanings should therefore be identified.

(C) Potential (more advanced)

- Role play. Sales talk comparing machinery: *This computer will do x/that computer can store more information* etc.

- Comparing objects in their past and present form: *The earliest cars could only do 4 mph.*

(D) Permission

This is best taught as a series of functional lessons on permission, using dialogue building and role play. Learners exchange roles in asking, giving, refusing, and begging permission. This may be based on an entertainments page for example. Students ask permission to attend different events. Those refusing may be asked to give reasons, or given grounds for refusing or accepting, or deciding which they will permit.

(E) Asking for things

This can be taught as part of a series on shopping/restaurants etc.

(F) Asking for information

- Role-play and dialogues on sight-seeing.

- Questionnaires in the classroom, asking other students about their holiday plans, for example.

- Information gaps (e.g. filling in a map, where each group has different pieces of information). *Can you tell me where the tropical forests are?*

- Quizzes written and run by students: *Can you tell me …? Will you spell …?*

(G) Requesting

- Allocating tasks; this may be role-play, or real tasks to set up a class-room activity.

- Rearrange classmembers (e.g. in order of height); *Can you stand by Naim, please* etc.

- Asking for services in a shop.

(H) Offering:

- Arranging a party (real or imaginary); *I'll bring the glasses. Shall I bring my tape recorder?*

- Offering services in a shop: *May I show you this one. Would you like me to get the manager.*

(I) Invitations: It is useful to set up reasons for accepting and declining: *Mary likes Sam, she doesn't like Peter. Peter asks her. Sam asks her but she can't go;* What is her reply in each case?

J, K & L Agreeing to a request and refusing/accepting it, with varying degrees of politeness. **Expressing reluctance;** once again identifying personalities and social contexts is important.

(M) Instant decision

- Role plays and dialogue building. Best taught by contrast with other futures (see page 76, Will/ Shall Future)

- The teacher sets up a class game, especially one in which forfeits are done by those making the wrong decision. Students decide what steps to take next. *We'll take a blue card We'll pass, We'll go on.*

(N) Volunteering: (builds on **H** and **M** above)

- Students are given a list of tasks to be done by a colleague who is absent, plus their own 'timetable'. Students work in groups to decide who can do the jobs on the colleague's list: *I could do that, I'm going to the post office.* This works best if some tasks cannot be undertaken by others, for example a dentist appointment, and if some are desirable, *I shall go to Paris to represent the firm.* (**See photocopiable page 3.**)

(O) Threatening

- Role-play: complaining about poor goods or services; *I shall write to the manager etc.* This offers revision for **H** and **N** above, *May I offer you a refund? I'll find you another room.*

- A parent getting angry about an untidy room: *I shall stop your pocket-money!* etc.

(P) Expressing determination

This can be introduced into role-play, dialogue or writing exercises. There is rarely enough substance for a whole lesson, though it can be useful then teaching negative probabilities: *You might not pass the exam. I will pass.*

(Q) Predicting certainty and likelihood

This should be taught as a series of lessons, building on each other, not all at once. The degree of certainty must be stressed at each point (Note: certainty is in the speaker's mind, it is not objective.)

- *Will/won't*: suggestions for possible contexts will be found on page 77, Will/Shall Future.

- *May/might*: students are given a list of possible future events, and asked to decide in groups if these are certain, likely, possible, or impossible: *will happen/might happen/may happen, won't happen.* (**See photocopiable page 14.**)

- Students are asked to create their own list about the future life of unknown people in photographs or sketches: *He won't be a jockey.* Other class members may challenge.

- *Mightn't (May not)*: Students are given, or asked to draw up a list of expectations about a future event. (for example the school's sports day): *Is it certain? No, it might be cancelled.* Then students suggest possible reasons:

  positive (unexpected possibilities): *The weather might be awful.*
  negative (expected things may not happen) *There mightn't be any electricity.*

- Shouldn't/should; this is often a useful last lesson in the series. Set up a context where the probability of the event occuring is high: I *have a cold. I've taken a cold remedy. Will I get better? Probably! I should get better.* (strong likelihood.) Then contrast this with the likely effects of other actions (certain, I *will*; possible, I *might*; unlikely, I *could*; impossible, I *won't.*)

R *Logical deduction about the present*

This should be taught as a series, not all at once. Any logical problem can be used.

- *Must be/can't be*: students are given a logical problem. A list of physical characteristics and three photographs are given to the students. Ask them to deduce the names/professions/who is the criminal etc: *Jim is taller than the doctor. Jim can't be the doctor. The doctor has red hair. Picture A must be the doctor.* etc.

- *Might be*: as above, but where the physical description fits more than one picture. Only by working through all the available information can one deduce identities. This is best with four or five pictures: *It might be A or it might be C. It can't be B or D.* Can be usefully done competitively, once the structure of modals is clear. (**See photocopiable page 15.**)

  All modals:

a The degrees of probability are shown schematically, then the teacher introduces a deductive activity as above, but the criminal is a master of disguise. The photographs show one man with beard and whiskers, one old man, one woman, one tall, one medium, one short. The students are given a photograph of the 'criminal' without disguise. Which is he? Is he any of them? Groups must reach a consensus, other groups may object: *It could be that one. It can't be that one. It needn't be any of them.*

b Giving possible explanations for inexplicable events, for example, selling a haunted house. Peculiar noises are heard. The vendor tries to explain the noises as the purchaser identifies them. A: *There's a whistle* B: *It must be the kettle.* A: *It can't be the kettle, it isn't switched on.* B: *It might be the wind* etc. Students can score points for plausible excuses, and for using a range of modals appropriately.

S *Obligation and compulsion* (rules, laws)

- Traffic regulations, traffic signs, *You mustn't exceed the speed limit, you needn't drive at 50 mph, you can drive at 60 mph, you can't/mustn't drive at 70 mph.*

- Inventing or noting rules for a game or competition.

- Airline regulations and customs controls.

- School rules.

- Suggested laws for new democracy.

T *Moral responsibility* (especially in conjunction with **S** above)

- Comparison of laws and customs in different cultures. This is especially successful in multiracial classes.

- A discussion on family responsibilities, parents' legal responsibilities, moral responsibilities, elicited and listed: *They must feed their children, shouldn't spoil them, can beat them, shouldn't beat them* etc.

- A discussion about laws e.g. taxes, capital punishment, traffic fines, wheel clamps, listing opinions as to what is necessary (*must*) and what is desirable (*should/ought to*).

U *Advice* (best as a series of lessons)

- Strongly felt advice, where there will be serious consequences if the advice is ignored: doctor to patient; advice on keeping pets; advice on precautions when travelling. In every case it helps to identify what will happen if the advice is not taken: *You'll be ill; it will die; you'll get lost.*

General advice:

- Each student is given a problem, *You have lost your passport*. Other students give advice. The student decides which piece of advice to accept and why.
- One student is given a physical problem (e.g. puzzle), other group-members advise.
- Role-play: Citizens' Advice Bureau. Students may be given 'problems' or invent their own.
- Written exercise: Agony aunt or problem page.

Advice to self: making New Year's resolutions.

Advice for enjoyment: roleplay, or short spoken reviews based on the student's own reading or film-going: *You must read this. You wouldn't enjoy that. I shouldn't bother with it.*

Ⓥ ***Insistence on undesirable habits***

Best taught as part of a series on complaints and most usefully tackled as a dialogue building exercise or roleplay:

- Complaining about the stranger in the next seat on an aeroplane, for example. Complaining about a teenage son/other family members. *He will keep coming home late.*
- Complaining to them: *I think you could make the effort, and come home on time*; *Must you come home so late?*

Ⓦ ***Habits of youth***

- Writing lessons on childhood memories, (e.g. family reunions, outings, activities, games)
- Historical information. The students are given the typical timetable of a medieval monk, Chinese emperor, or whatever is culturally appropriate. Students discuss the timetable, then produce a written account: *The monks would rise at four* etc.

Ⓧ ***Rebuke***

Probably required for recognition only.

Ⓨ ***Rhetorical devices***.

Probably required for recognition only, or possibly for formal debates, as they may become overused.

Learner Error: Form, Spelling and Pronunciation

1 Many errors arise from attempts to treat modals as main verbs:

a By creating an infinitive with *to*: *I must to go; He ought to can.*

b By creating a negative with *do*: *I don't must.*

c By creating a question form with *do*: *Do I must?*

d By combining modal with *will* to form a future, instead of substituting it for the appropriate form: *I will can* for I *will be able*; *I will must* for I *will have to*.

e By adding *s* to the third person singular: *He cans play the piano* or *He can plays the piano.*

f Occasionally, by attempting to create a continuous form for present action *I am canning* or attempting to form a passive *It is musted.*

2 Problems arise from contracted negative forms:

a *Won't* and *shan't* may be given as *willn't* and *shalln't*.

b *Mustn't* and *oughtn't* may be spelt *musn't* and *oughn't*.

3 Pronunciation problems:

a *Can't* may be pronounced on the pattern of *can*.

b Stressed and unstressed *can* are not differentiated.

c *Will/won't* /w/ is pronounced /v/ by many Germanic speakers.

d *Will* with a short *i* is pronounced *ee* by many students.

4 *I'd like to* may be interpreted and sometimes written as *I had like to*.

5 Other constructions may be substituted for modals, often in line with mother tongue usages: *He knows speak English* for *he can*; *It is possible he come* for *he may*.

Learner Error: Meaning and Function

1 *Mustn't* causes problems for many students. It may be substituted, as the opposite of *must*:

a for *needn't*, meaning no obligation: *I mustn't be in by ten o'clock* for I needn't be in by 10 o'clock.

b for *can't* meaning logical impossibility: *You mustn't be Dr Livingstone.*

c more rarely, for negative advice about enjoyment: *You mustn't see that film.*

2 *May not* and *mightn't* may be interpreted erroneously as meaning 'no possibility'; *She might not come*, however implies that there is a possibility that she might not come, not that she definitely won't come.

3 *Can* is sometimes mistakenly used as the opposite of *can't* for logical deduction *You can be Dr Livingstone.*

4 *Ought to* may be used by students as an equivalent of *should* in all cases: *If I ought to die,* see that my family is cared for.

5 Other constructions may be substituted for modals, often in line with mother tongue usages: *He knows speak English* for *he can*; *It is possible he come* for *he may*; *He won't probably come* for *he mightn't come*.

6 If students, especially Germanic speakers, recognise a 'past' form modal they may fail to recognise it as having future meaning or be unwilling to use it in this way.

7 The chief problems arise with differentiating functions. Learners often prefer to use *can, should, would, may* and especially *will*, to the exclusion of all other modals (for problems with *will* see page 73, Future section).

8 Learners may use *shall* and *must* with persons other than the first person, in inappropriate ways. *You shall be late*. *You must lose weight* may be produced for *You will be late* and *You ought to lose weight*.

MODAL AUXILIARIES; Perfect Form: analysis

Full Form		(Spoken Form)		Negative Form			(Spoken Form)	
I	will ('ll)	have ('ve) eaten	I	will	not	(won't)	have ('ve) eaten
	would ('d)			would		(wouldn't)	
	shall ('ll)			shall	not	(shan't)	
	should ('d)			should		(shouldn't)	
	may			may	not	(mayn't)	
	might			might		(mightn't)	
	—			cannot	not	(can't)	
	could			could		(couldn't)	
	must			—			
	—			need	not	(needn't)	
	—			dare	not	(daren't)	
	ought to			ought	not	(oughtn't) to	

Queston Forms	
Will you have eaten it? *(neutral question)*	Won't you have eaten it? *(expects answer 'yes')*

Tag Questions	
You will have eaten it, won't you? *(expects answer 'yes')*	You won't have eaten it, will you? You needn't have done it, need you?

(Meanings vary greatly with function, context, stress and intonation.)

Notes

1 The form is often referred to as a 'modal perfect'. Although the time reference may be similar to the present perfect, i.e. an action in the past, seen from the viewpoint of now, and affecting the present (I *must have left my gloves on the bus*, I *haven't got them now*), this is not always so. Modal perfects may refer to:

Actions in the simple past, with a past time marker: I *should have seen him yesterday*.
Note: *shall have* does not exist with past reference. However, *will have* does occur, indicating logical certainty, *I'm sure he will have seen her yesterday*.

Actions predicted for the future, with a future time marker especially with *by*: I *may have seen him by tomorrow*.
Note: *can't have/mustn't have/needn't have* do not exist with future reference. *Will have/shall have* are so often found with this meaning that they are regarded as future tense markers.

2 In the perfect form *must* refers only to logical necessity. There is therefore no negative. Logical impossibility is conveyed by *can't*, lack of necessity by *needn't*. The positive statement form of *needn't have* and *can't have* do not therefore exist, except in questions, question tags and hidden questions: *Need he have?*; *He needn't have, need he?*; *Do you think he need have?*; *Can he have left?*; *He can't have left, can he?*; *Do you think he can have left?*

3 *Daren't have* is included for the sake of completeness, and is omitted from the analysis which follows this note. *Daren't* has some existence as a modal (see 118 Modal simple forms) and *daren't have* is still occasionally found, with a distinct (present perfect) meaning: *He daren't have left* (therefore he must be here somewhere), compare: *He hasn't dared* (to) leave (so here he is). *Daren't have* has no future reference, and very rarely a past one. (The past form *durst* is now almost entirely obsolete.)

4 Any of the above modals may substitute for *will have* in any tense, with consequent changes in meaning and function. Equally, any of the past form modals above may substitute for *would have* in the third condition (see page 112, Conditional Section).

5 Past participles are formed exactly as for the past and present perfect.

Meaning and Function

A ***Logical possibility of past action affecting the present:***
I *will/won't/must/might/mightn't/may/may not/could/ couldn't/can't/needn't* have left them on the bus.

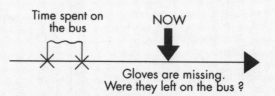

I'll have left my gloves on the bus

I'll have left them on the bus. (I haven't got them. I'm certain that is where they are.)
I won't have left them on the bus. (I haven't got them. I'm certain they are not on the bus.)
I must have left them on the bus. (I haven't got them. Logically, that is where they must be.)
I might have left them on the bus. (I haven't got them. It is possible that is where they are.)
I mightn't have left them on the bus. (I haven't got them. Possibly I didn't leave them on the bus.)
I may have left them on the bus. (I haven't got them. On reflection, it is possible that is where they are.)
I may not have left them on the bus. (I haven't got them. On reflection, perhaps I didn't leave them there.)
I could have left them on the bus. (I haven't got them. Physically possible that I left them on the bus.)
I couldn't have left them on the bus. (It was logically impossible that I left them on the bus, or colloquially, only an idiot would leave them on the bus, but I fear that is where they are.)
I can't have left them on the bus. (It is logically impossible that I left them on the bus, but I fear I did.)
I needn't have left them on the bus. (That is not a logical conclusion. I might have left them somewhere else.)

B ***Logical probability of scheduled actions affecting the present:***
Actions expected in the past:
He must/should/ought to/will/might/may/could have left by now.
He must have, (it is logically certain).
He will have, (I am certain).
He should have/ought to have, (it was scheduled).
He might have, (it is possible).
He may have, (on reflection, it is possible).
He could have, (it is physically possible).

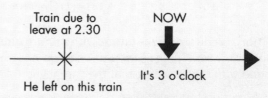

Actions expected in the future: (with a future time marker)
He /should/ought to/will/might/may/could have left by six o'clock.

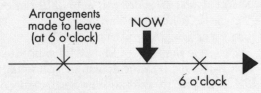

He should have left by then (by 6 o'clock)

In the negative form:
He can't/shouldn't/oughtn't to/won't/mightn't/may not/couldn't/needn't have left yet.
He can't have (it is logically impossible).
He shouldn't have/oughtn't to have, (it was not scheduled).
He mightn't have, (it is possible that he hasn't).
He may not have (on reflection, possibly he hasn't).
He couldn't have (it is physically impossible).
He needn't have (it isn't logically certain).

He can't have left yet

C **Logical probability of actions affecting a point in future time**: (with a future time marker)
I will/would/won't/wouldn't/could/couldn't/might/mightn't/may/may not/should/shouldn't/ought to/oughtn't to have finished by 5 o'clock.

I'll have finished by 5 o'clock

D **Altered Future potential:**
I would/should/could/might/may have seen him tomorrow (usually followed by but or if).
I would have, (it was certain or I wanted to).
I should have, (it was scheduled or I intended/promised to).

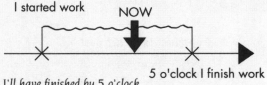

I would have seen him tomorrow but the appointment has been cancelled

I could have, (it was physically possible).
I might have, (it was a possibility).
I may have, (there was a rational possibility).
This construction is sometimes used in the negative, often to express consolation:
I wouldn't have/shouldn't have/couldn't have/mightn't have/may not have seen him tomorrow (anyway).
I wouldn't have, (it was certain that I would not see him, perhaps because I didn't wish to).
I shouldn't have, (I wasn't scheduled to see him, or it was impossible or inconvenient).
I couldn't have, (it was physically impossible).
I mightn't have, (there was a possibility that I would not).
I may not have, (there is a rational possibility that I would not).

E **Moral obligation which was not fulfilled in the past:**
You *should have/ought to have/written to your mother.* Colloquially also: *might have/could have.*
You *should have,* (it was your moral duty).
You *ought to have,* (it would have been polite).
You *might have,* (I expected you to; colloquial).
You *could have,* (it was the least I expected; colloquial).
You *shouldn't have/oughtn't to have been so rude.* Colloquially also: *needn't have been.*
You *shouldn't have,* (it was your moral duty not to).
You *oughtn't to have,* (it would have been polite not to).
You *needn't have,* (it was unnecessary to be rude).

F **Advice after the event.** Usually implies that the opposite was done.
(e.g. You *should have/ought to have bought it* (usually implies, but you didn't).
You *shouldn't have/oughtn't to have bought it* (usually implies, but you did).
I *would have bought it* (but you didn't).
You *needn't have bought it* (but you did, it was unnecessary).

Suggested Contexts

A *Logical probability in the past*

- The students are given a set of circumstances, some certain, some possibilities, and asked to express them. e.g.: *There is a bird in a locked room. How did it get in? It must have got in somehow. It can't have come through the door. It might have come down the chimney,* etc.

- Students are given a narrative in the past tense, containing some mystery, a person or object disappears for example (gloves, bank robber, pet). *What happened? He might have dyed his hair/it must have escaped* etc. (again differentiate degrees of likelihood).

- Ordinary misadventures, a flat tyre for example. *What happened? You must have run over a nail* etc.

B *Logical probablity of scheduled actions affecting the present.* It is important to set up a context in which both the present reference and the expectations are important:

- Students are given the situation in which a team is leaving to catch the train to the airport. They are told the time of the train, the distance from the station of each member, who has a car etc. Then the air-tickets are lost. The team must be informed so it is important to phone each member:
  What is the time now? Who can we contact? He mightn't have left yet; He must have left by now.

- Dialogue building exercise: A late shopper/caller at an office or shop, asks to see the manager. The staff member uses excuses and explanations to persuade the caller to return at a more convenient time:
  A *I'm sorry Madam, the manager isn't here at the moment.*
  B *He can't have left, his car is still outside.*
  A *Oh, he must have been called away unexpectedly.*

C *Logical probability for future time*

- Students are asked to predict their future: *In twenty years time I might have got married, will have left school, may have made a million.* Altering dates alters probabilities.

- Students are given a picture or blackboard sketch of various workmen engaged in building a house, at different stages of completion. They predict the state of the work at different future times: *By tonight the painter will have finished, the electrician might have arrived* etc. This can be made more communicative if there is a supposed 'right answer' monitored by another group.

D *Altered future potential.* This is for advanced levels:

- The teacher sets up the context of a cancelled VIP visit – if there is a real one, it is more interesting. Identify what the VIP *would have done/might have done* etc. These suggestions can be matched to a supposed list, and used for debate, what was likely/unlikely? (*Was going to* can be revised and use in conjunction with this construction.)

- Interrupted career: a sports person deciding on retirement, or suffering injury: *He might have been world champion.*

E *Moral obligation* (taught after *should/ought to* for present/future obligation)

- Students are given a narrative or picture sequence in which the 'rules' are transgressed, (for this usage it is better to avoid the context of crime). Groups identify the infringements: *He shouldn't have crossed the red light* etc. This can be done competitively.

- Use a video film, a situation comedy for example, in which someone behaves unkindly.

- Video films on driving lessons lend themselves to this activity.

- Retell a famous story. Elicit from the students instances where the characters' behaviour should have been different and ask them for explanations and suggestions for alternative plots. *He shouldn't have hidden the gun from the police. He ought to have told them the whole story.*

F *Advice after the event*

- The teacher gives a puzzle or difficult task to the class. One student or group (or the teacher, if that seems appropriate) attempts it, others watch, then they give retrospective advice. The task is reattempted, and the roles reversed; *You should have put the wire into the hole first.*

- As above, but the task is done incorrectly, deliberately. Students suggest improvements.

- The constructions can be used informally when correcting work in the class-room.

- Role-play. Returning goods after a long time, or complaining about a meal after it is eaten: *You should have sent it back. You ought to have kept the receipt,* etc. This works well in conjunction with other modals: *We can't give you a refund. You must produce the receipt,* etc.

Learner Error: Form, Spelling and Punctuation

1 Modals are often treated on the pattern of a full verb:

a they may be placed after have: *I have must* (compare: I have eaten).

b the negative is attached to have: *I haven't must* *I must haven't*.

c tags are made with have: *I must have, haven't I?*

d questions are made with have: *Have I must?*

2 Have is reduced to ve in speech. It may be heard as of, *you shouldn't of* and written as such.

3 Errors may be made with past participles, as in the present and past perfect.

4 Problems arise from contracted negative forms, as with simple modals:

a won't and shan't may be given as *willn't* and *shalln't*.

b mustn't and oughtn't may be spelt musn't and oughn't.

5 Pronunciation problems occur as for the simple modal forms:

a can't pronounced on the pattern of can.

b stressed and unstressed can is not differentiated.

c will/won't /w/ is pronounced /v/ by many Germanic speakers.

d will with a short i is pronounced ee by the majority of learners.

Learner Error: Meaning and Function

1 Learners may use must and mustn't in the perfect form for legal obligation or moral compulsion: *I must have seen him* for I have had to see the doctor.

2 Can (especially) is used in the statement form as the opposite of can't: You can't have seen him. *You can have seen him.* The nature of this error is not always recognised by teachers. (Compare: I don't think you can have.) The error may be inappropriately corrected to You may have seen him, whereas it may represent must have seen him. It is important to check the learner's intent.

3 Can may be used inappropriately for may, as above.

4 Mustn't may be seen as the opposite of must, and used instead of needn't or can't.

5 Learners find it hard to use apparently past and perfective forms for future reference or having once learnt this, to apply the form to past or present reference, (especially will/shall); *He will get there by now* for He will have got there by now.

6 Expressions such as I may/can well, I may easily cause problems with modal perfects. They are often inappropriately split: *He may have well gone, He well can imagine it, He may have gone easily*.

Passive Section

Points to Ponder

- ## For trainee teachers

  Which of these constructions would you describe as passive?
  I *have been arrested.*
  I *have been asked to go to London.*
  I *was followed.*
  I *have been to London.*

  The passive voice is often said to be an academic construction, useful mostly for academic and scientific purposes, and for newspaper reports. How far does this seem to you to be true? Do we use the passive in ordinary speech, and if so, in what contexts?

- ## For teachers' workshops

  In what ways can expressions like I *am tired* and *The window was broken* be considered passives? What problems, in your experience, do foreign learners experience with the English passive?

Introduction

The tenses and verb patterns mentioned previously in this book are in the active voice. The subject of the sentence or verb is the person or thing doing the action (*John hit Mary*). This is easy to conceptualise where the verb is an activity, clearly the 'doer' is active; but the same term can be used for other verbs as for example: It *happened.*

All the verb tenses in this book can also be produced in the passive voice, where the subject of the sentence is the 'victim' of the action (*Mary was hit by John*). Again, this is clearest when the action is something physical. The same construction with less dynamic verbs is classified in the same way; *Mary was met at the station* is also a passive construction.

The passive voice is made, in any tense, by using the appropriate form of the verb To *be* and adding a past participle. Hence the past simple passive of To *eat* will consist of the past simple of To *be*, (I *was* etc.) + past participle of To *eat* (*eaten*) to give I *was eaten* etc. This example, although grammatically correct, illustrates a widespread problem. Although it is theoretically possible to produce a passive form for any verb, many verbs do not lend themself meaningfully to the construction. (Anyone who *was eaten*, or *was killed* is unlikely to be in a position to say so.) Equally, the so-called 'intransitive verbs' very rarely make passives.

Since the structure of the passive is regular, the following pages concentrate chiefly on the uses of, contexts for, and problems arising from the passive voice. Contexts and problems are related to whether the structure is a simple tense, a continuous tense, a perfect tense, or a complex pattern using *used to*, *going to* or a modal auxiliary, and are not divided by time reference as in the active section.

SIMPLE PASSIVE TENSES: analysis

Base Form	
Present simple passive: French is spoken in Dominica. *Past simple passive*: Latin was spoken in Europe.	
Question Forms	
Is it spoken in Dominica? (*neutral question*)	Isn't it spoken in Dominica? (*expects 'yes', invites listener to agree or expresses doubt*)
Was it spoken in Europe? (*neutral question*)	Wasn't it spoken in Europe? (*expects 'yes', invites listener to agree or expresses doubt*)
Tag Questions	
It is spoken in Dominica, isn't it? (*expects answer 'yes, it is'*) It was spoken in Europe, wasn't it? (*expects answer 'yes, it is'*)	It isn't spoken in Dominica, is it? (*expects answer 'no, it isn't',*) It wasn't spoken in Europe, was it? (*expects answer 'no, it wasn't', or expresses surprise*)

Notes

1 In all passives, the past participle forms a kind of adjectival construction, and in simple forms it is difficult to determine where adjectives begin and passives stop. *The window is broken* for instance, has two meanings; it can describe an ongoing state, or a repeated process (*every cricket season*). The state is usually regarded as an adjective, the repeated process as a passive. In fact, it may be more helpful to the teacher to regard them as stative and dynamic forms of the same passive construction.

2 Reflexive verbs: A verb is said to be reflexive when the person or thing doing the action (the active person) is also the 'victim' of the action (the passive person). e.g. He *cut himself*. In this sentence *he* is both the subject of the action, and the object of it. As can be seen from the example, the construction is regarded as active. In other languages however the reflexive and passive form are similar as in *il s' est tué/ il est tué* which as a form parallels the English passive construction.

3 Conversational and informal English often replaces the passive form by an active form with *got*; *Mary got hit. He got cut*. This is especially acceptable where the verb would otherwise be reflexive, *He got dressed* etc.

M eaning and Function

Ⓐ *Present passive:*
a **Stative use**. To describe continuing states. Used exactly as an adjective: *She is tired. It is broken.*
b **To describe scientific or industrial processes**, where the speaker is interested in the product, or process, and not the people involved in the process: *It is heated in a large vat for three hours*.
c **To describe custom or ritual**, where the speaker is interested in the object and not those who use the object: *It is worn by the chief of the tribe.*

d **Academic objectivity**. To discuss scientific or academic truths: It is often said that ... used for stylistic reasons, to suggest objectivity and add weight to the statement; compare: Many people say that ...

e **To describe habitual or repeated processes**, when the speaker does not know who is responsible. The speaker is interested in the repeated nature of the process, not in the person responsible: Every night, a house in this area is broken into. Note also the construction with gets, ... A house in this area gets broken into... (Compare: Every night, someone breaks into a house in this area.)

f **To describe habitual or repeated processes** where the emphasis is on the activity not on the people performing the activity: My car is cleaned every Thursday.

g **To describe the daily routine of people or animals** who are not free to decide on, or to carry out this routine for themselves, (pets/babies, children etc.): The animals are fed at six.

B **Past passive:**

a **Stative uses:** She was tired. It was broken.

b **For past routines customs, habits and processes:** As b-g above.

c **Narrative**: Describing the fate of a person/animal/thing who was unable to control his own destiny: He was knocked down by a bus. It was destroyed by the volcano etc. It is often specifically used to draw attention to the role of the 'victim': Thousands were tortured by the secret police.

d **Official reports** of past events, when the outcome of the action is more important than the person who did it: A window was broken in the skirmish.

e **Official reports**, when the perpetrator of the action is not known, or not reported: A shop was broken into last night. A man was seen leaving the premises.

Suggested Contexts

A **Present passive**

a **Stative uses**

This usage does not require an individual lesson. Stative present passives are best taught as normal adjectives.

b **For scientific processes**

- Scientific experiments: The water is heated in the test-tube etc. Note that, in more modern scientific classroom teaching this formula has been replaced by a more personal active narrative; We heat the water in a test-tube.

- Describing how things are made/distributed etc. Students are given a flow chart, and asked to describe what is taking place: The letters are taken to the post office ...etc.
  (**See photocopiable page 9b**)

- Describing how things operate. Using a video, demonstration or diagram. This can be especially useful if the process is described in reverse: The door is opened by this lever. The lever is pulled by this cord etc.

c **To describe custom or ritual**

- 'Culture quiz'. Students are given a list or pictures of famous artifacts, and asked to describe what they are used for, or when they are worn. (e.g. orb, crown, veil, ring etc.) Note that the questions used to elicit the information are also in the passive.

- Using pictures of items used in unusual trades or occupations, elicit descriptions on the activities performed and the function of the instruments/tools used: This is used by doctors. This is used for taking temperatures.

d **For academic objectivity**

- Contrastive work. Students are given a piece of writing in 'personal' (active) style, and asked to transform it into a more 'objective' format. This is often best combined with past simple and modal passives: *Many people think this is his best novel. He wrote it in 1877, and a magazine published it in weekly parts*; becomes; *This novel, which is widely regarded as his best, was written in 1877, and published in weekly parts in a magazine.* This can also be combined with vocabulary work.

- 'Interpretation' exercise. Students are asked to match the passive construction with its 'hidden meaning': *It is often said that … I can't remember who said it.* This is most useful when combined with similar constructions in other passive tenses: *It might be thought that … but I am about to disprove this*,etc.

e **Habitual or repeated processes**, where the speaker does not know who is responsible:

- Crime statistics. Students are given a list of crimes, and some statistical information. Each student is asked to compile statistics by asking others: *How many cars are stolen every year?*

f **Habitual or repeated processes** where different people may be responsible for particular activities at different times:

- You might choose the routine of a large institution (e.g. hotel) where individual timetables for 3 or 4 employees have to be correlated: *Between 8 and 9:30 breakfast is served. At 9:30 the restaurant is cleaned, the dishes are washed* … etc. Deductions can be made from timetables: *The milk is delivered before* 8 a.m.

g **Describing the daily routine of people or animals** unable to decide for themselves.

- Choose an exercise, based on reading, video or listening, on the subject of animal care in a zoo or similar: *The animals … every morning at six. The straw … daily* etc.

B **Past Passive**

a **Stative uses**
With a past time marker. This can be usefully revised before introducing the passive as a tense: *The window is broken. It was broken yesterday. Who broke it? How? It was broken by a cricket ball.*

b **Past routines, customs, habits and processes**
With actions, objects and processes now no longer encountered (see **A** a–g present passive).

c **Narrative**, stressing the 'victim' role:
This is a common context using the past passive. It is often the best way to introduce the passive, if the group is not studying English for scientific or academic purposes.

- Use the context of a street accident, based on picture prompts or on a story elicited (in the active voice) from the students. This is then converted to the passive: *He was knocked over/taken to hospital/put to bed/examined/allowed to go home* etc.

- Criminal proceedings: *He was arrested, questioned, sent for trial, sentenced, imprisoned, fined, released* etc. This can be treated as above, or students can be given the sentences in random order, and asked to rearrange them to create the story.

- Natural disaster, (earthquake/volcano etc.). This can be derived from reading, film strip or video, or newspapers and current affairs when appropriate.

d,e and f **Official reports**

- Newspaper work. Students read an article in the newspaper (selected by the teacher.) They underline the passives, and retell the story in the active voice. Then they are given a simple narrative of a different event, and asked to write a report in the passive.

> - Role-play of a crime (e.g. bank robbery). This can be acted out or mimed by a group of students. Students may also simulate interviews with the 'reporters' using the passive (£3000 *was stolen*) in short written reports. Interviewees may use the active (I *lost £3000*). This activity combines well with the use of the passive for underlining the 'victim role.' (I *was taken prisoner*.)
> - Writing exercise. Students prepare a news bulletin. (This can be used for reading aloud, simulation, or other activities.)

Learner Error: Form, Spelling and Punctuation

1 Problems arising from the formation of past participles, or from the tenses of *To be* may be transferred to the passive; *It *was buyed*. I *weren't tired. Their eaten* etc.*

2 Where the past participle has an unstressed *ed* ending, students may hear and reproduce a base form of the verb in place of the past participle, especially before *by*; *I *was chase by a bus** (especially true of Chinese learners).

Learner Error: Meaning and Function

1 Learners are sometimes unwilling to use the past participle form for present meaning (especially in the stative sense). They often replace it by the present participle: I *am boring*, for I *am bored*.

2 Learners may attempt to make passive forms of verbs which do not meaningfully take the structure: *I *am died.**

3 Students may attempt to use a passive form for verbs or activities which they perceive as reflexive: *I *was dressed myself** (especially romance languages).

4 Some learners may perceive the passive as an alternative form of the perfect tense, especially with verbs of motion, where the mother tongue has a comparable structure (e.g. French, where *venir*, *aller* etc. form a composite past with *etre* instead of *avoir*). Hence, *I *am left.** (Note that forms such as I *am come* are encountered in English in literary, archaic and dialect forms).

5 Many students avoid the passive voice, because it is regarded as only scientific or academic in usage. This is an impression fostered by some course books. Hence A *bus knocked him down*, (suggesting volition), is mistakenly preferred to the more idiomatic, He *was knocked down by a bus*.

CONTINUOUS PASSIVE TENSES: analysis

Base Form	
Present continuous passive: The car is being mended. *Past continuous passive*: The car was being mended.	
Question Forms	
Is it being mended? (*neutral question*) Was it being mended? (*neutral question*)	Isn't it being mended? (*expects answer 'yes' or expresses surprise*) Wasn't it being mended? (*expects answer 'yes' or expresses surprise*)
Tag Questions	
It's being mended, isn't it? (*expects answer 'yes'*) It was being mended, wasn't it? (*expects answer 'yes'*)	It isn't being mended, is it? (*expects answer 'no', seeks confirmation or expresses surprise*) It wasn't being mended, was it? (*expects answer 'no', seeks confirmation or expresses surprise*)

Notes

1 Continuous passive forms are less common than simple passive ones.

2 Pronunciation:

a *being* is reduced in speech and often sounds like *been*.

b *ng* is produced as nasal / ŋ /. Some regional variations pronounce a / g / sound before a vowel: *being eaten*.

3 Past participle forms are created in exactly the same way as perfect tenses.

4 An emphatic form of the structure can be formed by stressing *is/was*, or by stressing the participle *being*, or both: It **was** *being mended*. It **was being** *mended*. It was **being** *mended*.

5 *Being* is replaced by *getting* in colloquial speech, where the subject of the verb is a person or animal: *I'm getting bitten*. In stative uses, the use of the continuous usually indicates that the process is progressive and *getting* is always preferred: *I'm getting sunburnt*.

Meaning and Function

As with all passives, continuous forms are used to underline the fact of helplessness or victimisation; where the speaker does not know who is bringing about the process, does not care who is doing it, or where it may be done by different people at different times, and where the process is more important than the agent. (There may sometimes be an element of self-importance suggested: *I am being photographed*.)

A *Present continuous passive*

a **For processes begun in the past**, and occuring continuously up to and across the time of speaking; expected to be transitory: *The car is being repaired.*

b **For processes recently begun**, and continuously repeated, but not necessarily occurring at the time of speaking; expected to be transitory: *I'm being invited to lots of interesting parties these days.*

c **For pre-arranged future processes**, with a future time marker, (passive diary future). To express future commitments: I *am being interviewed by the* BBC *tomorrow.*

B *Past continuous passive*

a **With a past point in time** specified by a time marker, or by an action in the simple past, when a process began before the point in time, continued across it and after it: *The car was being repaired when he came.*

b **With a period of past time** specified by a time marker, or by an action in the past or past continuous, where the process continued throughout that period of time. Attention is focused on the uninterrupted nature of the process: *We were being watched all the time we were there.* (Compare: *We were watched all the time.*)

c **With a point in past time, specified or implied, for processes repeated up to and after that time, and later discontinued**. Not necessarily occurring at that moment: *When he was six he was still being taken to school every day. When I last saw her she was being asked to do a lot of overtime.*

d **Discussing past plans**. To outline plans firmly entered into before the time in the narrative, but not yet carried out at that time: *We were being taken to London by a friend the next day.*

Suggested Contexts

A **Present Continuous Passive.** (Note, this is a construction for advanced students.)

a **Processes begun in the past** and occuring continuously up to and across the time of speaking.

- Excuses for things or people not being available. Role-play. Buying a house for example. Students are given a list of missing items or things that needed mending etc. The vendor has to make excuses: *There are no doors. They're being painted.*

- Debate on unfair treatment of an identified group (e.g. the employment of domestic workers). *They are being underpaid/ill-treated* etc. Passive forms can be provided as a check list for a discussion on employment conditions. It is better to avoid political discussions.

- Dialogue building for progressive stative use. A list of the discomforts experienced on the beach for example, can be elicited. *I'm being bitten.* (Note that I'*m getting* is more common in this context.)

b **Recent or current passive processes**

- A sick colleague. The teacher elicits a list of the extra duties which other people will be required to do. The jobs are distributed, and students complain using the *ing* structure: *I'm being asked to do extra typing* ... etc.). With verbs of asking, requesting, expecting etc.

- Students are given two pages, one past and one current, each showing a month's activities, from an imaginary celebrity's diary (e.g. pop-star). Then ask: *Is he getting more or less popular?* Students in groups or pairs consult the diary entries in order to answer: *He's being asked to open more supermarkets; he's not being interviewed on the radio any more.*

c **Pre-arranged future processes**

• Using two versions of 'tomorrow's diary', where events call for the passive form:
(e.g. *film-star, 9 a.m. make-up, 10 a.m. girl coming to measure for costume, 11 a.m. Interview with* BBC, *12,
Lunch, guest of director.*) Each member of the pair has different information. By means of question
and answer, students attempt to complete their own version of the timetable: *What is she doing at
10? She's being measured for a costume* etc.

B **Past Continuous Passive**

a **Excuses for past actions with past time specified**

• Students listen to a series of sounds on a tape, all made by the same object. They are asked to
guess what was happening to the object to create the sound; small stones for example: *They were
being shaken/rubbed together* etc.)

b **Past processes filling a period of time**
(There is probably not sufficient material for a whole lesson, but this usage may be taught in
conjunction with excuses for past actions, **B**a.)

• A series of 'cues' is produced, specifying a period of time in the past: *They couldn't have a bath last
night because* ... Students must complete the cues, using the passive structure: *The waterpipes were
being repaired/the tub was being cleaned/the room was being repainted.* This can be done competitivelyto
see who can produce most or most plausible reasons).

c **Repeated past processes**
Not a common use. Can be taught as part of series on expressing past habits.

d **Past plans**
Not a common use. Can coincide with lessons on writing narrative.

Learner Error: Form, Spelling and Pronunciation

1 Learners may hear, understand, and produce *been* for *being*; *I am been followed*, *I was been followed.*

2 Learners may understand the third person contracted form *he's* or unstressed *he was* as *he has*: *He has being
followed.* This may combine with 1 above to produce confusion with perfect passives: *He's been followed* for
He is being followed, and vice versa.

3 The past participle may be replaced by the present participle, in the present passive continuous: *I am being
biting* for I *am being bitten.*

4 The present participle of the verb may be substituted for the whole passive construction: I *am biting* for I
am being bitten. This tendency is compounded because some idiomatic usages permit this construction:
I *am burning* for I *am being/getting burnt.*

5 Learners may encounter any of the problems associated with past participles. These are dealt with more
fully under the section on the present perfect active (see page 23, Present perfect).

6 Very occasionally a deviant present participle of *To be* is created, perhaps because 'I *am being*' seems clumsy:
I amming bitten.

Learner Error: Meaning and Function

1 There is often a reluctance to use the present tense of To *be* with the present participle of To *be*. The initial auxiliary is often omitted, *I *being bitten** and the participle may be omitted, I *am bitten*. This has the effect of creating an apparently regular present stative passive.

2 Learners who have difficulties with the concept of active continuous tenses, continue to experience difficulties in the passive. For a fuller discussion of these, see the sections on the present and past continuous active (see page 12, Present continuous; page 40, Past continuous).

3 There is a strong tendency to avoid this structure altogether and use the simple passive construction at all times. In many instances this is a satisfactory substitution (I *am expected to do extra typing* for I *am being expected*) but not in all cases (*the car is repaired* for *the car is being repaired*). Students who avoid the tense may also have problems in interpreting it.

PERFECT PASSIVE TENSES: analysis

<table>
<tr><td colspan="2">Base Form</td></tr>
<tr><td>Present perfect passive:</td><td>He has been invited to the party.</td></tr>
<tr><td>Past perfect passive:</td><td>He had been invited to the party.</td></tr>
<tr><td>Future perfect passive:</td><td>He will have been invited to the party.</td></tr>
</table>

<table>
<tr><td colspan="2">Question Forms</td></tr>
<tr>
<td>Has he been invited?
(neutral question)</td>
<td>Hasn't he been invited?
(expects answer 'yes' or expresses surprise)</td>
</tr>
<tr>
<td>Had he been invited?
(neutral question)</td>
<td>Hadn't he been invited?
(expects answer 'yes' or expresses surprise)</td>
</tr>
<tr>
<td>Will he have been invited?
(neutral question or suggests a logical possibility about past actions affecting the present)</td>
<td>Won't he have been invited?
(expects answer 'yes', or provides an explanation for a present state)</td>
</tr>
<tr><td colspan="2">Tag Questions</td></tr>
<tr>
<td>He's been invited, hasn't he?
(expects answer 'yes')</td>
<td>He hasn't been invited, has he?
(expects answer 'no', seeks confirmation or expresses surprise)</td>
</tr>
<tr>
<td>He'd been invited, hadn't he?
(expects answer 'yes')</td>
<td>He hadn't been invited, had he?
(expects answer 'no', seeks confirmation or expresses surprise)</td>
</tr>
<tr>
<td>He'll have been invited, won't he?
(expects answer 'yes')</td>
<td>He won't have been invited, will he?
(expects answer 'no', seeks confirmation or expresses surprise)</td>
</tr>
</table>

Notes

1 Forms containing the structure *be being* are possible, but uncommon. These are usually reduced to the nearest parallel form. Hence I *have been being followed* is almost always reduced to I *have been followed*. The form does occur however, when the speaker wishes to indicate that a state has been progressively arrived at, *Why haven't you had the car? It's been being repaired*. With people or animals *getting* is almost always substituted for *being* in this construction, to avoid the duplication: *I've been getting bitten*.

2 Future continuous passive forms, with the additional modal, are extremely rare. The construction does occur, however, as in 1 above, with other modal auxiliaries: *He may have been being interviewed*.

3 Past participle forms are created in exactly the same way as for the perfect tense: *It has been eaten*.

4 *Shall* may sometimes be substituted for *will* in the first person in the future perfect: I *shall have been given the new timetable by then*.

5 A common use of *will have been* is for logical probability relating to the present: I *don't think it will have been Mark*. All other modal perfect forms which are used for logical probability can be substituted for *will have*: I'm *sure it can't have been sold*.

6 All perfect forms explain a state of affairs at a specific point in time, by explaining the actions which led up to it and affected it: *It has been mended* (it now works); *It had been mended* (it worked then); *It will have been mended* (it will work then).

7   Passive forms are used when the speaker wishes to emphasise the helplessness of the 'subject', or when the agent is unknown, or unimportant, or where the process may be brought about by different agents at different times (e.g. in academic or scientific contexts). Continuous forms stress the ongoing and uninterrupted nature of the process at a given moment in time.

Meaning and Function

(For general guidance see diagrams under parallel active tenses.)

(A) *Present perfect passive:* (a very common form).Used to explain a present state of affairs, in terms of what happened to things or people immediately beforehand: *He isn't here, he's been called away.*

(B) *Past perfect passive:* As **A** but relating to a specified past moment in time: *He wasn't at the meeting, he'd been called away.*

(C) *Future perfect passive:* As **A** but predicting events relating to a specified future moment in time: *He won't be there when you get there. He'll have been called away.*

(D) *Future perfect passive:* As **B** but relating to present time, where the past process is not known for certain, but it is a matter of speculation or logical possibility. Any other modal perfect may be substituted: *It will have been sold by now. It might have been/must have been sold by now.* Note that with negative sentences, *by now* and *already* become *yet: It can't have been sold yet. Will have been* is often reduced to *will be,* but other modal perfects occur frequently with the full form.

Suggested Contexts

(A) *Present perfect passive*
For present states:

- Role-play: Selling a house/car etc. Student A asks about possible faults or problems. Student B gives the salesman's assurances that these have been dealt with: *It has been rewired/repapered/ repaired/repainted* etc.(**See photocopiable page 8.**)

- Dialogue building exercise. Complaints: a hotel guest draws up a list of complaints about his room. The hotel manager reassures him the next day that these have been dealt with: *The TV doesn't work. It has been mended now.*

- Students are given a series of manufactured objects and asked to describe how they are finished, using the passive structure: *It's been varnished, polished, carved* etc.

- Academic and scientific writing: *Shakespeare has long been regarded as the greatest English poet. Experiments have recently been carried out which show* ... etc.

(B) *Past perfect passive*
For past states:

- Students are shown two pictures or cartoon drawings of a house and its contents for example, before and after a burglary during the owners' trip abroad. They are asked to compare the two pictures: *When they came back it had been broken into/the windows had been broken* etc.

- Reading or listening comprehension on the development of a city or building for example. Students are given diagrams of the different stages of development. Working together, they must assess which diagram refers to which date: By 1860 *a new wing had been built* etc.

- As for the previous activity but students are only given the diagrams, and are asked to comment on the development of the city/building through the years.

- Logical puzzles: Students are given statements about the past and asked to pick out those which are false. This can be based on general knowledge, *Guns hadn't been invented*, or deduction, *The detective didn't know about the new evidence because he hadn't been told* … etc.

C *Future perfect passive*

- Promises of future action, where a salesman or manager promises future action before the customer will buy/take the room: *Don't worry sir, it will have been replaced by this evening.* etc.

D *Future perfect passive* (and other modal perfects for logical deduction)

- Guessing the results of experiments: a small coin is left in the corridor at the beginning of the lesson. Students are asked to consider what will have happened to it by the end of the lesson. Suggestions are recorded and the outcome checked when the lesson ends. This can be done using a range of modals: *It will have been picked up/moved/handed in*, etc.

- As for the previous activity but with fictional objects: *Mary left her passport on the bus. What do you think will have happened to it?* Groups compete to provide the maximum number of plausible possibilities for each object.

- Each student is given a diagram of a process (e.g. production line, or the postal system) and they are then asked to describe the process: *I posted a letter this morning. What will have happened to it since then?* (certainties with *will have*, possibilities with *might have* etc.) (**See photocopiable page 9b.**)

Learner Error: Form, Spelling and Pronunciation

1 Both the order and form of auxiliaries are often confused, especially where a wrong order results in a similarity to another known structure: *He was had been taken*, *he has will be taken* etc.

2 *Been* and *being* are often confused: *I have being followed* or even *I have being been followed.*

3 Third person *he's* (*he has*) in the present perfect passive is often interpreted as *he is*: *He is been followed.* This sometimes produces confusion with the present continuous passive: *The car is being repaired* for *has been repaired* and vice versa.

4 Problems with the past participle may arise in exactly the same ways as for the present and past perfect.

5 Difficulties may occur with *will* and *shall*. (For fuller notes, see page 73, Will/Shall Future)

Learner Error: Meaning and Function

1 Problems may occur with the interpretation of any perfect tense in exactly the same way as for the active equivalent. For fuller notes see relevant active tenses.

2 Many students are unwilling to perceive *will have been* as having present reference for logical deduction: *It will have been sold by now*, creates confusion.

3 Many students attempt to add other modals rather than substitute them for *will*, especially *may*: *It may will have been lost.* This appears to be compounded because of the native speaker idiom, *It may well have been lost.*

4 Students may not perceive the present perfect passive as relating to a present state, especially as it appears to equate with past passive forms in some languages (e.g. French *il a été vendu* which can be translated as *it has been sold* or *it was sold*).

COMPLEX PASSIVE TENSES: analysis

Base Form		
Future	Will/shall passive:	They'll be told.
	Going to passive:	They're going to be told.
Modals	Present form:	He can be told.
	Past form:	He could be told.
Past	Used to passive: (discontinued habit)	He used to be driven to school.
	(Was going to be) passive: (altered past plans)	He was going to be trained as a doctor.

Question Forms	
Will they be told? (neutral question, or asking about logical possibility)	Won't they be told? (expects answer 'yes', seeks confirmation)
Are they going to be told? (neutral question)	Aren't they going to be told? (expects answer 'yes', seeks confirmation)
Can he be told? (neutral question, or asking about logical possibility)	Can't he be told? (expects answer 'yes', can be a suggestion)
Could he be told? (neutral question or asking about logical possibility)	Couldn't he be told? (expects answer 'yes', can be a suggestion)
Did he use to be driven? (neutral question)	Didn't he use to be driven? (expects answer 'yes')
Was he going to be trained? (neutral question)	Wasn't he going to be trained? (expects answer 'yes')

Tag Questions	
They'll be told, won't they?	They won't be told, will they?
They're going to be told, aren't they?	They're going to be told, aren't they.
He can be told, can't he?	He can't be told, can he?
He could be told, couldn't he?	He couldn't be told, could he?
He used to be driven, didn't he?	He didn't use to be driven, did he?
He was going to be trained, wasn't he?	He wasn't going to be trained, was he?
(expects answer 'yes', seeks confirmation)	(expects answer 'no', seeks confirmation expresses surprise, can express disquiet)

Note: For completeness the following forms have been included and although theoretically possible, are uncommon:

Future Continuous	:	will/shall	:	He will be being coached for the Olympics.
	:	going to	:	He's going to be being coached over that period.
Present Continuous	:	modals	:	He may be being coached at that time.
Past Continuous	:	modals	:	He could be being coached at that time.

Notes

1 Complex continuous forms, requiring *be being*, are relatively rare. The longer the verbal construction, the more uncommon the continuous form. Hence I *may be being followed* is unusual; I'm *going to be being followed* is even more unusual. In practice the form is usually:

a contracted to the parallel simple form: When I *come*, I *may be followed*.

b rephrased into an active construction: They *may be following me*.
Note that the use of the continuous suggests not only that the process is ongoing or progressive (which are the usual meanings of the continuous form), but also that the subject cannot prevent the process. This may be because of helplessness or importance, or both:
I *may be being followed* (they are sufficiently interested in me to follow me. There is nothing I can do to prevent this).

2 Present form modal passives (including *will*) have a possible present meaning as well as a future one. Hence Can *it be eaten?* means is it possible for anyone to eat it in future, is it safe for anyone to eat it at any time, or, rarely, is it logically possible that someone has already eaten it? Compare: Will *it be repaired*?

3 All past form modal perfects have possible present, future or past reference depending on the context: *Should it be eaten*?

4 *Used to be* is replaced in formal speech and in formal writing by *would be*, when the passive verb is used in a dynamic sense: When *it snowed, we would be taken to the park*. This replacement is not always possible when the passive has stative or adjectival force: He *used to be interested*.

5 For the use of *will/shall* see the relevant section (page 73, Will/Shall Future)

6 The past participle is created in exactly the same way as the perfect tense.

7 For the use and meanings of modals see page 117, Modal Auxiliaries.

8 Where the subject is a person or animal, *get* may be substituted for *be*: You'll *get burnt*.

9 As with all passives, these complex constructions are used where the speaker wishes to stress the fact that the subject is helpless, or where the agent is unknown, or unimportant, or where a variety of agents may perform the process at different times, and that process is more important than the agent.

M eaning and Function

Complex future and modal passives

A **Will/shall:**

a **Predicting future processes**, with timetables: They *will be met at the airport*.

b **Promising future processes**, with a time marker: It *will be collected tomorrow*.

c **Warning of future possibilities**: You'll *be hurt*. You *might be hurt*. (Note *get* is often preferred in this usage: You'll *get hurt*.)

d Occasionally, **for oaths and exclamations**: Well, I'll *be damned*!

e **Deducing logical present possibility**: the passive acts as an adjective: It'll *be repaired by now*.

B **Going to:**

f Occasionally used **for general intention, or plan:** We're *going to be collected at the airport*. Other futures are more common. Compare: We'll *be collected at the airport*. We're *being collected at the airport*.

g **As a warning or threat** (of events which are evident now): *You're going to be bitten.* Get is often preferred in this usage: *You're going to get bitten.*

h **Expressing determination**: *I'm not walking. I'm going to be driven!*

C **Present form modals:**

i As a–c **with different degrees of permission, probability/possibility and desirability**: *You must/may/be met at the airport* etc. with appropriate modals.

j As e **logical possibility** with differing degrees of certainty: *It must be repaired by now.*

D **Past form modals:**

k As a–c **with differing degrees of permission probability/possibility or desirability:** *You could be met at the airport.*

l As e with differing degrees of certainty: *It should be repaired by now.*

m **For past habitual processes**, especially in conditional sentences, with could/would/might: *When we were young we might be taken to the pictures on Saturdays, if we were lucky.*

Complex past passives:

A Used to, for habitual past processes: *I used to be taken to school.*

B Was going to for changed plans: *I was going to be collected at the airport, but the car broke down.*

Suggested Contexts

Complex Future and Modal Passives

A **Will/shall**

a **Predicting future processes**:

- Information gap exercise. A visit to a pet parlour, or similar. Each student is given part of a timetable and asked to fill in the gaps, using *What will happen to the dog at x o'clock? It will be collected, trimmed, bathed, combed, exercised* etc.

- A description of a proposed new factory. Students are given a flow chart or diagram and asked to trace the development of the product: *Raw material will be brought in through this door. It will be emptied into the vats, boiled* etc.

- Role-play. A boss outlines the requirements of a new job: *You will be required to ...*

- Each student is given two pictures or diagrams, one of a house or site as it exists, the other of the architect's proposals. Students, in groups or pairs, list projected changes: *The door will be painted blue* etc. (**See photocopiable page 8.**)

b **Making promises**:

- Role-play. A customer complaining that services or goods are not satisfactory. The company promises amendments: *That will be mended when we have finished the walls. That will be done straight away.*

- Reading/writing exercise based on advertisements for beauty products: *Old skin will be renewed* etc. This can lead to interesting discussion on the use of the passive. Why is the passive form preferred to an active form? For example; *This will renew your old skin.*

c **Warnings**:

- Making objections. Role-play. A teenager wants to do things (*ride a bicycle/go to the disco* etc.). The parents make objections: *You'll be/get hurt. You'll be/get overtired.*

- Students are shown a strip cartoon or video, where a threat can be logically deduced: *It will be/get caught by the cat.*

d **Oaths and exclamations**:

Probably best not taught, but the question is occasionally raised by advanced learners.

e **Logical possibility**:

Best taught as part of a series on logical possibility: *It may be mended by now; It'll be mended by now* etc.

B **Going to**

f **Plans and intentions**:
As part of general work on plans and intentions. Requires the revision of the 'Going to' future.

g **Warnings and threats** (which are evident now):
As c but add incidents where the danger is immediate and visible: *He's going to be/get squashed.*

h **Determination**:
The context can be set up using the example of a spoiled child: *I'm not going to walk, I'm going to be carried.* This can be compared with I *want to be carried*, to highlight different degrees of determination.

C and **D** **Present and past form modals**

With modals expressing permission, probability/possibility and desirability (i and k)

- With modals expressing permission. Using the context of pet parlour, give the students the list of activities which are proposed for the pet but ask them to change it according to the desirability of any activity for their particular pet: *The dog can be washed, but its coat must not be trimmed.*
- With modals expressing desirability. Students are given the ground plan of a building (a private house for example), and asked, in groups, to work out the necessary/desirable/possible changes to convert the building into a hospital for example. *The doors must be/will have to be widened; more windows could be put in* etc.
- With modals expressing possibility. Role-play. A customer is asking about delivery/services. The tradesman is unwilling to make outright promises: *It must be fitted tomorrow. I can't promise, madam. The parts may be delayed.*
- With modals expressing possibility/probability, as c but with the mother advancing hypothetical problems: *You might be/get run over.*

Logical possibility: (j and l)

- For academic and scientific hypotheses: *New techniques may be discovered. It may be argued that ...* etc.

m **Past habits**:
Best taught as part of a series on conditionals: *At Christmas we would/might be taken to the pantomime, if we were lucky; In Elizabethan England if someone was caught stealing a sheep, he would usually be executed.*

Complex Past Passives

These are probably not common enough to warrant an entire lesson. They may be touched on if encountered, or if learners raise the topic. The form rather than the meaning creates difficulties.

Learner Error: Form, Spelling and Pronunciation

1 *Been* is often substituted for *be* (perhaps on the pattern of the perfect passive) *I will been followed.*

2 In continuous forms *be* may be omitted altogether: *I may being followed.* (Note that omitting *being* produces an acceptable form, I *may be followed.*)

3 Other modal verbs may be combined with *will/shall* instead of replacing them: *I may will be followed.* Note that this error may be reinforced by the English idiom I *may well be followed.*

4 Learners may attempt to create deviant past forms using *was/were*, on the pattern of the past perfect: *I used to was taken*. I *might was taken to school in a cart.*

5 Learners occasionally attempt to create deviant forms by combining *get* with *be*, instead of substituting it: *You will get be sunburnt* You *will be get sunburnt.*

Learner Error: Meaning and Function

1 Learners may not understand past modal forms to have present or future meaning: I *could be shot*, may thus be perceived as having past reference.

2 Learners may attempt to substitute *would* for *used to* in the stative sense: My *father would be interested* for *he used to be interested*, and vice versa.

3 Many learners avoid complex passives altogether if possible, or regard them as merely literary or scientific devices.

Appendices

- Emphatic tenses
- Tag questions and tag answers
- Prepositional and phrasal verbs

Points to Ponder

- **F**or trainee teachers

  What is the difference between these sentences:
  I *like fish*. I *do like fish*.

  If someone asks It *isn't raining, is it*? does he think that it is raining or that it is not? What answer is expected? Does the tone of voice make any difference to the question?

  Look at these two sentences:
  She ran up a big hill.
  She ran up a big bill.
  Now rewrite the sentences using *it*. (*She ran up it*. etc.) Does this pose any problems for EFL learners?

- **F**or teachers' workshops

  How important is it to allocate specific lessons to dealing with:
  – stress and intonation?
  – emphatic tenses?
  – tag questions and short answers?
  How do you prefer to teach prepositional and phrasal verbs, grouping them by the base verb, the preposition, by meaning or not grouping them at all?

Emphatics

Introduction

An emphatic version of every tense in English can be created by stressing the auxiliary. In tenses where there is more than one auxiliary, the stress is placed on either, or both:

I **have** been eating. I have **been** eating. I **have been** eating.

In the negative, the usual stress is on the negative marker:

I have **not** eaten.

When the spoken contracted negative is used, the stress falls on that form, and sometimes also on the main verb:

I **haven't** eaten. I **haven't eaten**.

Where a second auxiliary follows the spoken negative, the stress may be transferred to that, together with the main verb:

I haven't **been** eating. I haven't **been eating**.

Emphatics are used to express contradiction, surprise, or insistence, and rely heavily on stress and intonation for their function. By using irregular stress patterns, learners may inadvertantly produce emphatics, especially when concentrating on the auxiliaries required to create a tense. With elementary learners, this is unimportant, but as grammatical fluency and intonation improves, learners should be made aware of emphatic variations.

Since there are emphatic versions of all tenses, and the force of an emphatic is much the same in any tense, it is obviously unnecessary to list them all. For most tenses too, the emphatic is created exactly as the ordinary tense, with the addition of stress on the auxiliaries. However, there are two English tenses where there is no auxiliary in the full statement form, the present and past simple, and for these a separate emphatic form exists.

In the following pages, the present and past simple emphatic forms are examined in more detail, with particular reference to the role of stress and intonation. The meanings and functions could be mirrored for all other tenses, with alteration in the appropriate time reference, and appropriate adaptations.

PRESENT EMPHATIC: analysis

Full Form	(no contracted Spoken Form)		Negative Form	(Spoken Form)	
I you we they	**do**	walk	I you we they	do **not**	(**don't** walk) (don't **walk**) walk
he she it	**does**		he she it	does **not**	(**doesn't** walk) (doesn't **walk**)

All full verbs except *to be* form the emphatic in this way. Modal verbs have no separate emphatic form.

Question Forms

Do you walk? (*speaker thinks the listener doesn't usually walk, cannot walk or does not enjoy walking for pleasure*)

Don't you walk? (*speaker thinks the listener usually walks, or walks for pleasure*)

Do you **walk**? (*speaker previously thought the listener usually travelled by some other means, but now thinks he walks or now believes that walking may be his hobby*)

Don't you **walk**? (*speaker previously thought the listener often, or usually walked, but now doubts this*)

You **do walk**? (*speaker thought the listener had decided never to walk, or couldn't walk/ walked for pleasure, but now believes otherwise*)

Question Forms are often strengthened; **Do** you **really** walk?'

Another form, derived from the present simple, is also used emphatically:

You **walk**? (or You **run**?) (expects answer 'yes', but expresses surprise)

You don't **walk**? (*speaker believes the listener does, but is greatly surprised/delighted/disapproving; requires strong stress and intonation*)

Tag questions

You **do** walk, **don't** you? (*I claim that you do, please confirm this*)

You **do** walk, don't you? (*I though you had, but suddenly I doubt it*)

You **don't** walk, **do** you? (*I claim that you don't, please confirm this.*)

You **don't walk**, do you? (*I suddenly think you do, and regard this as extraordinary.*)

Questions to draw the target

Why don't you (+verb)?

Why *don't you walk?* ⎯⎯⎯⎯⎯⎯⎯⎯⎯⎯⟶ I **do** walk.

What emphatics, statements are often a better way to draw the target. The emphatic form in these contexts suggests contradiction or self-defence:

You should walk. ——————————————→ I **do** walk.

I thought you usually walked. ——————————→ I **do** walk.

You told me that you walked to school. ————→ I **do** walk.

(The short answer form I *do*, I *don't*, for the present simple may be seen as deriving from this tense).

Notes

1 Form: Negative and question forms appear identical to the present simple, but are differentiated by stress. In writing stress is often marked informally by capital letters or underlining. In speech the stress is very evident. The verb *To Be* has no emphatic form – emphasis is given by stress alone.

2 Stress: In the positive form, the stress is almost always on the auxiliary (*do/does*); in the negative usually on *not*, or *don't/doesn't* in the contracted form; or may carry a double stress. (The form I **walk**, does of course exist, but insists more on the nature of the action, rather than contradicting a supposition, or emphasising the fact of the action. In the present simple version, the use of stress is exactly parallel to all other uses of stress for emphasis: e.g. It's **you**.)

3 Intonation: As emphatic tenses rely on stress, intonation becomes very important. There are many variations of intonation pattern, but the following gives a sample of the possible range: I *do walk* can be: an affirmation (**I do walk**); an angry contradiction (I **do** *walk*); a reminder of the circumstances (I *do* **walk**).

Tag questions can also vary greatly in meaning with intonation and stress shifts. In general the greater the rise/fall patterns, the more emotive the content. (See page 169, Tag questions, for fuller information.)

You **do** walk, **don't** you? (Expects 'yes' and seeks confirmation.)

You **don't** walk, **do** you? (Expects 'no' and seeks confirmation.)

You **do** walk, **do** you? (I strongly believed that you never walked, but now discover that you do.)

Meaning and Function

As with all emphatic tenses, meaning relates to the attitude of the speaker and supposed attitude of the listener.

(A) To **express reassurance or reaffirmation** that action actually occurs, or of the general truth of a statement.

a Habitual actions:
I **do** *turn off the lights* (although you think/fear that I don't).
They **do** *serve tea at that restaurant* (although we believed/we were told that they didn't).
I *do eat* **fish** (although I don't eat meat); compare: I *do* **eat** *fish* (although I don't like it much).

b Scientific, natural and mathematical truths (often as a warning, or reassurance):
The leaves **do go** *brown if the plants are watered in hot weather* (so don't do that).
The tablets **do make** *some people feel giddy* (so don't worry if this happens to you).
Some people **do go** *bald early* (he isn't the only one).

c With Stative verbs for states of mind, possession, etc.:
You **do** *have a black tie* (although you appear to have forgotten about it). Compare: You've got a black tie (so you don't need another); You **have** *got a black tie* (although you say you haven't).
He **does** *live here* (although you seem to doubt it/there is no sign of him at present).

Note: With verbs of involuntary sensation (hearing/seeing etc.) British English prefers an emphatic form with can, for the present moment;

Compare I **can** hear bells (*now*) (although you doubt it); I **do** *hear bells* (habitually, although you doubt it).

B **To express contradiction:**

You **do** *break the speed limit* (although you claim you don't).

Three and three **do** *make six* (and not seven as you claim).

I **do** *like icecream* (although you claim that I don't).

C **To express enthusiastic reinforcement** (or disclaimer in the negative):

I **do** *like your hat*. Stress on *hat* (I do like your **hat**) suggests ... *but not your dress.*)
I **don't want** *to disturb you* (but I have to); I *don't want to disturb you* (sorry, if I am).

D **With verbs of hoping, wishing** etc:

a   Where the stress is on the auxiliary to express enthusiasm or strong feeling:

I **do** *hope I can come* (but it is possible that I won't be able to).

I **do** *want to see that film* (may suggest, please invite me).

I **do** *think you should go to the doctor* (that is my strong advice).

b   Where stress is on the main verb, often implies a suggestion or warning. This use is fairly specialised and advanced:

I do **wonder** *if that's wise* (but you will probably do it anyway).

I do **hope** *the new headmaster agrees with you* (but I privately doubt it).

c   Where there is a double stress: expresses very strong emotion, often effusive:

I do hope *you can come* (pressing invitation, over-polite for most situations).
This usage can be employed with verbs of emotion also:

I do hope *Beethoven.*

E

a   **To express invitation**: especially where the verb expresses a hobby or activity. The pronoun may be stressed:

Do you *play chess*? (i.e. would you like to play chess with me?)

Do *you* **ride/sail/climb**? (polite way of asking *Can you ride?*, implying invitation).

b   As a way of seeking an invitation. The speaker expresses a strong desire, leaving the way open for the listener to make an offer:

I **do** *want to see that film* (expecting *Well, come with us!*).
Asking for an invtiation, even indirectly, is not considered polite. The exception is where one seeks an invitation to do something flattering or helpful to the listener:

I **do** *want to see the new baby* (expecting, *Well come and see him now*).

Suggested Contexts

The emphatic form is probably best reserved for more advanced levels, and is often best introduced as part of a series of lessons on stress, intonation, and expressing emotion. This is also true of tags and questions. (Note: It is rare that an entire context can be set up using the present emphatic.)

(A) **To express reassurance or reaffirmation**.Role-play; rival salespersons try to persuade a customer to select a service (hotel/restaurant/tour/photocopier) rather than another: *Our hotel **does** have a swimming pool; that one **doesn't** allow children* etc., based on brochures, printed material. Use the best suggestions for a dialogue building exercise.

(B) **To express contradiction**

- Comparative reading exercise on the life-styles of stars/footballers. This can be drawn from differing sources on the same subject; *Paper A says he **does** use a backing group; Paper B says he* **doesn't.**

- Use a fact-sheet (information on a particular country, for example) containing errors. Check the real facts against the fact-sheet. This can be done with mixed-nationality groups. Students make 'guesses' under given headings, *What do most people eat for breakfast/grow/wear/do for a living in China/ Italy?* etc. Students of that nationality can correct others. This may lead to heated debate between people of the same nationality (good use of the emphatic) and arbitration may be necessary!

- Debate on an environmental subject: 'Nuclear Energy is a danger to health.' (This type of discussion usually divides classes into those strongly for and those strongly against the premise, and may include a wide use of future tenses also.)

  Note: It is important for all contexts that there should be some statement of facts, a simple conflict of opinion will not suffice.

(C) **To express enthusiastic reinforcements** and **D** a and b **with verbs of hoping and wishing**. Can be taught as part of lessons on expressing enthusiasm (being a guest etc.) or polite advice.

(D) c and **(E)** **To express invitation**.

  Probably best not specifically taught, although advanced learners may be interested to study the double stress form as part of a discussion in expressing strong emotion and invitations etc. for passive recognition.

Learner Error

1 An emphatic form may be produced instead of the present simple by some learners:

a In the full (statement) form, especially in answers: I ***do** walk* for example, might be produced instead of I *walk*, as though it were a simple statement.

b In negative and question forms by stressing the auxiliary.

2 Students may produce the emphatic form of *To Be* as I *do be* which no longer exists except in dialect forms.

3 Problems may also arise with stress and intonation:

a Students may produce inappropriate stress and intonation patterns, thereby changing the meaning of the sentence. (Especially true of Germanic-speaking students.)

b They may fail to produce a strong enough intonation pattern, thereby removing the force of the emphasis. (Especially true of Far Eastern students.)

4 There may also be a misuse of the tag forms, usually caused by failure to understand the implied viewpoint.

PAST EMPHATIC: analysis

Full Form	(no contracted Spoken Form)		Negative Form	(Spoken Form)	
I you he she it we they	**did**	walk	I you he she it we they	**did not** **didn't**	walk

All full verbs except *to be* form the emphatic in this way. Modal verbs have no separate emphatic form.

Question Forms

Did you walk? (*speaker expresses surprise*) **Didn't** you walk? (*speaker seeks confirmation*)

Did you **walk**? (*speaker previously thought the listener arrived by some other means, but now thinks he walked*)

Didn't you walk? (*speaker previously thought the listener walked but now doubts it*)

You **did** walk? (*speaker though the listener had decided not to walk, but now believes you didn't*)

Question forms are often strengthened. **Did** you **really** walk?

Another form, derived from the past simple, is also used emphatically:

You **walked**? (or You **ran**?) etc (*expects answer 'yes', but expresses surprise*)

You **didn't walk?** (*speaker is greatly surprised/delighted/disapproving; strong stress and intonation*)

Tag Questions

You **did** walk, didn't you? (*seeks confirmation*)

You did **walk**, didn't you? (*expresses doubt*)

You **didn't** walk, did you? (*seeks confirmation*)

You didn't **walk**, did you? (*expresses surprise*)

Questions to draw the target

Why didn't you walk? ⎯⎯⎯⎯⎯⎯⎯⎯⟶ I **did** walk.

With emphatics, statements are often better ways to draw the target. The emphatic form in these contexts suggests contradiction or self defence:

You should have walked? ⎯⎯⎯⎯⎯⎯⟶ I **did** walk.

I thought you were going to walk? ⎯⎯⟶ I **did** walk.

I expected you to walk. ⎯⎯⎯⎯⎯⎯⟶ I **did** walk.

The short answer form I *did*, I *didn't* for the past simple may be seen as deriving from this tense.

Notes

1 Form: Negative and question forms appear identical to the past simple, but are differentiated by stress. In writing, stress is often marked informally by capital letters or, underlining. In speech the stress is very evident. The verb *To Be* has no emphatic form – emphasis is given by stress alone.

2 Stress: In the positive form, the stress is almost always on the auxiliary *did*; in the negative usually on *not*; *didn't* in the contracted form; or may carry a double stress.
(The form I **walked**, does of course exist, but insists on the nature of the action, rather than contradicting a supposition, or emphasising the action. In the past simple version, the use of stress is exactly parallel to all other uses of stress for emphasis: e.g. It **was** *you*.)

3 Intonation: As emphatic tenses rely on stress, intonation becomes very important. There are many variations of intonation pattern, but the following gives a sample of the possible range. I *did walk* can

be: an affirmation; I **did** walk a contradiction; I **did walk** an angry contradiction; I did **walk** a reminder of the circumstances.

Tag questions can also vary greatly in meaning with intonation and stress shifts:
You **did** walk, didn't you?   Expects answer 'yes' and seeks confirmation.
You did **walk**, didn't you?   I expected you to walk, but now suspect you didn't.
You **did walk**, didn't you?   It suddenly occurs to me that perhaps you didn't and this was foolish to you.

(For fuller notes see page 169, Tag Questions.) In general the greater the rise/fall pattern, the more emotive the content.

M eaning and Function

As with all emphatic tenses, meaning relates to the attitude of the speaker and supposed attitude of the listener.

(A) **To express reassurance or reaffirmation** that action in the past actually occurred;
a Single actions:
I **did** *turn off the fridge* (although you think/fear that I didn't).
You **did** *leave the keys on the table* (I told you that you had, and you did not believe me).
b Repeated or continuous action:
I **did water** *the flowers* (although they are now dead and it appears that I did not).
You **did have** *a red car* (although you appear to have forgotten about it).

(B) **To express contradiction:**
You **did** *break the speed limit* (although you claim you didn't).

(C) **To express enthusiastic reinforcement** (or disclaimer in negative):
I **did** *like the flowers*
I **didn't** *want to disturb you.*

(D) **With verbs of hoping, wishing** etc:
a Where stress is on the auxiliary; expresses disappointment that the wish/plan has not been fulfilled:
I **did** *hope we could come* (but now I know we can't).
I **did** *want to see that film* (but now its too late).

b   Where there is a double stress, the form expresses disapproval that the wish/plan was not fulfilled, because of the listener. There is usually a very high emotional content:

I **did want** *to be part of the team* (but you didn't chose me).

I **did hope** *you would visit your mother* (but you didn't).

c   Where stress is on the main verb the form is used to express tentative suggestion, or little expectation of success:

I did **wonder** *whether you would like to come* (but I didn't expect you would).
This use is fairly specialised, and often has the effect of withdrawing the suggestion/invitation.

E **To express invitation:** The speaker implies that the wish has not been fulfilled, leaving the way open for the listener to make the offer:

I *did want to see that film* (expecting, Well, *come with us!*).
Asking for an invitation, even indirectly, is not considered polite, in English. The exception is where one seeks an invitation to do something flattering or helpful to the listener.

I *did want to see the new baby* (expecting, Well *come and see him now*).

 Suggested Contexts

The emphatic form is probably best reserved for more advanced levels, and is often best introduced as part of a series of lessons on stress, intonation, and expressing emtoion. This is also true of tags and questions.

(Note: It is rare that an entire context can be set up using the past emphatic.)

A

a   **To express reassurance or reaffirmation**. Groups A & B are given a problem set in the past (e.g. Group A: *You lost your passport on holiday. You didn't find it, but what steps did you take?*) Elicit a list of possible ways in which they could have found it. Group B must make their own list of suggestions and then compare with Group A. Group A gets a point for each sensible strategy, Group B did not think of, and vice versa. (Group B: *You should have rung the police*; Group A: We **did** *ring the police.*)

b   Complaints role-play: (e.g. hotel service, elicit a list of complaints). The manager reassures, reaffirms, excuses: We **did** *take £3 off the bill*. We **did** *replace the television*. Use the best suggestions for a dialogue building exercise.

B **To express contradiction**. Use two sets of facts which contradict each other (picture story and text for example).

*   Testing evidence against statements *Your partner said that you **did** go to the restaurant.*
*   Use an historical fact-sheet containing errors, check real facts against the fact-sheet, eliciting the differences.
*   Debate: elicit a topic for debate or supply one, e.g. "The quality of life was better before television."
*   Role-play, mistaken identity: The police arrest someone they mistake for a criminal: I **wasn't** *in London*, I **didn't** *go to London*.

Note: It is important for all contexts that there should be some predetermined position, a simple conflict of opinion will not suffice.

C To express *enthusiastic reinforcement*. As part of a lesson on expressing enthusiasm (being a guest etc.) or polite disclaimers (office situation?), **I did enjoy** *that concert; Could you do some overtime?* **I didn't want** *to be late tonight.*

D With verbs of *hoping, wishing etc*. Part of a lesson on irritation, disapproval and squabbling, (contrast with the simple forms to practice the stress: I *hoped we could go out tonight;* I **did** *hope we could go out tonight;* I **did hope** *we could go out tonight.*

E To express *invitation*. Probably best not specifically taught.

Learner Error

1 An emphatic form may be produced instead of the past simple by some learners:

a in the full (statement) form: I *did walk* for I *walked*.

b in the negative and question forms by stressing the auxiliary.

c students may produce I *did walk* (emphasising the fact of the action) for I *walked* (emphasising the nature of the action) or vice versa.

2 Students may produce the emphatic form of *To Be* as *I *did be** or *I *did was.**

3 Problems may also arise with stress and intonation:

a students may produce inappropriate stress and intonation patterns, thereby changing the meaning of the sentence. (Especially true of Germanic-speaking students.)

b they may fail to produce a strong enough intonation pattern, thereby removing the force of the emphasis. (Especially true of Far Eastern students.)

4 There may also be a misuse of the tag forms usually caused by failure to understand the implied viewpoint.

TAG QUESTIONS: analysis

Throughout this book you will find the 'tag questions' given as part of the analysis of every tense. Tag questions are questions in which the speaker makes a statement (e.g. <u>You eat fish</u>) and then adds a short interrogative form (e.g. <u>don't you?</u>). If the statement is negative the tag question is usually positive, and vice versa: *You eat fish don't you? You don't eat fish, do you?* (but see Notes below). Tag questions are always formed with the auxiliary, not the full verb, in the interrogative part.

a   In tenses which already contain an auxiliary, that auxiliary is used in the tag question. Thus, tags are formed in continuous tenses with the appropriate part of *be: You're not coming, are you?*; in perfect tenses with *have: You haven't seen him, have you? You hadn't seen him, had you?*; in emphatic simple forms with *do: You don't swim, do you?*; in modal forms, with the modal: *You can't come, can you? You will come, won't you?*

b   The present and past simple forms use *do* as the auxiliary: *You eat fish, don't you? You went shopping, didn't you?* except for *To be*, which forms a tag question directly, *You aren't John, are you?*
Note: *To Do* may be seen as following this irregular pattern, but the result is the same as if it were regular (*You didn't do it, did you?*).
To have may also follow this pattern, *You have a car, haven't you?* but is frequently replaced by the present perfect in British English, *You have got a car, haven't you?* or by the regular form in American usage, *You have a car, don't you?*

c   In tenses which have more than one auxiliary, the tag question is formed from the first of these: *You won't be meeting him, will you? You won't have met him, will you? It might have been sold, mightn't it?*

Notes

1   Form: The base form of the tag question is usually given as above. It has the effect of, literally, questioning the original statement. With neutral intonation (see below) it indicates what assumptions the speaker is making, and what he expects the response to be. The expected response applies to the first (statement) half of the question. Hence *You eat fish, don't you?* breaks down into two halves: *You eat fish* is what the speaker believes, and *don't you?* requests confirmation of that assumption. The answer, therefore, is expected to be *Yes – Yes, I do eat fish*.
The negative form expresses the speaker's belief that the negative statement is true, *You don't eat fish, do you? You don't eat fish* is the statement which the speaker believes, *do you?* checks that assumption. The expected answer, therefore, is *No – No, I don't eat fish*.

• Tag questions may be formed, where both halves of the question are in the positive form: *You're John, are you? You've seen it before, have you?*
In this case the speaker has usually just arrived at the conclusion expressed in the statement half of the sentence (often because he has just been told) and is surprised by it. This form may be challenging, or even hostile, but this depends heavily upon stress and intonation.

• The form in which both halves of the sentence are negative is theoretically possible, but extremely rare. Where it does exist, it represents a hostile challenge to a negative statement which has just been made by another speaker: *You don't like it, don't you?*

2   Tag questions commonly require a *yes* or *no* answer, or a short tag answer (see page 172, Tag Answers). The answer, however, is made to the question, and not to the statement section of the tag. Hence *You're not John, are you?* is really equivalent to: *I don't think you are John. Are you John?* The answer, therefore could be No (I am not John) or possibly Yes (I am John), but not Yes, (you are correct) I am not John.

3   Tag questions can also be constructed with *there: There's nothing wrong, is there?* and with negative words such as *nobody, Nobody really knows the truth, do they?*

4   All tag questions depend heavily for meaning and function on stress and intonation patterns.

M eaning and Function

The use of tag questions is greatly influenced by pitch, intonation and stress which can in turn greatly vary the meaning. Here is a sample of the most common variants. Tag questions can be produced for any tense and with any model form. As far as regards intonation, in general terms if the speaker seeks confirmation to something he believes to be true or not true the intonation will fall. In expressing surprise or incertainty the intonation will tend to rise.

(A) *Seeking confirmation:*

You've met Jane, haven't you?	(expects 'yes')
You don't like horror films, do you?	(expects 'no')
They don't allow dogs into the park, do they?	(expects 'no')
Nice day, isn't it?	(expects 'yes')

(B) *Seeking support:* (when there is an element of contention)

I didn't say anything of the kind, did I?	(To third party.)
I didn't say anything of the kind, did I?	(To listener directly.)

(C) *To express doubt/concern:*
You are coming, aren't you?
You don't think she overheard, do you?

(D) *To express surprise/disapproval:* (a previously held belief is suddenly questioned)
She isn't 60 years old, is she?
You don't smoke, do you?

(E) *In situations of confrontation:*
You weren't telling the truth, were you?
You haven't done your homework, have you?

(F) *For expressing requests and invitations:*
You can't help me with this box, can you?
You haven't got the time, have you?
(Compare: Haven't you got the time?)
You wouldn't like to go to the cinema, would you?

The tag can also be used with commands to express request:
Sit down, won't you? (Compare: Do sit down, won't you?)
Let's go, shall we?
Give me a hand, will you? (Orders with: will; would; can; can't.)
Sit down, can't you?
With will you:
Don't make a noise, will you?

(G) *With double positive verbs:*

a   To express surprise:
Oh you're going to Australia, are you?
You've met Jane, have you?

b   To express hostility/disapproval:
So, you think you're clever, do you?
It's you that makes all that noise, is it?

c   To express doubt:
You do eat meat, do you? (Possible, but a negative tag is more common.)

Tag form used for real questions:
You're sisters, *are you?*
This is the right queue, *is it?*
You haven't seen my gold pen, *have you?* (It is possible that you've seen it, but I doubt it.)

Suggested Contexts

It is very difficult to set up realistic contexts for most tag questions as a systematic lesson. However, much useful work can be done by:

- giving a series of tag questions (as an exercise or as part of a listening comprehension) and asking about the speaker's assumptions. This can be done as a multiple choice exercise; presented with a list of possible interpretations, the student must tick the appropriate one.

- giving students a question tag and asking them to produce it with varying stress and intonation. to give different meanings.

- introducing them as part of a series on stress and intonation.

- using them as part of a listening comprehension. (What answer does the speaker expect?)

Learner Error

1 Learners often fail to understand the implied assumptions of the speaker and may treat tag questions as merely a version of the interrogative. However, *Do you eat fish?* is not equivalent to *You eat fish, don't you?*

2 Some learners regard *isn't it* as a universal tag (derived from the mother tongue pattern, especially French (*n'est-ce pas?*) but also Spanish (*verdad*). It is used:

a with inappropriate tenses: *He will come, isn't it?*

b with inappropriate persons: *You are John, isn't it?*

c with negative statements: *It isn't here, isn't it?*

3 Even when the auxiliary is correctly used, learners may produce a negative tag even when the first part of the sentence is negative: *I'm not cold, aren't I?*

4 Learners may create a tag question from the wrong auxiliary, or from more than one auxiliary: *He shouldn't have come, hasn't he?* *He shouldn't have come, should have he?* *He shouldn't have come, should he have?*

5 Occasionally tag questions are created from whole expressions especially with idioms: *I may as well, may as welln't I?*

6 Frequently tag questions are answered with the inappropriate short answer, especially when the statement part of the tag question is negative: *You're not coming, are you?* *Yes*. No would be the appropriate reply, but what the learner is expressing incorrectly here is agreement with the statement part.

7 There may be difficulties with interpreting differences of meaning which depend on stress and intonation.

8 Students may inadvertently create wrong meanings by incorrectly using stress and intonation.

TAG ANSWERS: analysis

These are formed from the auxiliary, in exactly the same way as tag questions. They can be used to amplify short answers (*yes* or *no*). Hence *Yes, I do/am/have/might/will*; *No, I'm not/I don't/I won't/I haven't* etc. are used to amplify *yes* and *no* when:

1 Expressing enthusiasm (emphatic): *Do you like chocolate? Yes I do.*

2 Reassuring: *I'm not sure that you like chocolate. Yes, I do.*

3 Contradicting an assertion: *You won't like this cake. You don't like chocolate. Yes I do.*

4 Contradicting an assumption, especially when expressed in a tag question: *You don't like chocolate, do you? Yes, I do.* (This can often be impolite without careful intonation. It can be softened by the use of expressions such as *actually*: *Well, yes, I do actually.*)

5 Grudgingly agreeing with an assertion or assumption: *You like chocolate, don't you? Yes, I do* (but not much).

6 Tag answers may be used as a reply without *yes* and *no*, but this is formal. In conversational speech, the speaker usually goes on to give additional information:
Do you like London? I do. (very formal, may appear unfriendly)
Do you like London? I do, but I find it very crowded. (conversational)

7 They may be used without *yes* and *no*, not as a reply, but as a commentary upon actions, events or utterances. This is especially true of modal forms: *I don't want to go. You must.*
In British English this is very common, especially for expressing delight, thanks etc. Stress and intonation are extremely important, to the extent of altering the meaning to what appears to be the direct opposite of the grammatical meaning:
e.g. *I bought you a present. You didn't!* (meaning: You did. How very kind of you).
I bought you a present. You shouldn't have! (meaning: I am absolutely delighted).

Learner Error

1 Learners may produce unamplified *yes* or *no* answers when fuller tag answers are required: *You don't like chocolate, do you? Yes.*

2 Learners may produce too much of the verb in the tag answer: *Are you going to wash your hair? Yes, I'm going to.*

3 Learners may produce inappropriate answers in response to tag questions. *You're not going, are you? *Yes, I'm not.**

4 Students may fail to comprehend the force of stress and intonation in the 'comment' usage, and may understand the sentence only as a grammatical unit. Hence *You shouldn't have* may be interpreted as a rebuke.

5 Learners may attempt to produce meanings without the accompanying stress and intonation patterns. Hence *You shouldn't have!* which may express a rebuke or express thanks, must have the intonation appropriate to the intended meaning.

PREPOSITIONAL AND PHRASAL VERBS: analysis

No book about teaching verbal patterns would be complete without some mention of phrasal and prepositional verbs. English has a large number of these and whole books have been written on the subject so these notes can only be a brief outline.

Prepositional and phrasal verbs consist of verb and preposition (and noun phrase). Three main categories can be identified:

a where the meaning of the individual parts is retained:
   Look away; stand up; walk across.
b where the preposition is used to strengthen the verb:
   Drink up; wear out; tire out.
c where the meaning of the verb as a whole differs from the meaning of the individual components.
   Look up (seek information in reference work).
   Let down (disappoint).

Students should however be made aware of the verb as a whole rather than as a set of individual components. Thus in the sentence: *He looked the dates up in a history book,* to *look up* is the whole verb.

1 A prepositional verb is one where the particle is a simple preposition:
   Look at the pictures.
   He **came through** the window.
   He **rowed across** the lake.

2 A phrasal verb is one where the particle behaves like an adverb:
   At last things are looking up.
   He kicked up such a fuss!
   He's fallen out with his partner.
   These verbs can be intransitive (no object):
   The plane took off,
   or transitive (+object):
   He took over the company.
   If the object is a noun phrase (*the company*) it can also come between the verb and the particle:
   He took the company over.
   If the object is a pronoun it can only come between the verb and the particle:
   He took it over (not *He took over it*).

   (Note: Since the problem of positioning the object does not apply to intransitive verbs, these can be taught simply as idioms.)

3 Phrasal verbs can often look like prepositional verbs because the same prepositions can be used in both, (i.e. *about, across, along, around, by, down, in, off, on, over, through, under, up*).
   If we introduce a pronoun as the object it will help to distinguish between them:

   In phrasal verbs the preposition can follow the noun object:
   I **looked up** the word or I **looked** the word **up**

   and must follow the pronoun:
   I **looked** it **up** (not *I looked up it* which has a different meaning.)

   Let's now look at prepositional verbs:
   I *looked after the cat.*
   I looked the cat after and * I looked it after * are nonsensical. The correct sequence is I *looked after it.*

   We may thus deduce that *look after* is a prepositional verb because it is only with phrasal verbs that the pronoun can come between the verb and the preposition.

4 Phrasal prepositional verbs:
These are a combination of both types of verb:
I get on with him very well.

Suggested Contexts

A Phrasal verbs can be taught purely functionally, as they arise in reading comprehension passages, for example. However, the particular grammatical problems posed are possibly best resolved by specific work on the difficulties. Also the change in meaning of the verb makes phrasal verbs a candidate for vocabulary lessons.

B Phrasal verbs to be taught can be selected according to the preposition. Some prepositions tend to create phrasal verbs (e.g. Up: *look it up/make it up/drink it up/pick it up*; Out: *sort it out/make it out/put him out/let it out*; In: *let him in/take it in/throw it in*; Over: *make it over/put it over/take it over*; Down: *put it down/take it down/let him down*. This does not, of course, mean that the prepositions do not occur in normal verb patterns (*I ran up the hill*; *I ran up it*).

C Phrasal verbs could be selected according to the base verb. Some verbs tend to attract chiefly phrasal constructions. (e.g. Make *it up/it out/it over*; Put *him up/it down/it away/it out*.) However, it will be seen that many of these constructions involve the prepositions in **B** above, and these verbs are occasionally found in non-phrasal constructions. (*Make for it*; etc.)

D They can be selected as opposite pairs, because phrasal verbs often occur as opposites: *take in/ let out*; *take it up/ let it down*; *open it up/shut it down*. (This can also help with intransitive verbs i.e. those with no object: *I rang him up, but he rang off*.)

E Where one phrasal verb has a range of meanings, a text can be prepared in which alternative expressions are used, and the phrasal verb substituted, or vice versa. (e.g. *Put out a light/a cat/ a hand/a distress call/to be put out* etc.)

F Phrasal verbs could be arranged around a basic topic (e.g. shopping: *try it on/take it off/put it back/ take it in/let it out/wrap it up*; but note: *pay for it*).
All of these can be found in course books. The most efficient method is probably to combine one or more of the above, so that the items become more memorable. Topic-related 'families' are very useful, especially as it enables other language work (role-play etc.) in the same lesson, but they obviously cannot cover all possible phrasal verbs. One important consideration is not to have too heavy a load for one's students at any one time.

Learner Error

1 The learner may not appreciate that the phrasal verb means something more, or other than, base verb and preposition. Hence *look out* means *pay attention*, and not literally *look outside*.

2 Learners may attempt to place the object pronoun as though phrasal verbs followed the normal pattern: **I looked up him.**

3 The learner may treat a normal verb and preposition, or non-phrasal prepositional verb, as though it were phrasal: **I looked it after.** This latter mistake occurs when the learner perceives a verb to be phrasal.

4 Many learners use latin-based vocabulary to avoid the use of phrasal or prepositional verbs (especially where the mother tongue is romance-based): *I extinguished the light* for *I put it out/switched it off*.

5 Germanic speakers may attempt to place the preposition before the verb, especially where the resultant verb does exist in English: **I output it**.

Photocopiable Section

	Activity	Language practice		page
1.	Daily Routines (Regular verbs)	Present simple: Past simple:	She cooks breakfast every morning. She cooked breakfast yesterday. *some verbs take *es* or *ies* in the present simple but are all regular in the past. (*brush, wash, cook, walk, type, phone, post, finish, play, visit, study, watch*)	177
2.	Daily Routines (Irregular verbs	Present simple: Past simple:	He gets up at 7 o'clock. He got up at 7 o'clock. *verbs are regular in the present simple, but all irregular in the past. (*get up, eat, take, drive, buy, swim, make, write, run, read, sing, drink*)	178
3.	Planned Activities	Present continuous: Diary future: Will/shall future: Future continuous: Future perfect: Conditionals: Modals:	I'm sorry, he's having lunch at the moment. No, he won't be in at 1 o'clock. He's having lunch with Charlie. I'll check the computer print-out for Anne. She'll be having lunch with Anne at 1 o'clock. She'll have done the photocopying by 3 o'clock. If you do the print-outs, I'll do the bookings. If I did the print-outs before 10 o'clock, I would have enough time to do the booking for you,Sally. I can/could send Mrs Green the flowers, I'm free at that time.	179
4.	Spot the activity	Present continuous: Past continuous:	He's asking someone the time. He was asking someone the time.	180
5a b.	Guess the activity Complaining	Present perfect continuous: Past simple: Past perfect: Past perfect continuous:	He's been playing football I only used it once when.... I had only painted half the wall when.... I had only been wearing the shoes for five minutes when....	181
6.	Picture sequence	Past simple:	He woke up and found it was a lovely day.	182
7.	Changes to planned activities	Was going to:	We were going to have a holiday by the sea but...	183
8.	Comparisons	Used to: Passive:	The garden used to be completely over grown. The grass has been cut.	184
9a b	Activities about to happen Flow chart	Going to: Passive:	He's going to ring the doorbell. The letters are stamped and posted.	185

10.	Map-planned activities	Timetable future: Diary future: Future continuous: Future perfect: Future perfect continuous:	*He visits the pyramid on the fourth day of his journey.* *He's visiting....* *He'll be visiting....* *He'll have visited....* *He'll have been visiting....*	186
11.	Map-giving directions	General Condition: First Condition:	*If you carry on straight down Long Lane, you get to....* *If you turn right at the bottom of Parkway Hill, you'll....*	187
12.	Questionnaire	Second Condition:	*If you were in a space bubble....*	188
13.	Picture story	Third Condition:	*If he'd got up earlier, he would have....*	189

14.	Predicting the future	Modals, simple forms:	*We may/ might endanger....The world will....
			               increase....
			               cause....
			We can/could recycle....
			should/ought to prevent
			must avoid*
				190

15.	Logical deduction	Modals:	*We can't/couldn't be.... It would be.... It may/might be.... It must be....*	191

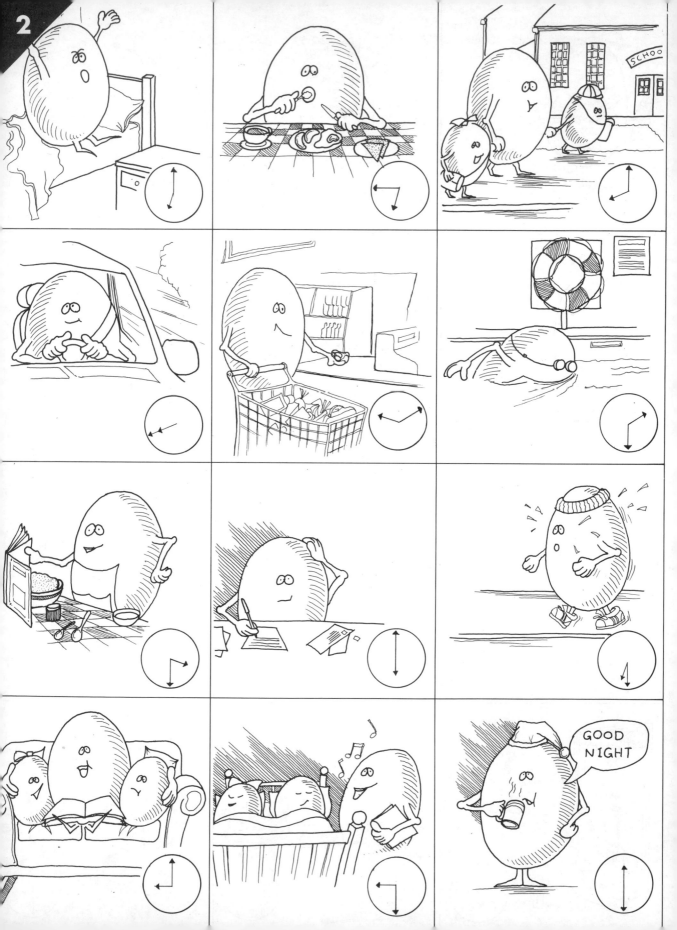

Anne is ill and can't go into the office.
Could Sally and Mike do her work for her?
How could they divide the tasks
between them?

Anne's Diary

AM	
7	Fax Hong Kong with details of conference.
8	Book accommodation for conference. Book restaurant. (Dinner, 18th March, 9pm-10 people)
9	Check preparations for lunch (1 o'clock).
10	Check computer print-outs.
11	Send flowers to Mrs Green (Newgate Hospital, ward 2).
12	Book taxi for Mr King for Airport (5.30pm).

PM	
1	Buffet lunch introduce new staff to managers.
2	
3	Show new staff around the building
4	Reply to job applications – check dates for interviews.
5	Remember to check birthday arrangements with restaurant. ('Chez Pierre') Remember to buy present for Sally.

Sally's Diary

AM	
7	
8	Meet Chris at office- remember report.
9	Meeting with Mrs Kean-163 Clifton Street, Tel 071 111
10	
11	Collect travellers cheque for New York trip.
12	

PM	
1	Lunch with Jane.
2	Do photo copies for conference.
3	Update mailing list.
4	Dentist appointment.
5	Post new catalogues.
6	Buy new dress for dinner.

Mike's Diary

AM	
7	
8	Cancel appointment with Mrs Spencer.
9	Arrange flight and hotel for Mr Peters.
10	Book 3 places for theatre and dinner.
11	Send price list to clients.
12	

PM	
1	Lunch with Charlie.
2	Photo session at studios.
3	
4	Drive Mary to Waterloo-leave 5.30.
5	
6	Buy present for Sally-dinner at 8

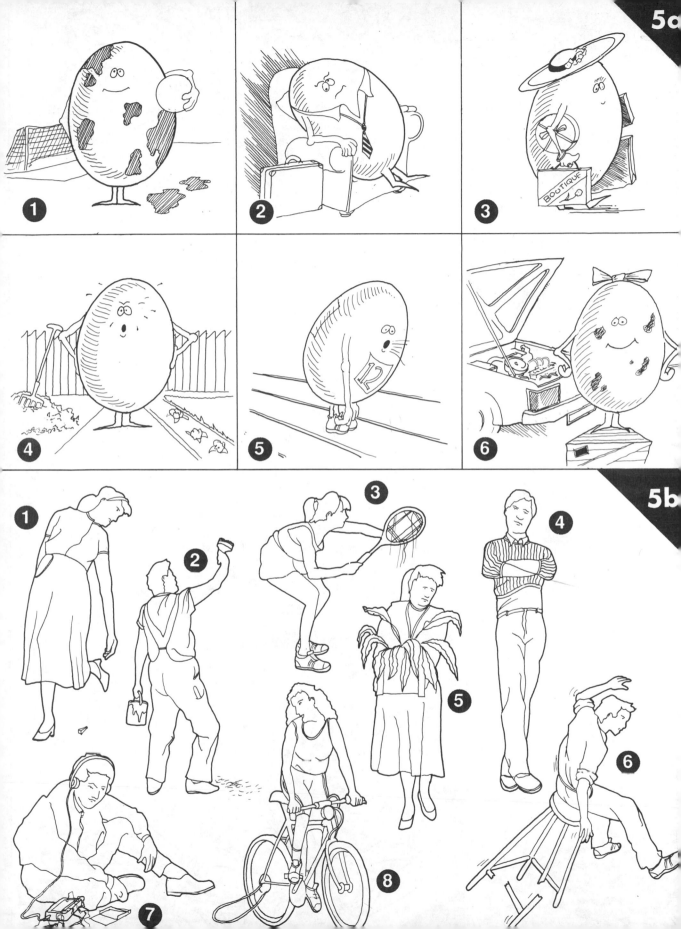

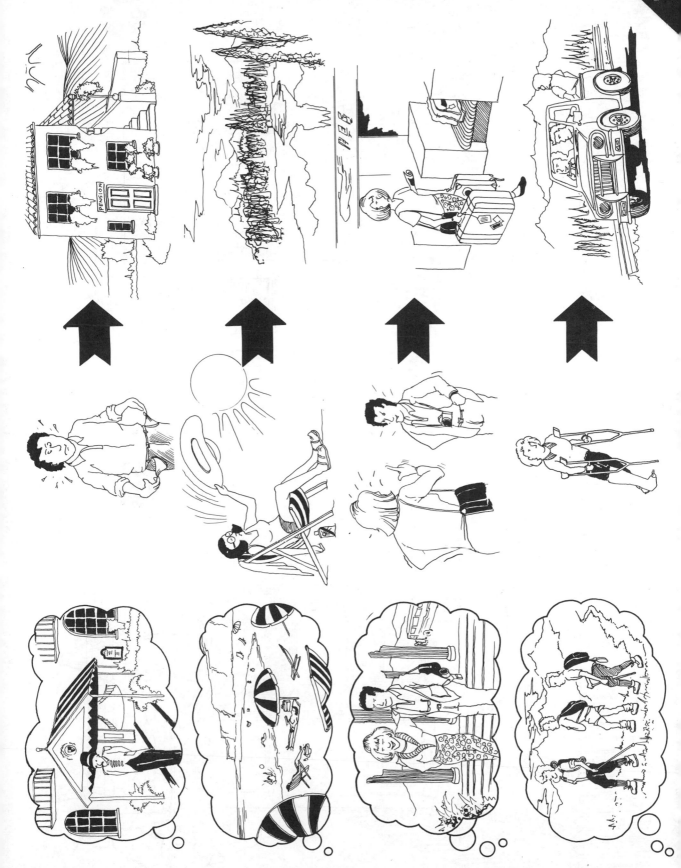

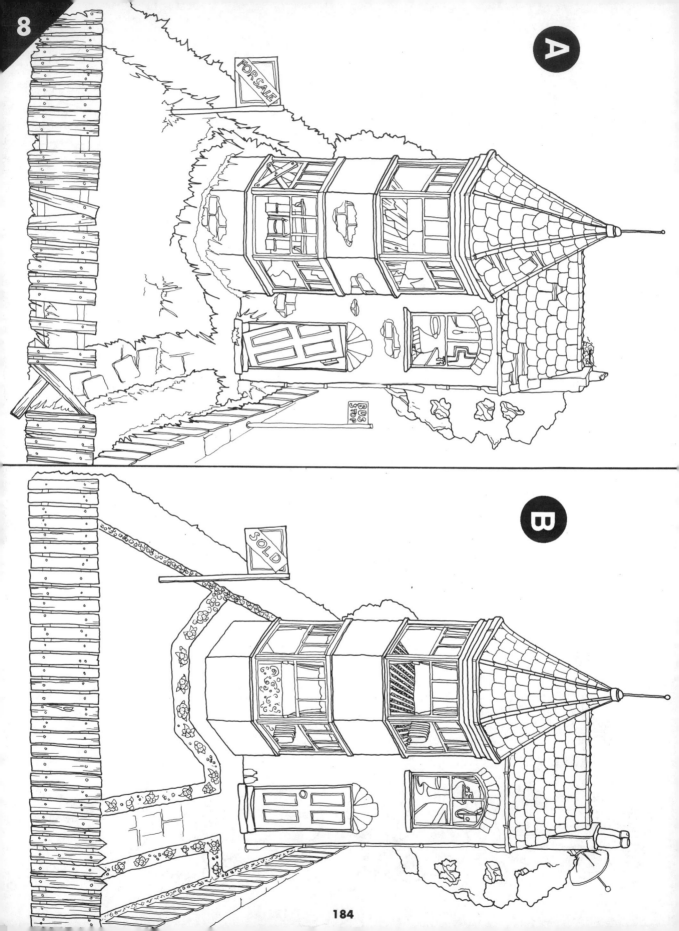

POST OFFICE

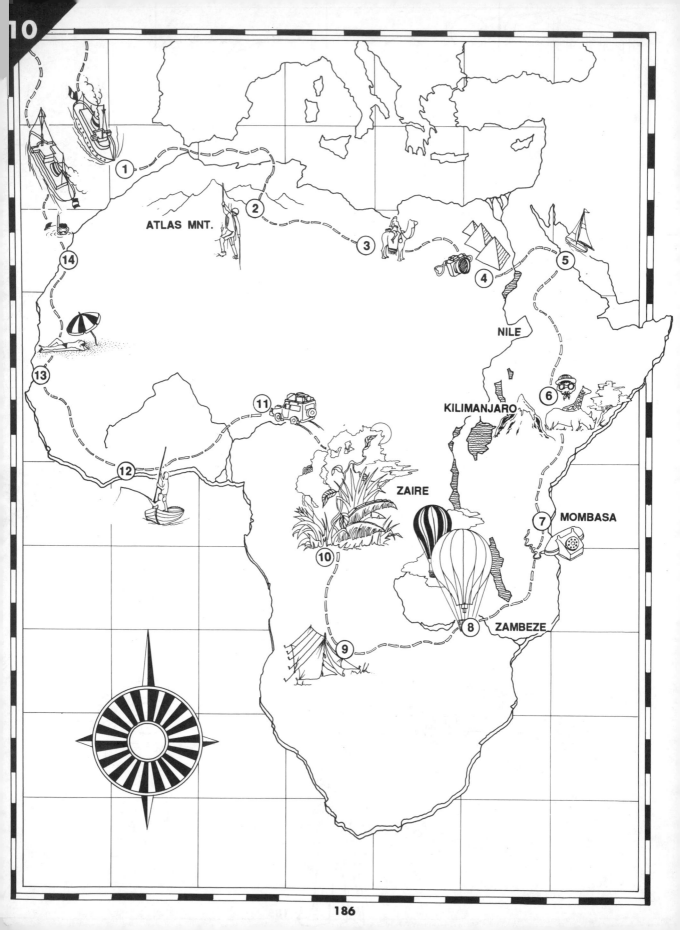

ATLAS MNT.

NILE

KILIMANJARO

ZAIRE

MOMBASA

ZAMBEZE

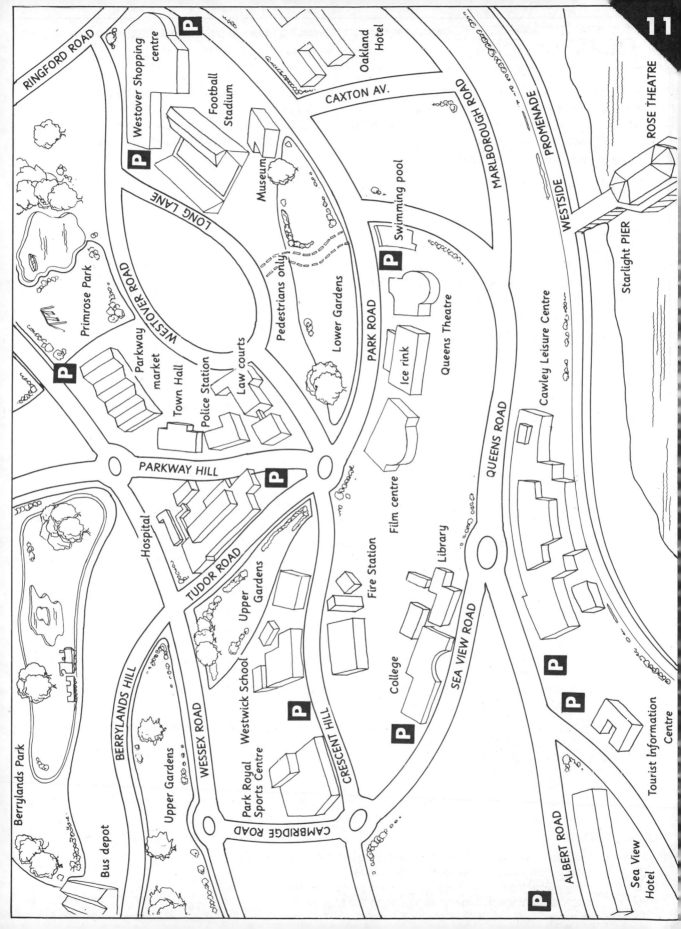

Questionnaire

More and more 'ordinary' people are travelling in spacecraft, and their survival depends not only upon knowledge, but also on good decisions. How would you survive in space?

1. You are in a space-bubble, outside of the earth's atmosphere, and a small meteorite makes a little hole in the wall of your bubble. You must stop the air from escaping. Would you

a) put a plastic bag over the hole?

b) put your finger in the hole?

c) put your metal dinnerplate over it?

2. You land safely on the moon, and set off on your £1m moon-buggy to explore parts of the moon no one has ever seen before. The battery on your buggy fails, so that you have no transport and no radio. Would you

a) light a fire to attract their attention?

b) walk back without the buggy and try to find base?

c) wave and shout?

3. You survive your adventures with the moon buggy and your exploration takes you into a valley in the moon-mountains. You look up and see a rock, half as big as you, slipping gently towards you. Would you

a) jump?

b) run?

c) blast it with your laser gun?

d) put out your hand and try to stop the rock?

4. You leave the moon, and begin to orbit a planet in deep space. Your companion leaves the space-bubble to do some repairs, but his battery-pack fails, and is just too far away for your life-line to reach. Would you

a) wait until you pass him on the next orbit?

b) throw him a parachute?

c) climb down the life-line and try to reach him?

d) tell him to throw his battery pack away?

SCORE

1. a) 0 points — The bag would also be sucked out. The problem isn't solved.
   b) 3 points — You are very brave. The suction of the vacuum would probably damage your finger, but perhaps your colleague would have time to find something to put over the hole.
   c) 5 points — A good temporary solution. The suction would hold the plate against the wall and seal the hole while you and your friend look for a better solution.

2. a)) points — There is no air on the moon. Your fire would not burn.
   b) 5 points — Your moon-buggy tracks would make it easy for you to find your way back. You could return for your moon-buggy later, with a new battery.
   c) 1 point — Without air your shouts could not be heard. Your friends might see you wave however.

3. a) 5 points — This would be a good idea. On the moon you could jump much higher than on earth.
   b) 3 points — This is possible, but in the low gravity you would not be able to run very quickly, especially in a spacesuit, and the rock would probably catch you.
   c) 2 points — A dangerous solution. Now there are lots of small rocks coming towards you! Also the blast might cause an avalanche.
   d) 0 points — The moon has little gravity, but a big rock would still be impossible to stop and heavy enough to squash you.

4. a) 1 point — You wouldn't pass him. If he was working near your spacecraft, he would be orbiting too. All the same, you would have time to make a nother choice!
   b) 0 points — A parachute would not help him in space. If he caught it, that would push him slightly further from the spaceship.
   c) 4 points — This is dangerous, but it would be possible.
   d) 5 points — This would be sensible. If he threw his pack away from the spaceship, his own energy would push him backwards, towards you, so that the lifeline might reach him.

HOW TO SCORE

0 - 5   Perhaps it would be better if you did not go to the Moon this year?

6 - 10   Good. You made some sensible decisions.

11-15   Very good. You would keep calm in dangerous situations.

16-20   Excellent. When would you like to go to the Moon?

The environment - What might happen in the next years ?
Is there anything we could do to save our planet ?
Will the situation get worse ?

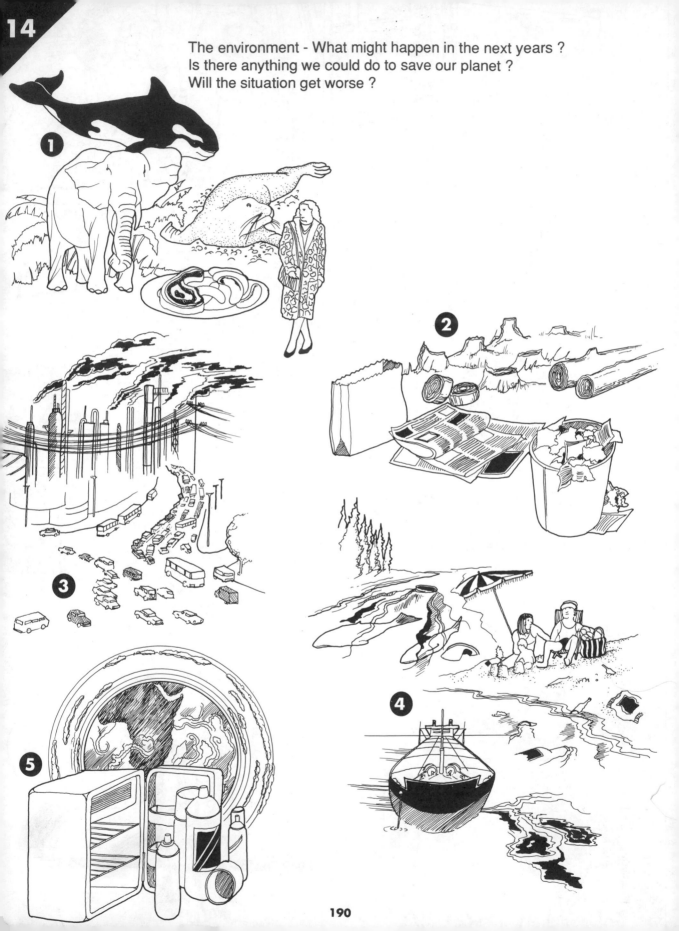

You are on a desert island and you are lost. There is very little to eat on the island but you do manage to find five kinds of grasshopper. Luckily you have a book on insects which explains that only one type of grasshopper, the earth-hopper, is in fact edible, the others are all deadly poisonous. Which of these five insects is the earth-hopper and when are you most likely to catch it?

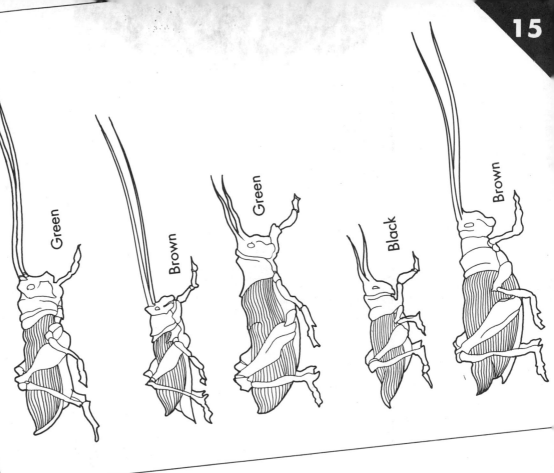

Green

Brown

Green

Black

Brown

GRASSHOPPERS

The grasshoppers on this island can be identified by their size and colour and by the length of their antennae. Both the sand-hopper and the bush-hopper have bodies which are longer than their antennae. All the other kinds have bodies which are shorter than their antennae.

The bush-hopper and the long-hopper both jump long distances but they are smaller than any of the other grasshoppers.

The sand-hopper and the digging-hopper are green and come out at midday. The other grasshoppers, which are either black or brown, come out in the evening.

Only the earth-hopper can be eaten, all the other kinds of grasshopper are poisonous.